SOVIET LITERATURE
IN THE SIXTIES

SOVIET LITERATURE IN THE SIXTIES

An International Symposium

Edited by

Max Hayward *and* Edward L. Crowley

Published for the
Institute for the Study of the USSR

FREDERICK A. PRAEGER, Publisher
New York • London

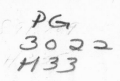

Frederick A. Praeger, *Publisher*
111 Fourth Ave., New York 3, N.Y., U.S.A.
77–79 Charlotte Street, London W. 1, England

Published in the United States of America in 1964
by Frederick A. Praeger, Inc., Publisher

This book is Number 139 in the series
Praeger Publications in Russian History and World Communism

PREFACE

The essays in this volume were originally given as papers at a symposium held under the auspices of the Institute for the Study of the USSR in Bad Wiessee in September, 1963. They are concerned with various aspects of recent Soviet literature, such as the political background, the merits of Soviet literature in relation to the earlier Russian and West European background, the evolution of the Soviet literary language in the years after Stalin, a study of the little-known non-Russian literatures of the Soviet Union, and some problems of Soviet publishing. It is hoped that this symposium will contribute to an understanding of an important aspect of Soviet intellectual life.

M. H.

Contents

SOVIET LITERATURE
IN THE SIXTIES

RUFUS MATHEWSON

The Novel in Russia and the West

I

Hemmed in by orthodoxies, Russian writers have had to fight harder than others for the mere right to exist and to work. The struggle for survival has brought repeatedly into the foreground the question of the *preconditions* for a sophisticated literature. It can be proposed as an axiom that the fortunes of Russian writing depend directly on the degree of success with which these elementary conditions are defended. In the nineteenth century the writers found an area of autonomy between government hostility which would silence them and the strident radical critics who would recruit them in the service of social change. After the October Revolution, these two forces, in effect, became one, and the situation for literature became far more precarious. The preconditions, here considered simply as the artists' right to explore experience, to organize their findings in literary forms and to gain access to the public — all reasonably free of dictation or persecution — have been imperilled throughout Soviet history and for long periods of time obliterated.

If we add one more precondition, the full extent of the Soviet assault on the literary sensibility becomes clearer. This is the right fully to participate in the world literary community — to read, study, debate, accept or reject the works and the criticism of the rest of the world. If the classical Russian writers had not taken part in this dialogue, they would not have made their startlingly original gift to the world. Soviet chauvinism has assumed that the new society would generate its own culture: in the 1920's the "Proletkult" held that its sources would be found in the newly victorious class; Stalin substituted "socialist" for "proletariat" and "realism" for "culture" and insisted that the new, self-sufficient society would accomplish the same thing. Generations of Soviet writers have been cut off partially or completely from the evolution of modern European literature.

True, Soviet literature, with some access to the Russian past, knew the great current of realism that had carried European prose forward during the past century and a half. But genuine realism has never been contained for long in any codified program, and the novel has never remained true to any exclusive definition of its properties. If we may speak with some assurance of a number of permanent variables in the history of the form,

we also know that the one irreducible constant is change — the incorporation of new kinds of experience, the steadily renewed challenge to en-
crusted attitudes, the permanent evolution of forms and techniques to
contain the new subject matter. The direction of change has depended
on the next pioneer who adds his new word and his new vision to the
history of the form, never on legislative programs drawn up by interested
politician-critics.

The new directions the novel has taken have almost always been
subversive of an established order. It has moved steadily into new or
forbidden areas of experience, challenging convention, decorum, dogma,
ideologies — shocking the respectable, exposing misconceptions, ridiculing
the sacrosanct. The novel has registered its great achievement as a mode of
knowledge by being "iconoclastic, mythoclastic, rationalistic, analytic, self-
critical."[1] Its work has been the steady undermining of misconceptions,
the penetration of surfaces, the search for the human in the midst of —
often in contrast to — the society's self-justifying description of itself. Its
authors have traditionally known the experience of alienation, its heroes
are very often outsiders, interlopers, nobodies, scoundrels, from Uncle Toby
to Stavrogin, and, more recently, prisoners trapped in the absurdities
of society, of consciousness, of existence. In its constant action as critic
and challenger the novel has always had a disreputable air. It has often
disturbed the peace.

The growth of "modern tragic realism," as Erich Auerbach has
indicated, has depended on the incorporation of more and more complex
views of human life.[2] The necessary combination of the ordinary and the
sublime has been achieved with the aid of the historian's vision, or of
metaphors derived from the natural and political sciences, or of new
theories of consciousness. But its use of the new intellectual discoveries
has never made it subordinate to the inner workings of other disciplines.
It avoids all such "certainties" in its own perilous, uncertain quest for
the order of the universe. The novelists have exercised the authority of
explorers on the frontiers of experience; they have had to assume that
their findings are uniquely necessary for mankind, and are coterminous
with the findings of no other disciplines.

The writer's claim to autonomy has assumed the validity of many
truths, and of many means of access to them. Henry James' investiga-

---

[1] Harry Levin, *The Gates of Horn: A Study of French Realists*, New York, 1963,
p. 470.
[2] Erich Auerbach, *Mimesis: The Representation of Reality in Western Literature.*
Translated from the German by Willard Trask. New York, 1957, p. 404. I would
cite here as relevant to my argument his most effective description of the mission
of realism: "(to press) unswervingly on from the random data of the phenomenon
itself to the ultimate depths of existence." (P. 375.)

tions in the nature of evil or Balzac's *etudes des moeurs* were intended as new discoveries about life and society, which could be made only through the art of the novel. The protagonist learns by unlearning, as misconceptions are overthrown in a process which Harry Levin has called "the literary technique of systematic disillusionment."[3] The exploration is conducted through the steady play between "innocence and experience, sense and sensibility, appearance and reality."[4] The play between these contrary elements moves always toward the truth, toward knowledge of reality through the *loss* of illusions. The area of the unknown has been reduced, but it always looms large and forbidding and challenging for the serious novelist. The relativism which permits the novelist to work assumes both the existence of the unknown and the right of access to it.

Marxist critics are not the only ones to point out that the novel is the product and expression of bourgeois civilization. Auerbach and Levin have formulated impressive new arguments in support of this truism, showing how the novel's foundation rests on an intellectual pluralism that rests in turn on theories of representative government, indicating that its authors and its heroes are individualists who take full advantage of the privileges granted to the venturesome in capital investment and, by extension, in the realm of feelings and ideas. Money, property, class, marriage, the family, the laws and customs that define and protect them are the stuff of the bourgeois novel. Its steady criticism of the society's values is seen by the Marxist as a prelude to a saner and juster society. Foregoing prediction, Levin has proposed that the novel stands as an impressive monument to the relentless search by the middle class for self-knowledge. In any case, the origin of the form in a distinct social order, no matter how it is characterized—as bourgeois, capitalist, democratic, exploitative, pluralist or individualist—raises questions about the acceptance of the form in the USSR that have never been fully investigated. That it has survived at all in Soviet society suggests that the novel has its deepest roots in an ineradicable curiosity about human behavior, and in certain conditions of modern life that transcend social arrangements.

The French novel predominates in the brief, general description I have given here. The two scholars I have relied on insist on the centrality of the Stendhal-to-Proust continuum in the history of the form. Both have approached the Russian frontier in their summarizing chapters but have declined to cross it. A few qualifications should be made about the special achievement of the great Russian realists, the family legacy, as it were, of the Soviet novelists.

The Russians' "criticism of life" covered as vast a range as the Western novel, but far more of their energy was spent attacking current doctrines of

---

[3] Levin, *op. cit.*, p. 48.
[4] Levin, *op. cit.*, p. 48.

progress and social change — utilitarianism, socialism, nihilism, positivism.
Flaubert's *L'Education sentimentale* and Dickens' *Hard Times*, it is true,
indicate that Western writers were as aware of the dehumanizing aridity
of the ideologies of progress. But for the Russians the radicals' vision of the
world and of themselves was a primary object of skeptical investigation.
Fictional inquiries into the Napoleonic ego (*War and Peace* and *Crime and
Punishment*), into the related sin of rational pride (Bazarov and Ivan
Karamazov), into the arrogance of those who would reorganize mankind
according to a blueprint (Pasternak was enunciating in *Doctor Zhivago*
a time-honored theme, first set forth in *Notes from Underground*) discredited the questionable ideologies through the flaws in the characters
who advocated them. Indeed, they called into question the validity of any
ideology as a sufficient description of life. The sense of life as a thing lived
beyond the boundaries of rational doctrine or of reason itself constituted
their rebuttal to their own optimistic reformers and, as a grateful Europe
later learned, their gift to modern thought. The Russian celebration of the
irrational has been acknowledged in the tributes Freud, Nietzsche, Kafka
and Gide paid to Dostoevsky.

Auerbach has suggested that the Russians enriched realism's continuous
search for new kinds of experience by incorporating a religious reality in
the novel. Religious or metaphysical, it is true that the Russians used the
novel — as the Americans did also and the French and the English did not —
to order all dimensions of experience, to approach the ultimate meanings
of existence. Again Europe has acknowledged its debt. Konstantin Levin's
quest for the final answer and the drama of the Dostoevskyan sinner were
stripped of their religious references and taken into the very heart of
modern fiction as the French — Malraux and Camus, above all — would
freely admit.

The Soviet gamble — whether or not the risks have ever been understood — was that they could transfer this form from the social system that
generated it, separate it from its milieu and its tradition, and compel it to
serve new and radically different ends. Merely to list the properties of the
form and of the conditions under which it grew is to suggest the extreme
difficulty, perhaps the impossiblity *a priori*, of accomplishing it. The
Soviet writer is not free to explore, to experiment, or to challenge his
milieu. He dare not risk alienation; he is not able to draw freely on the
resources of the past, or on the discoveries of a rich, discordant and ever
changing intellectual life. He is asked to make the novel accomplish what
it has never successfully accomplished before: to affirm a rigid set of
political and social values into which all the variety and pain of human
experience must be fitted. Stated in these general terms, it would seem that
the brash Soviet literary experiment could only fail. Abram Tertz's defini-

tion of the irreconcilable elements in socialist realism — theological purpose and the lifelike representation of reality — would seem to summarize the hopelessness of the situation in one swift insight.[5]

II

Tertz's pessimism would certainly be justified if the rulers' view of socialist realism had been enforced in its fullest application through the whole of Soviet history. But this, of course, is not the case. Writers have been free enough, at times, to explore their world, or have been clever enough or lucky enough to bypass the apparatus of restriction. It cannot be said that there is a Soviet novel *sui generis*, but there is enough genuine work to permit the isolation of certain properties of the novel as it has developed on Soviet soil.

According to Auerbach's measure of literary progress — the successful incorporation of new kinds of reality — it is immediately clear, I think, that the world that confronted the Soviet writer was a radically different one. Two immense new themes presented themselves to him — social revolution and the building of the new society — the struggle to accomplish the first, the labor to accomplish the second.

The most compelling theme, of course, has been the Civil War, the social apocalypse. Writers from Furmanov to Pasternak have returned to it in search of the meaning of modern life at the moment of its first definition. What does it offer the working novelist as a new kind of experience? Man *in extremis*, in a maelstrom of suffering and violence, naked and hungry before the absolute, broken loose from his moorings, wandering over the face of the land, moving in his feelings from a radiant vision of the new world to the limits of despair and depravity. The "facts" of this disordered world were elemental: the struggle for the gross necessities of existence, the disfiguring restrictions of military life, deprivation, murder, torture, solitude, pain, death.

The novel has seldom dealt with the apocalypse. The challenge confronting Soviet novelists is the more formidable if we consider the traditional ingredients they were deprived of. A thick-textured social existence has been central in the novel from Jane Austen to Dostoevsky. In the Soviet Civil War society itself had ceased to exist. The novel of manners, *l'étude des moeurs*, obviously had nothing to teach the new Soviet writer. There were no small movements of men within and across the barriers of a solid social structure. The drama of the rebel against society, Julien Sorel or Raskolnikov, is equally inapplicable: there is nothing to challenge, nothing to conquer, and nothing to punish the deviator or the interloper.

---

[5] Abram Tertz, *Socialist Realism*, Pantheon Press, Boston-New York, 1961.

Society-as-enemy has solidified into the anonymous face of the White Army. There is violence aplenty but of a totally implacable and impersonal kind; even when the enemies are brothers or friends, there is no modulation, no possibility of exchange. Without a social order to contain them, personal relations are deprived of continuity, or of the kind of slow development that permits nuance, intimacy or depth. Families were smashed or they hung together with animal stubborness. Private life had very nearly disappeared; the Soviet writer stood somewhere between the elemental and the metaphysical, deprived of the human stability that might connect the two in an artistic synthesis.

Chaos was not total, of course. The fact of Bolshevik victory meant that "a divine purpose," historical inevitability, was moving through the maelstrom. A final order was imposed on the novelist by history but he has felt free at times to make it invisible to the participants or to hide its ultimate benevolence behind the harsh mask of terror, arbitrariness, or indifference. Individual fates were not always made to coincide with the pattern of historical events. There was dignity to be found on occasion, in the destinies of the revolution's honorable casualties — Melekhov in Sholokhov's *The Quiet Don*, for example, or Mitka Vekshin in Leonov's *The Thief*.

The special formal challenges imposed by the new subject matter have not yet been clearly defined by criticism. A Soviet scholar in a recent article on the "typology" of the novel has recognized the centrality of the Civil War to the Soviet literary imagination, and has sought to classify the novels about it according to period and to the method of handling the experience.[6] But his categories — the "journalist" and the "philosophical" are the principle ones — although they mark the distinction between lower and higher forms of imaginative organization, are not very helpful, finally, since they make too little allowance for the full range of the moral experience or for the various technical solutions to new literary problems. Yershov's indifference to formal matters is made most evident by his scorn for all twentieth century "avant-garde" literary tendencies.

We can agree that it was easier for the untalented — the "journalist" — to stick to the "facts" as Furmanov does in the first Soviet diary-novel, and safer to dissolve the moral questions of terror and violence in the pieties of the cause. But other writers ventured much more. Isaac Babel, yielding to the fragmented nature of the experience as he had known it, sought to define certain plain verities — beauty, courage, justice — in the swift glimpse of the short story. Novelists Fadeev, Leonov, Sholokhov, Fedin, and Pasternak confronted the challenges of moral inquiry and fictional

[6] L. Yershov, "Tipologiya sovetskogo romana," *Russkaya literatura*, Moscow, No. 4, 1962.

order with varying degrees of success. The experience of dispersal and rupture is ordered by A. K. Tolstoy in *Road to Calvary* by parallel narratives describing the fates of several individuals. The multilayer structure is held together by coincidental encounters across the face of Russia. Pasternak endows the accidental meetings of his characters with a kind of enchantment and contrives out of his central pattern of coincidence an idyl of private experience which is meant to refute the social engineers. Sholokhov was able to dramatize in a grand tragic design the great moral questions that arise from the collision between History and a decent confused man. By shifting his focus between the military struggles and the Cossack village, Sholokhov fixed his historical narrative in a thick web of human experience. These few swift examples suggest that serious writers were able to incorporate the new reality history offered them into viable novel forms.

The fact of Bolshevik victory in the Civil War became the myth of immutable Party victory in all its peacetime enterprises. The myth imposes predetermined outcomes, robs the novel of surprise, prevents searching inquiry or criticism, restricts human experience to situations of endless warfare, to the neo-military vocabulary of the governing Soviet rhetoric. It freezes the main outlines of structure, permitting variation only in the details of the formula. And these variations require an ingenuity so labored that it further endangers spontaneity, energy, surprise and freshness. (Leonid Leonov's *Road to the Ocean* is an example of talent crippling itself with contrivance: the formula is still there, unchanged by the technical *tours de force*.)

In the novels of construction and production the resistance of the material itself is added to the other obstacles. Of the literature of construction in the late Stalin era Yevtushenko has said in his *Precocious Autobiography*: "The heroes of novels smelted steel, built houses, sowed wheat, but never thought and never loved — or if they did, it was as lifelessly as puppets."[7] This was the fault, he said, of the writers who accepted Stalin's view "that people were the little cogwheels of Communism." To exonerate Stalin of *this* crime, I would suggest that the same deadness entered the Soviet novel with the first work of the 1920's that celebrated industrial process and defined individual destinies through their relationship to the blast furnace, cement mixer or milking machine. In placing technology at the heart of the novel, Soviet writers were reversing a tradition nearly as old as the novel itself. The nineteenth-century writers' dread of machines, factories, and the industrial wasteland,

[7] Yevgeny Yevtushenko, *A Precocious Autobiography*. Translated from the Russian by Andrew MacAndrew, New York, 1963, pp. 75—6.

was based on aesthetic grounds, but in the broadest sense the new ugliness meant the reduction of the human, the mechanization of the soul. Matthew Arnold held that great poetry, centered in great ideas, was needed to combat the meanness of spirit, the hegemony of practical minds that accompanied the industrial revolution. The American writers of the mid-century looked to nature — to the sea, to the woods, to the frontier — as the true realm of the human while an ugly and, they feared, dehumanizing civilization was taking shape.

The victim of urban industrial civilization — the artist, the child, the worker or the merely honest man — is an archetypical figure in modern fiction. It is difficult to name a major novel that celebrates the relationship between man and machine. C. P. Snow, in his *The Two Cultures*, censures the literary intellectuals for their reactionary attitude toward modern technology, the one indispensable instrument of human betterment. The grandeur of its promise underlies the Soviet cult of labor. But the Soviet novelists who have embraced technology would seem to have demonstrated that the nobility of the collective enterprise is not enough to convert the experience itself into viable literary forms. The "reactionary" Westerners may or may not oppose the industrial age, or may merely hope to keep certain traditional values alive. Marx blamed capitalism for men's alienation from their human potential, but the industrial process is the same in any social system, no matter what kind of rhetoric is used to explain its goals. I am not here claiming that the industrial process is intrinsically antiaesthetic, or that the relationship of a man to his industrial labor is *a priori* a demeaning one. But the Soviet effort to demonstrate the contrary in hundreds of novels is surely unconvincing. The novel with a machine at its center confers moral worth on the men who tend it, according to the success with which they make it work. Men become appendages of the machine, "tools of their tools," in Thoreau's phrase. Relationships — love, friendship, hatred — are formed around the machine, actually in a sense, *pass through* it, and bear its impress, as the pursuit of the whale shapes the relationship in *Moby Dick*, or the beauty of the rain-drenched garden in Tolstoy's *Family Happiness* colors the characters' emotion in the proposal scene. But relationships that bear the aesthetic impress of the machine cannot fail to demonstrate its tonelessness, its unvarying geometry, its statistical uniformity. Lives measured by R. P. M.'s, bricks laid, bushels picked, or percentages of butter fat are lives scarcely measured at all. The machine may require the devoted application of energy (physical exhaustion in the machine's service is one of the most common "emotions" in this kind of fiction), but when it dominates a novel it reduces the scope for heroic action or self-sacrifice appropriate to the victory myth, diminishes the intellectual range for a radical inquiry into the values of society, rules out the amplitude of feeling, the sense of a universal perspective, gained from setting man against the natural world. In Chekhov's universe, through the beauty and indifference of nature man touches the ultimate boundaries of his existence — the gift of life and the fact of death. Through the machine Soviet man touches the five-year plan, or History's blueprint, with his individual fate absorbed in the eventual collective achievement. Nature is less a source of beauty than a brute force to be conquered and made into a supplier of raw materials for shelter, food, clothes and the gadgetry of modern material well-being. Yevtushenko has said that Soviet industrial literature should be read by machines, not by men.

Nature has not entirely disappeared, of course, from Soviet writing. Prishvin's appreciations of the natural world find an audience of nature lovers. Pasternak, solitary in all he did, made his special perceptions of the natural world the source of his major poetic statements. The forests give to Leonov's accounts of localized problems a sense of the permanence of Russia. Sholokhov, alone among major Soviet writers, has treated nature traditionally. It is the spiritual habitat of his hero, the source of his attachment to life and of whatever meaning he can discover in the turbulence around him. Melekhov responds as a farmer to the rhythms of the seasons; he is the aesthetic creature of the Don landscape. His tragedy in its full dimensions may be read, quite apart from political labels, as the downfall of pastoral man before the assault of the new industrial society.

While Soviet novelists were struggling with these intractable themes in the period between the wars, Western novelists moved into vast new areas of experience, revolutionizing language and form as they went. The gap between Soviet and Western writers is very large. Merely to list the names of the authoritative voices in Western literature suggests the distance that separates them: Proust, D. H. Lawrence, Kafka, Mann, Joyce, Forster, Faulkner, Hemingway, Virginia Woolf, Malraux, Gide. For reasons largely irrelevant to literature, Soviet cultural magistrates have preferred Theodore Dreiser, Upton Sinclair, Erskine Caldwell, Romain Rolland, Henri Barbusse, Halldor Laxness, Howard Fast.

It is enough, I hope, to point to a few general themes, present in the modern European novel, and almost entirely lacking in Soviet writing: the movement inward into the workings of consciousness — Proust's into memory, Virginia Woolf's, and of course, Joyce's, into the process of association — was not duplicated in Russia. The artist's self did not become a primary object of investigation. D. H. Lawrence's pioneering in the sexual dimensions of experience has been ignored in the USSR. The absence of Freud, and of the whole movement that grew out of his work, has deprived Soviet writers of one of the great achievements of twentieth-century thought. Pavlovian reflexology has placed consciousness itself beyond the reach of scientific investigation.

The very broad approach to experience, which I would call the existentialist, is also largely unavailable to Soviet writers. Western literature asks religious questions, even if it returns no religious answers. To appreciate the breadth of this category, think of Kafka, Malraux, Faulkner and Camus. They have in common the examination of mystery as their central concern. The hero is often a prisoner — of time, of consciousness, of absurdity, of an insatiable destiny, of a dehumanized society. His efforts to escape, to achieve self-definition, to discover values in a blind, hostile universe form the substance of the novel and provide the universal statement which is the object of the writer's quest. It is a literature of men *in extremis*, and its findings are often devastatingly bleak.

This is a category so indistinct that it comes into relief only in contrast to Soviet literature. The essential difference is in the presence of mystery, of the unknown. Soviet man's spiritual adventures have been *conformist*, occuring within the known and the given, that is to say, within a fixed set of social values. They come to an invariable and predictable conclusion. Under the shallow rationalist scientism of Soviet Marxism there have been few unanswered questions outside the sphere of the natural sciences. The humanist curiosity has had little to concern itself with: the novel as an art of exploration is obsolete. Soviet literature has not been free to examine the ironies and the tragedies of existence. Basic loyalties have remained beyond anyone's right to question.

The nineteenth-century novelist whose influence weighs most heavily on Western writing is Dostoevsky. His explorations of the lower limits of consciousness and his existential dramas have become the common property of modern literature. But there is no room for the Underground Man in the Crystal Palace.

III

The French Romantic rebellion against neo-classicism in 1830 sought emancipation from a system of convention-bound forms. A new way of looking at the world, and a new sensibility, required new forms, new themes and a new language. The rebellion of Soviet writers after Stalin's death may have equalled the French movement in seriousness and intensity. But neo-classicism was one of the world's great artistic systems, with a highly developed and subtle program; socialist realism was a crude, self-contradictory *political* doctrine which, if fully enforced, guaranteed the death of art. The aim of the Soviet rebels was more fundamental than Victor Hugo's; it was to regain the right to exist, to reestablish the preconditions for a genuine literature. Artistic questions were secondary.

A police system, not an artistic doctrine, was the target. The lack of challenge in the enemy's ideas was reflected in the new movement's lack of sophistication. Wordsworth and Coleridge felt that a new literature would gain greater access to the important truths of experience, but the Soviet writers were demanding the right *not to be forced to lie.* Elemental words — "truth," "sincerity," "privacy," "freedom," "justice," — constituted a plea merely to be allowed to remain alive as artists.

The artistic outburst of 1830 coincided with the overthrow of the Restoration monarchy. No such political change occurred in the USSR in 1953. Bonds were loosened but not broken. This accounts for the curious if incomplete quality of the Soviet literary rebellion. A great deal of ground has been regained in the sense that many forbidden subjects can be written about, and the myth of Soviet victory has lost some of its control over internal artistic order. But these are tentative gains. The restrictive mechanism has not been dismantled nor has the restrictive ideology been repudiated. If the limits have sometimes seemed indistinct, a sharp counter-attack indicates that the writers have inadvertently crossed them. We may not doubt, I think, that if Ehrenburg, Nekrasov, Tendrya-kov, Yevtushenko and Voznesensky were given their heads, not only as writers but as cultural legislators, the new Russian literature would be far more varied, more venturesome and more brilliant than it is.

In asserting the right to breathe, the writers commit a political act, implicitly calling for a redefinition of the relationship of the citizen to his compatriots, and to the authorities. In Hungary and Poland the cry for literary freedom coincided with the grievances and aspirations of an entire nation. In the USSR no such conjunction has taken place, but the attack on bureaucracy, cruelty, careerism, emotional stagnation and violation of privacy which the new literary voices express cannot fail to have important social consequences. As "criticism of life" in Matthew Arnold's sense, it represents a classic instance of the humanist intelligence at work in an oppressive social atmosphere. The cant, smugness, hypocrisy, the deadening of language and of thought — the evils Arnold attacked in newly industrial England — are the targets of the young Soviet writers. They are qualities of the moral atmosphere, at one remove from political institutions. But in a closed, unitary society where the Party supervises everything men think and do, institutions are called into question even when they are not named.

Since the loyalty of Soviet citizens is meant to extend to every corner of social and intellectual life, criticism of any part may seem to jeopardize the whole. Since the unfinished conflict with the authorities compels the writers to be tentative and evasive on questions like this, it is not possible to know how much of this hope for change in the moral and aesthetic quality of Soviet life extends to political institutions, to the system itself. Is it possible that Tertz and Pasternak complete the others' inarticulated intentions in their own openly subversive attacks on the assumptions of Soviet life, and in their celebration of the life of the heart and the imagination? There is more evidence to suppose that their hopes for change would be fulfilled in cleansing the air of all of Stalin's indecencies. If this is so and it seems more likely — it remains a dispute within the church against usurpers of the dream.

At first glance, the new Soviet writing has an unmistakably old-fashioned look. It is still untouched by the experimental currents in Western writing, unaffected by the revolutionary discoveries of the new psychology, or of the vision of modern painting. Imprisoned in a pedestrian rationalism, it is deprived of genuine mythic or metaphysical dimension. The narratives of a Tendryakov or a Nekrasov or a Solzhenitsyn are deployed in an orderly manner through time, do not "distort" experience in order to see it freshly, do not shift point of view in any radical manner or divert the steady gaze of the observer-narrator. Language does not attempt to reproduce the actual flutterings and oscillations of consciousness but is "logical" in the sense that it is a rational, ordered description of event, scene or feeling. There is little symbolism, no *arrière-plan* of meanings, as in Thomas Mann's novels, nor does one find the electric prose of Flaubert or Tolstoy in which every commonplace detail is charged with significance and made a "working" part of the main narrative development. It is instead low-tension, plain-spoken, photographic, confined on the whole to surfaces.

At the same time it is a prose of great moral seriousness which no doubt speaks to its contemporary audience as a fresh and authoritative commentary on experience. A wider area of moral choice and of self-definition may be the biggest single gain Soviet writers have made since Stalin's death. Honest men in Tendryakov's stories face personal moral challenges and cannot rise to them; or they speculate on the discrepancy between legal and moral guilt in a hunting accident; or they quail before a vision of human malevolence for which there is no official explanation or cure. The protagonist in the new fiction is often caught, trapped or unjustly punished as a result of a local breakdown of the system; he is the victim of bureaucrats, unscrupulous police officials, unjust superiors. But these instances of pain and humiliation are generally represented as "abuses," not as flaws in the system itself, and it is reasonable in most cases to assume that the writer's intention is to expose the "abuse" in order to eliminate it and make the system work better. In the gradual revelation through fiction of the systematic criminality of Stalin's police system — in Nekrasov's *Kira Georgievna*, for example, or in Bondarev's *Silence* or in Solzhenitsyn's *One Day* — the intention has rather been to call on the nation to confront a moral catastrophe in order to remove its after-effects from the collective conscience. The injustice in question is more than an "abuse," but the works are retroactive self-examination: the shame is assumed to have been removed, and there is no head-on confrontation with the responsible authorities. Stalin is dead, after all.

A literature concerned with guidance in moral problems has predictable defects, some of which, no doubt, are accentuated by habits passed on from the Stalin era. Sentimentality, schematism, "patness," banality, an absence of irony and a tendency toward false clarity are to be found in works by some of the prominent new writers. Dudintsev's inventor in *Not By Bread Alone* is the wooden emblem of a problem; the restless young people in Aksyonov's *Ticket to the Stars* are fresh, charming figures in Soviet fiction but they risk very little and discover less in their flight from home. Nekrasov's veterans in *Native Town* are "good guys" who earnestly find their way back from military to civilian life, search for — and find — true love, careers, and a purpose in life. The action in all three novels occurs outside the strict control of Party precepts, but the final solutions all coincide with a broader definition of conformist expectations and there is no very strenuous moral inquiry, and few difficulties that cannot be solved if one means well.

Occasionally, moral concern, character and situation coincide in a memorable way. When the concentration camp graduate in Nekrasov's *Kira Georgievna* asks himself how he should feel about his imprisonment, why he is not more bitter, whether there is some ultimate satisfaction in having shared the people's agony, he has reached an impressive level of moral utterance. Solzhenitsyn's controlled understatement in "One Day" is impregnated throughout with irony which flares up with compelling effect in the final lines. The carefully modulated steps in the hero's process of self-discovery in Granin's *A Personal Opinion* transcend the Soviet scene as authentic disclosure of character, unsweetened by pious assurances.

The novel's traditional figure, the outsider, has reappeared in Soviet writing. In presenting ordinary, fallible men who live on or beyond the edge of respectability, writers no doubt hope to restore a note of plain human veracity in order to wipe out the memory of the victorious automatons who for so long dominated literature. Idlers, drunks, ex-convicts, alienated artists are not perhaps "typical" in the sense of the quintessential or of the average, but they are of much greater human and literary interest. Their situation on the margins of society gives the writer a vantage from which to present society's victims or its rebels, or, if he must, to point the way back to respectability. On the whole the Soviet outsider is not asked to carry the burden of protest of his famous predecessors, the scoundrels, criminals, and rebels against the order of the universe. There is no Chichikov wriggling out of the hands of the law, forever beyond redemption, no Huck Finn, heading for the frontier, leaving behind a civilization he has learned to despise, no Julien Sorel going to his death in calm defiance of the contemptible society he has invaded and conquered. The Soviet outsider is not an instrument of radical inquiry or protest. Kazakov's drunken buoy-tender in *The Outsider* is presented as thoroughly reprehensible by socialist and by human standards until we are told that he and his slatternly mistress possess the folk's magic gift of song. We are also confronted here, I suspect, with a parable about the situation of the artist, as we seem to be in other stories by Kazakov.

The individualist hunter, Teterin, in Tendryakov's *The Trial* promises to express in a traditional way the natural man's distaste for industrial progress in a traditional — perhaps Tolstoyan — sense, but it is clear at the end that his function in the story is simply to record the complexities of the moral tangle from a neutral vantage point. In Kazakov's *Adam and Eve*, the outsider is not reconciled or punished or redeemed or finally explained. The alienated artist repudiates the world he knows: the critics in Moscow, his fellow artists, even the sympathetic girl who travels to the island retreat with him. It may be that his vision of the earth hurtling through space, or his attraction to the life of the local fishermen, are meant to suggest that he has touched some new and authentic layer of experience. But the fictional presentation of his situation — even if it is meant to be understood as confusion or as ambivalence — yields no final insight. Only Solzhenitsyn has made full use of the outsider. His modest convict, an accomplished but fastidious scrounger and a good comrade, calls a whole civilization into question (whether or not Khrushchev realizes it) precisely because he is too simple to see the political dimensions of his problem.

The outsider in modern Western writing has gone far beyond anything imaginable in Soviet literature, in his exploration of the lower limits of experience. He has become the outcast — a sexual deviate, a professional criminal, a dope addict. It seems evident that the search for revelation in a movement downward — Jean Wahl has called it "trans-descendence"[8] — will eventually exhaust the literary possibilities of depravity. The world of the addict, for example, is so remote from ordinary life that its comment on the normal is irrelevant or incomprehensible.

The exploration of sex in Western writing has gone, in one direction, toward the mere contemplation of depravity, but it has also clearly established itself as a central concern of the best modern writing. Joyce,

---

[8] Quoted in Lionel Abel, "Beyond the Fringe," *Partisan Review*, New York, Spring 1963, p. 110.

Miller and Lawrence in their distinct ways have legitimized the language, the physical details and the extra-sensual dimensions of the sexual experience. Post-war writers have assimilated this legacy and pushed the exploration still further. Norman Mailer has recently said that sexual experience is the last frontier open to the novelist.

There is no need to labor the contrast between Soviet and Western literature on this score. Isaac Babel made sexual experience an integral part of his striking stories. But the prevailing movement until Stalin's death was toward decorum and finally toward prudery. Since 1953 Soviet writers have begun to acknowledge that sex exists, that it is an essential part of a good marriage, indeed of genuine love in or out of marriage. The casual affairs of soldiers, lumberjacks, and war veterans on the town have been alluded to. But the experience itself has not been investigated. The central dramatic situation in the new writing, the serious triangle, has been treated with a turn-of-the-century solemnity and reserve.

The key questions concerning the treatment of sex and of all other taboo subjects in Soviet writing must be directed toward the future. Should we assume that Soviet writers will have to duplicate the long difficult search of Western writers for new subject matter, including the false starts and the lapses into vulgarity and sensationalism? Or will they rejoin the main stream of literary evolution by leap-frogging the painful process of discovery — as the Russians have done so often in so many fields — and draw on the best of it for their own purposes? Or — and this is a melancholy third alternative — will prudery and chauvinism, enforced by political decisions, return Soviet literature to its former isolation and paralysis?

If Soviet thaw writers have been unable or unwilling to follow their colleagues in the West, what use have they made of the available past? They have bypassed their own experimental writers of the period between the wars, most notably Babel and Olesha, who had found new formal resources to express their personal visions. The absence of Proust and Joyce from the Soviet canon symbolizes the lack of response to Western writing in the same period. Nor does one feel the presence of the Symbolist movement (in either its French or Russian manifestations) which Edmund Wilson has so persuasively shown in *Axel's Castle* to be chief source of modern literature. The old-fashioned quality of the new writing must be attributed finally, I think, to its dependence on the classical tradition, a dependence which to date is more imitation than creative repossession. Without suggesting that the new writing displays his delicacy or his toughness, his insight or his irony, I would consider Chekhov as the historical point of departure of the new writing.

The Russian classics are an incomparably good place to go to school, but none of the new writers has written anything to match Tolstoy's

account of Anna's carriage ride or the first pages of Chekhov's *Enemies*.
The world that supported his splendid prose has given way to a totally
new one which has not yet been permitted to generate a style appropriate
to the contours and pressures of its life.

IV

Nathaniel Hawthorne complained in the preface to *The Marble Faun*
that it was difficult to write in a country "where there is no shadow, no
antiquity, no mystery, no picturesque and gloomy wrong, nor anything
but a commonplace prosperity in broad and simple daylight." Tocqueville
had argued persuasively two decades before that there could be no serious
American literature. But Hawthorne found the magic combination of
"firelight and moonlight" he sought; American writers discovered no
lack of picturesque and gloomy wrongs, beginning with the institution of
slavery; the broad and simple daylight, itself, has been shown to be a
harsh, malevolent glare. Tocqueville was proven wrong for all time in the
period between 1850 and 1855 which saw the publication of *Leaves of
Grass*, *Moby Dick*, *The 'Scarlet Letter*, and *Walden*.

I would not expect the Soviet writer or critic to sympathize with
Hawthorne's (and James') nostalgia for the past. He would think of such
a list of conditions as "remnants" — in his vocabulary "bourgeois survivals."
And the possibility that men should confront each other in a broad and
simple daylight is for the Socialist not a grievance but a dream, and a
dream of great dignity. But in a world where "should be" is arbitrarily
confounded with "is," the peril for the novel in the Soviet writer's own
terms is that it cannot measure the distance between existence and the
dream.

And when he does look around him, the bleakness of present-day
Soviet life, the technological rawness, the institutionalized ugliness, would
seem to offer no more promise to the imaginative writer than did Hawthorne's America. And yet it may be as quickly conquered. (Modern
Russia has its share of gloomy wrongs!). Auerbach has shown us that the
conditions for the existence of modern realism can be established in
alsmost any environment.

Provided, of course, that certain *pre*conditions are met. (I have been
making a distinction throughout this essay between the conditions of the
life lived in a society; that is, the writer's material, promising or un-
promising; and the preconditions which must be established if the writer
is to work at all.) A freely inquiring, intellectually charged, morally
vigorous literature cannot fail to appear both as an affront and a challenge
to the governors of a social system who claim to be infallible. The fresh,

precise, evocative use of language plays havoc with the rhetoric of justification and threatens the ideological ties that bind each Soviet citizen. Every genuine novel or story threatens to establish a center of independent judgment on questions the Party has not considered open to discussion. Certain preconditions have been partially established in the past decade, but they exist only at the sufferance of the Party. It is difficult to believe that any compromise on this issue can be a lasting one, that a free literature and an infallible political party can coexist indefinitely. But if the conflict is a mortal one, the odds are not so heavily in favor of the holders of power as it would seem. The Party is defending an intellectual vacuum. The liberal party in the arts, speaking through Ehrenburg, Nekrasov, Yevtushenko and others, knows very well what the conditions for its survival are: a guaranteed autonomy, unlimited access to all the world's art, the right to experiment. It may be that the Party will have to meet these demands if it wants any art at all. On the other hand, the *kind* of literature the new Soviet writing promises to become when it has reached full growth requires rights as broad and as well-anchored as our own if it is to survive.

There seem to me to be two tendencies in the Western approach to Soviet literature: to dismiss it out of hand, through a depressing sense of the precariousness of the preconditions I have mentioned, or to celebrate the fact that the Russians are writing again — to be grateful for small favors. In listing the deprivations and inhibitions under which this fledgling literature has come into being, I have meant to describe it, to fix it at several points in relation to world literature, but not to pass a final judgment on it. I have long hoped that a dialogue could be established between East and West, not a political wrangle, but a genuine discussion, not excluding sharp but honest disputes. No such exchange is possible with men like Yermilov, but there is an area of common interest, literature itself, and there are men, we now realize, who know what literature really is.

A. GAEV

The Decade Since Stalin

Unlike political events, which can change the structure of a state in a single day, events in the world of art require some interval before works begin to express the spirit of a new era. Consequently, while the death of Stalin could immediately inaugurate a new political stage, it could not in a single day change the character of Soviet art, particularly literature which had for so long played an ignominiously subservient role. Nevertheless, in a fairly short time, even before the refurbished political line had been more than vaguely outlined, literature began to reflect a long imminent tendency toward liberation from the harsh restrictions which had been established under Stalins' thirty-year dictatorship.

First, however, one should take a brief look at those long years which preceded the events to be reviewed in this paper.

By 1953, after years of Stalin's bloody terror which extended even to the field of creative art, a perceptible thinning of the literary ranks had occurred. Pages could be filled with the names of original and independent writers of integrity who perished. The slight respite provided by the Second World War was brought to an abrupt end by the Party Central Committee decree of August 14, 1946, when M. Zoshchenko and Anna Akhmatova were expelled from the Union of Writers and the editorial boards of the journal *Zvezda* and the almanac *Literaturny Leningrad* were sharply censured as a warning to the editors of other Soviet literary journals. The long reign of terror even left its mark on those writers who survived physically. Fear shackled creative thought, clipped the wings of imagination and confined creative writing within an incredibly narrow framework. A situation has developed which the writer and critic, Aleksandr Voronsky, had accurately prophesied years before, when, in January 1925, appearing unexpectedly at the House of the Press where the First All-Union Conference of Writers was in session, he delivered a speech which was not on the agenda. In these bold words he said:

> They seek to stand with a bludgeon and brandish it over your heads. If someone's head stands a little higher, that head will be struck down. With the same bludgeon they will dictate to you subject, ideas and style. I fear that in a few years time literature will become as

spiritless as an accountant's ledger. Novels and poems will be scribbled off on line with a set standard. Idyls and odes will be cooked up according to a strict recipe, regardless of reality, regardless of artistic truth.[1]

Due to the systematic suppression of creative thought, by the time of Stalins' death Soviet writers comprised two basic groups — the "Time-Servers" and the "silent ones." To the first category belonged thousands of authors who assidously carried out all Party directives and went out of their way to laud Stalin. The "silent ones" were considerably fewer in number. The term was first used in 1934 during the First Congress of Writers with reference to I. Babel because of his literary silence. Later it was applied to Yuri Olesha and other writers none of whose works had appeared for a long period in Soviet literary journals. As time went on the number of "silent ones" grew, and included such names as Boris Pasternak.

Between these two groups there was another, still smaller one, consisting of such writers as Mikhail Prishvin and Pavel Bazhov who circumvented Party control because their works were so apolitical in form and content that Party requirements, however exacting, were as inapplicable to them as they were to a textbook on differential calculus or pharmacopeia.

Stalin's death did not immediately serve as a turning point, because his basic policies remained in force. The inertia of Stalinism was fairly strong and even such events as the changes in the system of political control and the first amnesties could not be regarded as signs of the disintegration of public life in the Soviet Union.

Nevertheless, by the fall of 1953 certain works of literature were appearing which bore witness to the emergence of a new trend in creative thought and, consequently, in public opinion. At the beginning of 1954 this trend became more clearly defined. It was at this time that Leonid Zorin's play *Guests*, showing the renaissance of Soviet society, was published. The author's bold ideas initially passed without comment and it was only on June 15 that *Literaturnaya gazeta* printed a sharp criticism of the work in typically Stalinist style.

By this time Ilya Ehrenburg's short story *The Thaw*, the title of which was a year later to become a catchword, had already been published. At the end of 1954 came the Second Congress of Soviet Writers which had been preceded over a period of eight months by congresses and conferences of writers in the provinces at which problems of literature had been discussed and delegates to the all-union congress chosen. Yet the inertia of Stalinism was still all-pervasive, as witnessed by purges in the same year

---

[1] Quoted from *Literaturny sovremennik*, Munich, 1951, No. 2, p. 84.

of the Union of Soviet Writers and the expulsion from its ranks of such undesirables as N. Virta who were thereby prevented from attending the all-union congress.

The spirit reigning at the congress was also significant. In the main the congress was dominated by aims laid down in the Stalin period. Yet, at the same time there were a number of speeches reflecting new ideas among the writers. Of the 720 delegates to the congress, 522 were Party members. The tone of the proceedings was set by an appeal from the Central Committee which stressed the requirement that the works of Soviet authors should adher to the spirit of socialist realism. The main speaker, Alexei Surkov, stuck strictly to the Central Committee appeal, but some of the other speeches were of a markedly critical nature. Only major writers dared to make independent speeches. These included Ilya Ehrenburg, Kornei Chukovsky, Mikhail Sholokhov, Olga Berggolts and Valentin Ovechkin, who indignantly declared that the Soviet book market was flooded with a turbid flow of tendentious rubbish.

Sholokhov in particular spoke out so sharply and unexpectedly that F. Gladkov took the floor to make an impromptu statement regarding the inadmissibility at the congress of "criticism which was non-Party in spirit." The criticism leveled at Sholokhov was that he had spoken of the calamity represented by the "grey stream of colorless mediocre literature which had in recent years been flowing from the pages of journals and flooding the book market." Sholokov had also hurled a serious reproach at Soviet literary criticism:

> In critical literature not a single article has been printed without deletions and a glance over the shoulder.[2]

Ehrenburg touched on the most festering sore points in Soviet literature:

> We know some contemporary authors who quite sincerely write untruth . . . . Such authors prettify the outward appearance of their heroes . . . . They do not spare the gilt in depicting a communal apartment, in their works machine shops look like laboratories and collective farm clubs like boyars' mansions, but this tinselly sham world is populated with primitive creatures.[3]

Despite the strictly Party spirit of the congress as a whole, such sharp condemnations of debased Soviet literature provided evidence of intellectual ferment.

Soon after the congress the well-known literary scholar Professor L. Timofeyev published a bulky collection of articles entitled *Russian Soviet*

---

[2] *Literaturnaya gazeta*, December 26, 1954.

[3] *Ibid.*

Literature in which a great deal of space was devoted to the congress and to the phenomena in Soviet literature to which the delegates had alluded in their speeches. The orthodox professor referred to the appearance of "seditious" literature:

It is known that shortly before the congress several works appeared (*The Destruction of Pompeii* by N. Virta; *The Guests* by L. Zorin; *Man of Action* by S. Gorodetsky, *The Crown Prince* by A. Mariengof and others) in which Soviet life was depicted in a distorted manner and our people were slandered. The conflicts which formed the basis of these works (the contrasting of simple people with state institutions, the older generation with the younger, etc.) are figments of the imagination, forgeries, and bear no relation to Soviet reality. [4]

The articles in the collection particularly stressed the fact that the slightest deviation from socialist realism would lead writers onto the road to ruin:

Discussing the problems of socialist realism, congress participants sharply criticized objectivism — as one of the deviations from socialist realism — and works in which, to a greater or lesser degree, objectivist and naturalistic tendencies were expressed. *The Seasons* by V. Panova and *The Thaw* by I. Ehrenburg. [5]

Timofeyev presented his recipe for Soviet satire: in the past satire had the task of destroying the state system but Soviet satire must reinforce the Soviet state. It is significant that in the first article in the book the Zhdanov decree of August 1946 was described as a measure which had stimulated the normal development of Soviet literature:

The decisions of the Central Committee of the All-Union Communist Party of Bolsheviks of 1946 on literature and art, in summarizing the basic features of the new historical period in the life of the country, set Soviet literature new creative goals. [6]

From the above it may be seen that the inertia of Stalinism continued to influence the Party line on art and literature in 1955. Despite distinct shifts in the system of the dictatorship, the Party in no way changed its attitude toward creative art. Yet this inertia was meeting resistance which evolved spontaneously from life itself.

It should be noted that at this time a fierce struggle was going on in the highest quarters over the leadership of the Party. As a result, Party

---

[4] L. I. Timofeyev (Ed.), *Russkaya sovetskaya literatura* (Russian Soviet Literature), Moscow, 1955, p. 680.

[5] *Ibid.*, p. 681.

[6] *Ibid.*, p. 38.

control over art, and in particular literature, was considerably slackene
The Party leaders quite unjustifiably assumed that the resolutions adopt
by the Second Congress of Soviet Writers would become a program
action for writers. As it turned out, these resolutions had no effect wha
soever, and the congress was quickly followed by the appearance of mo
and more works dealing with controversial problems of Soviet life, i
cluding some which it would have been impossible to broach earlie

It should be added that the official proceedings of the Twentieth Par
Congress held in 1956 did not in themselves provide the impetus f
revelations about the evils of the Stalin period, since the more startli
sections were not published and were accessible only to high-ranki
Party members. Even those writers who had participated in the congre
had no right to refer to the sins of the Stalin period in their works. Neve
theless, many of the secret details at once became known and Khrushche
condemnation of Stalin encouraged the writers to produce works of hither
unprecedented frankness.

The "thaw" now began in earnest. The two main publications in whi
"seditious" works appeared were *Literaturnaya Moskva* and *Novy m*
The editorial board of *Literaturnaya Moskva* gathered together auth
of nation-wide fame: Anna Akhmatova, Konstantin Simonov, A. Tvard
sky, Konstantin Fedin, K. Chukovsky, N. Aseyev, Ilya Ehrenbu
V. Shklovsky, S. Marshak, N. Zabolotsky, Ye. Kazakevich, V. Kaver
M. Aliger, V. Grossman and representatives of the younger generati
such as Yu. Nagibin, A. Yashin, N. Zhdanov, Yevgeny Yevtushenk
and D. Granin.

It was these publications which printed A. Yashin's "Levers," N. Zhe
nov's "A Trip Back Home" and Yu. Nagibin's "Light in the Window" whi
were subsequently subjected to severe criticism. *Literaturnaya Mosk*
also published Ehrenburg's article on "The Poetry of Marina Tsvetayev
which was intended as a foreword to a collection of the poetess' ver
which was in preparation but provoked a number of attacks includi
a special feuilleton in *Krokodil* under the title "The Death Worshipper
after which the collection was published without it.

The most sensational work of this period was Dudintsev's novel *N
by Bread Alone*, published in *Novy mir*.[7] The main feature of this wo
was not so much the detailed description of crude illegality under t
Soviet regime but rather placing on a high pedestal a man not link
with a collective, a lone genius, a man who had in fact set himself agai
the common herd. Another feature of the novel which failed to me
Party requirements was that the positive characters belonged to t
category of pure idealists and, what is more, their idealism had nothing

---

[7] *Novy mir*, 1956, Nos. 8, 9 and 10.

common with Communist ideology which was described in the novel as "bourgeois Communism."

Dudintsev's novel was a major work but hardly possessed glittering artistic qualities. It had no fresh images, critical situations, flights of creative genius or wealth of language. The value of the work was further diminished by the happy ending which took place, incidently, while Stalin was still alive — in 1951. However, the mediocrity of the presentation was redeemed by the fact that the author dealt with many important aspects of Soviet life.

During the same period controversial problems were being dealt with even more boldly in certain briefer works. Here one must refer again to Yashin's short story "Levers" which ran to no more than half a dozen pages. Why is this story so notable? The plot is simple: four Communists in a rural area are criticizing the local leadership at a Party meeting, comparing their quite sincere views on the heartlessness and arrogant attitude of officials to ordinary people. A little while later the local school-mistress arrives and the Party meeting begins. In the course of the meeting, as though a magic wand has been waved over them, these same persons are transformed into heartless petty officials, repeating trite phrases. The significant thing is that as soon as the meeting was over they once again became real people:

> When collective farm chairman Kudryavtsev and farm worker Ivan Konoplev went out of the office into the dark muddy street, the conversation turned again to life, everyday affairs, work — the same as it had been before the meeting . . . And once again they were simple, warm-hearted, upright people — people, and not levers.[8]

These few short pages told the terrible truth of how the Party turns people into soulless dummies, destroys a man's feelings, his thoughts and all manifestations of individuality — in other words precisely what is to be valued in a man.

No less characteristic of the "thaw" period is the short story "A Trip Back Home" by the young writer N. Zhdanov. It is based on a single episode: an important official learns of the death of this mother and leaves the capital for the remote village from which he himself had come. The story centers around the hours which this man spends in his little wooden cottage after the funeral, while he is waiting for a train. He sees the appalling poverty and squalid way of life of a collective farmer. In conversation with the neighbors he learns that all collective farmers are doomed to such a miserable existence. Finally comes the tragic question which is put to him by one neighbor, a friend of his dead nother: "Have

---

[8] *Literaturnaya Moskva*, 1956, No. 2, p. 513.

they done right to us?'' The question goes unanswered, but it and the
entire situation once again underline two terrible truths: the bottomless
gulf that separates the regime and the people, and the absurdity of break-
ing up the way of life of the peasants, a break-up which has not improved
their lot in any way.

These few examples give some idea of the nature of literary works
published during the "thaw" and the reaction they provoked.

One very important event, typical of the emergence of independent
thinking in those years, was the debate on socialist realism which started
in 1956. True, at first it applied only to painting, but it soon spread to
literature too. The term "socialist realism," which is still today inscribed
in the Party commandments, was severely questioned during the "thaw.''
Many venerable practitioners and theoreticians of art expressed the view
that socialist realism, far from being an esthetic concept, was purely
political and therefore had no place in art. There were quite open declara-
tions that the concept must be dispensed with. The attack was so strong that
even Communist theoreticians surrendered to it. Perhaps the best example
was an article published in *Kommunist* under the title "A Book on the
Problem of the Typical in Esthetics." Nominally this was merely a review
of V. A. Razumny's book *The Problem of the Typical in Esthetics*, but
since it was printed in the central Party organ the review became a
directive. In this lengthy article the term "socialist realism" did not
appear once and instead it was stated:

> Until recently in esthetics there was a widely accepted attitude
> that, in creating his work, an artist should first and foremost find an
> essence, a general theme, and only then individual phenomena in
> which to express this essence. This attitude did great damage to our
> art, it encouraged schematic, lifeless works. [9]

The attitude here castigated was, in effect, socialist realism. This was
precisely how it had been interpreted over a long period: proceed from the
general, ignoring individual phenomena. The example given illustrates
how shaky the Party's hallowed requirements had become and how strong
the attack launched by the champions of free creative art was.

On the basis of those works which achieved the greatest popularity
at that time, one may point to the following features of the "thaw"
period: first, the loud protestation about the crying injustice which
prevailed in the country; second, the assertion by a number of authors
that an immense rift had occured between the regime and the people;
and third, the questioning of the viability of socialist realism.

---

[9] *Kommunist*, 1956, No. 7, pp. 101—02.

The first two features, it should be noted, to some extent corresponded with the still secret line of Khrushchev's Central Committee, but the fact remains that, in broaching them, the writers were acting on their own initiative and were not simply adapting themselves to the aims of the new Party leaders. The third feature, on the other hand, was a clear manifestation of opposition to the Party line. Attacks on socialist realism were an act of mutiny, a manifestation of free thought running entirely counter to the fundamental demands of the Party.

The campaign against free thinking in art had already begun by the end of 1956 following the revolts in Hungary and Poland. In 1957 the assault on "sedition" in literature became more resolute, but still took the form of admonitions. In May of that year a number of Party leaders attacked the inadmissible free thinking of writers. With the direct participation of Khrushchev himself the Central Committee condemned the works of such writers as Dudintsev, Yashin, Granin, Yevtushenko, Aliger, Martynov, Kazakevich, Slutsky, Zhdanov and Kaverin.

It should be remembered that this period has been an exceedingly critical one for Khrushchev and his supporters and, as a result, the Party leaders had little time to spare for literary affairs. In June 1957 the struggle for power among the Party hierarchy came to an end with the expulsion from the Central Committee Presidium of Malenkov, Kaganovich, Molotov and Shepilov, and, although it remained a secret at the time, the removal from power of Bulganin, Voroshilov and other prominent figures. This change in the leadership which put Khrushchev in indisputed command, was marked by more resolute action against free thinking in art. Alarmed by the role of the writers in the Hungarian revolution, the new master resolved to restore order on the literary scene. At the end of August, after a delay of three months, Khrushchev's speech "For a Close Link Between Literature and Art and the Life of the People" was published.[10] This was, in effect, a directive for a ruthless and systematic campaign for the subordination of literature to the requirements of the Party and the complete restoration of the subservient role of art.

However, before speaking of the Party campaign against the free thinking of the "thaw" period, mention should be made of certain events which coincided with the "thaw." One of the most important of these was the rehabilitation of many writers, living and dead, who had become "unpersons" under Stalin. Rehabilitations were more often of the dead than the living, but even so did not apply to all of them. In 1957 there appeared a volume of selections from the writings of Babel who had been struck from the list of Soviet writers twenty years before. The collection

---

[10] *Pravda*, August 28, 1957.

ran to 376 pages and contained almost all the main works of the author.[11] The Soviet reader could once again flavor the creative fragrance of this writer, an honest and objective depictor of reality.

At this same time the emigre I. A. Bunin was admitted to the classics of Russian literature. Then too there appeared V. Shklovsky's book *For and Against* on Dostoevsky, whose works, although not suppressed, had long been officially regarded as harmful.[12] However, it must be remembered that a number of writers who had earlier been condemned did not benefit from the amnesty. These included Boris Pilnyak, Panteleymon Romanov, Nikolai Klyuyer, Osip Mandelshtam, Mykola Khvylovy, G. Kosynka and D. Falkovsky.

Although the generally known facts about the struggle for artistic freedom during the "thaw" were linked primarily with the literary organizations in Moscow and Leningrad, the literary revolt was not confined to these centers. The "thaw" was felt to a greater or lesser degree in almost all the Soviet republics. An indication of this can be found in the report of a conference of Georgian writers and artists, at which Georgian Central Committee First Secretary Mzhavanadze spoke of "erroneous tendencies" which had recently emerged in art.[13] He cited V. Gabeskiriya's plays *On the Edge of the Precipice* and *The Snowclad Mountains of Guriya* as examples. In Armenia, Central Committee First Secretary Tovmasyan in a speech to a conference of writers and artists, said:

> Here in Armenia... there have been people who, relying on the erroneous theses of D. Shepilov, have asserted that the Party leadership is hampering the development of literature...[14]

Similar signs of the "unfortunate" state of literature were also noted in Tadzhikistan, Kirgizia and other republics.[15]

Symptomatic of this period was the appearance of contradictory reviews of the same works in various Soviet publications, *Novy mir* for example, published a favorable review by Boris Slutsky of a book by the Kazan poet Rafgat Dovletshin, who writes under the pseudonym of Mikhail Lvov. A month later *Pravda* came out with a devastating review which berated the author and Boris Slutsky in the same breath.[16]

Another notable literary event of this period was the publication outside the Soviet Union of Boris Pasternak's novel *Doctor Zhivago*.

---

11 I. Babel, *Izbrannoye* (Selected Works), Moscow, 1957.
12 V. Shklovskiy, *Za i protiv* (For and Against), Moscow, 1957.
13 *Literaturnaya gazeta*, October 8, 1957.
14 *Kommunist*, Yerevan, December 3, 1957.
15 *Literaturnaya gazeta*, November 19, 1957.
16 *Pravda*, November 24, 1957.

The Party leaders' onslaught on the "seditious" writers was fairly resolute, but the suppression of the "revolt" was only nominal. This is borne out by the proceedings of the Fourth Plenary Session of the Board of the Union of Soviet Writers held in February 1958. S. Smirnov, a member of the editorial board of *Literaturnaya gazeta* speaking of the inflexibility of these writers, said that they had adopted the pose of people who had "not laid down their arms." Thus even jealous supporters of Communist law and order, who had tried to conceal the true situation, were forced to admit that the opposition had not been broken. Evidence of the true situation was provided by the increasing campaign of censure. On March 8, 1958 *Literaturnaya gazeta* accused Ye. Kazakevich of distorting reality in his story "The House on the Square"; on April 3 the same newspaper printed a critique entitled "Living Truth and Poetic Skill," which censured the poets Yevtushenko, Slutsky and Martynov. The February issue of *Inostrannaya literatura* repeatedly attacked Dudintsev, Kaverin and Zhdanov in an article on "Literature and Reality"; on April 8, *Literaturnaya gazeta* printed an article fulminating against Yevtushenko's fourth book of verses. At the Thirteenth Congress of the Komsomol, First Secretary of the Union of Soviet Writers A. Surkov commented pointedly:

> Is it really normal that here in the Moscow organization we have only one poet of Komsomol age and that one is Yevtushenko?[17]

The pressure on free thinking in art assumed various forms. One, for example, was the failure to award any Lenin Prizes for literature in 1958. This was the first such case in the history of state awards. In all preceding years writers had been well represented. Since the institution of the Stalin Prize on December 20, 1939, 2,339 prizes had been awarded for literature and art, between 15 and 20 percent of them for literature. In 1958 it was decided to punish the writers. This is borne out by the Soviet press itself. It was obviously no coincidence that, two days after the announcement of Lenin Prize winners, the critic V. Yermilov published an article in which he said:

> It must now be particularly clear to each of us that the award of a Lenin Prize is at the same time both a form of encouragement and a form of criticism. Today writers have felt this particularly acutely. But such criticism is fatherly, it does not dismay, but provokes a desire to work better, to give of all our strength, to dedicate our talent to the service of Party and people.[18]

---

[17] *Komsomolskaya pravda*, April 20, 1957.
[18] *Sovetskaya Rossiya*, April 24, 1958.

It was during this time that the ideological problems besetting Soviet youth began to receive more attention in the Soviet press. There have been many crises in the Soviet Union, but those of an economic nature — in industry or agriculture — never constituted such an acute danger. If the reorganization of the economic councils or the Machine Tractor Stations did not have the expected effects, at least it was possible to try other experiments and hope for better results. With ideology, however, it is a totally different matter: a crisis in this field cannot be solved by any amount of experiments or unorthodox measures.

The existence of an ideological crisis was mentioned in the Soviet press itself. In June 1958, a *Pravda* editorial referred to the problem. First admitting that

> ... this does not mean that we are already finished with survivals of the past, out-dated views and customs inherited from capitalism.

It went on to sermonize about the "amoral" misdemeanors of certain Soviet young people:

> Among young people there are those who lead an idle life, adopt a disdainful attitude toward manual labor, and worship the glitter of the capitalist world.[19]

All these phenomena were organically linked with the work of young writers who were now frequently expressing independent views. At this point it is fitting to refer to Yevtushenko's book of verse *The Promise* which appeared at the beginning of 1958. The collection began with a "Prologue" in verse, in which the poet expounded his credo:

> Long live travel, and scorching heat
> And greed, triumphant greed!
> Frontiers hamper me . . . I find it awkward
> Not to know Buenos Aires, New York,
> I want to roam to my heart's content around London,
> To talk to everyone, even if it be in broken speech!
> Like a child, hanging over the side of a bus,
> I want to drive through early morning Paris!
> I want art — as varied as I![20]

The poet has discarded the materialistic approach to life, he has his own concept of life and expresses this concept in his verses:

> History is not just wars,
> Inventions and toil;
> It is smells and sounds too,
> And the tremor of boughs and grass.[21]

---

[19] *Pravda*, June 15, 1958.

[20] Ye. Yevtushenko, *Obeshchaniye* (The Promise), Moscow, 1957, p. 6.

[21] *Ibid.*, p. 20.

In Yevtushenko's poetry one finds very specific references to people who have returned from concentration camps. To one of them he devotes a poem in which the prisoner of yesterday is depicted thus:

> Avidly he listens to the radio,
> Pores through the press.
> Everything in him breathes character
> And buzzes with interest. [22]

It is significant that in the last line of this poem the poet says of himself that he fears nothing. Yevtushenko's credo is particularly clearly underlined in a short verse about a little boy with an apple in his hand who follows up every rustle of life and has his own great destiny. It is clear that the poet is posing the problem of the new generation which desires to build its life in its own way, not as somebody lays down. He foresees a serious collision between this younger generation and its predecessors:

> But I dread the moment
> When, realizing its rights,
> It will rise, recognized, over the world
> And utter new words. [23]

The zealous champions of law and order he treats virtually as personal enemies:

> Many do not like me,
> Blaming me for much,
> And brandish thunderbolts
> On my account.
> Sullen and splitting their sides
> They laugh at me,
> And their unkind glances
> I feel on my back.
> But all this pleases me.
> I am proud
> That they do not hit it off with me,
> There's nothing they can do. [24]

In another case he inveighs with great assurance against orthodox Communists, likening them to the Greeks at Troy who gave praise and gifts to gain their end, although they were concealing brickbats under their cloaks.

---

[22] *Ibid.*, p. 21.
[23] *Ibid.*, p. 36.
[24] *Ibid.*, p. 25.

> Let the spleen lie in your entrails,
> Let them condemn you and upbraid you,
> But let them not buy you with their honors,
> Prevail on you with comfort . . .[25]

Some lines in his poems may even be interpreted as a call to revolt. To judge from his writings, the poet regards as personal enemies those who adhere to the officially approved pattern in art and life. Naturally the Party could not pass lightly over such mutinous poetry. *Literaturnaya gazeta* published an article by the critic A. Dymshits in which he said:

> This book has already been subjected to serious and businesslike criticism in the press. But in order to speak of it with journalistic enthusiasm it was necessary to go beyond its limits and turn one's thoughts to those whose attitudes the poet has been trying to express in a number of his verses. Then it would be clear that Ye. Yevtushenko is far from being alone in his views, that he is spiritually linked with a small, but sufficiently unpleasant stratum of variously disposed young people who think not so much of what they can give society as of what they can take from it.[26]

In this article the "Prologue" was subjected to a detailed critique and Yevtushenko himself was scornfully compared with the poet Igor Severyanin. In the tones of a prosecuting counsel the critic came down upon the poet for setting at the center of many of his works a character unacceptable in a socialist society. In addition the poet was accused of decadence, of taking an individualistic view of the world, and of glorifying negative human traits.

> Indeed, such poems of Ye. Yevtushenko as the "Prologue" and the like deserve not simply critical appraisal, but a heated journalistic rebuff, angry and harsh words.[27]

But Yevgeny Yevtushenko and his poetry were far from being isolated phenomena at this period. Almost simultaneously the voices of poets A. Voznesensky, R. Rozhdestvensky, B. Akhmadulina, B. Slutsky, B. Okudzhava and others of the younger generation rang out. The eve of the sixties was marked by a mass influx of young writers. The only parallel had been forty years before when, seized by revolutionary romanticism, such poets and prose writers as A. Fadeyev, M. Svetlov, M. Golodny, I. Utkin, V. Katayev, A. Bezymensky, S. Kirsanov, I. Katayev, I. Ilf, Ye. Petrov, E. Bagritsky and Yu. Olesha crossed the literary threshold.

---

[25] *Ibid.*, p. 42.
[26] *Literaturnaya gazeta*, July 12, 1958.
[27] *Ibid.*

These set up literary organizations which competed quite legally with those of the recognized masters of the time. But, we would repeat, these young writers were moved by revolutionary romanticism, whereas those who have emerged in the last few years have quite a different orientation. First, however, one must remark on their numbers. To the list of poets already mentioned may be added the names of V. Kostrov, G. Kalinovsky, V. Korzhikov, R. Kazakova, S. Sorin and N. Solntseva. Young prose writers are no less well represented: V. Aksyonov, A. Kuznetsov, E. Shim, Yu. Shcherbak, Ye. Shatko, Yu. Semeyonov, M. Rozovsky, A. Gladilin, V. Alminsky, I. Zverev, N. Dolinina, Yu. Kazakov. The younger generation has also produced a literary critic, Stanislav Rassadin, who has introduced fresh ideas into this aspect of literature.

A further notable fact is that the majority of these young writers have had a full and thorough education. Some of them have graduated from literary institutes and many are representatives of the professions: Aksyonov is a doctor, Kostrov a chemical engineer, Dolinina a teacher, Rozovsky an art scholar, Shcherbak a doctor, and Kuznetsov a constructional engineer.

The young writers began to express new attitudes at times quite unexpected in Soviet society. Nikolai Ageyev, for example, wrote a poem, "Lights on the Chusovaya," in which the hero was a peasant who had fought against Kolchak in the Civil War but returned home to the Urals with the dream of setting up his own one-man farm. A lengthy review of the poem in *Znamya*, showed that the reviewer was puzzled as to how to assess such an unexpected plot. [28]

Of course, by no means all writers became "rebels." Many continued to write in the same spirit as before. Free thinking was rarely to be observed among the elder generation who had so recently witnessed the disappearance and liquidation of so many of their colleagues. But a group of more flexible and adaptable writers did emerge who set about producing works designed to reflect the new leadership by the simple device of introducing heroes somewhat reminiscent of Khrushchev. The first to do this was that most adept of Soviet writers A. Korneychuk. His specially written play *Wings*, which appeared in 1954, portrayed the leader of an oblast Party organization, a countryman whose sister still worked on a collective farm. This character was made to express views which Khrushchev had already expounded in speeches. In 1956 the disgraced N. Virta, who had been expelled from the Union of Writers, published a long novel, the basic aim of which was to show how the change in the Party leadership was leading to changes in a collective farm village which had previously been in a perilous state. With his great artistic flair and an adequate sense

[28] *Znamya*, 1958, No. 1.

of proportion, Virta succeeded in making his novel absorbing to read and fashioned it in such a manner that the first two-thirds could be interpreted as a daring criticism of collectivization.

It is significant that such a writer as Mikhail Sholokhov, who had spoken out so boldly at the Second Congress of Soviet Writers and was perhaps even the unwitting cause of Fadeyev's suicide, proved unequal to the occasion when the opportunity occurred for asserting creative freedom. His novel *They Fought for the Fatherland* was published in 1959. It should be remembered that in the previous year Sholokov's name had been put forward for the Nobel Prize. He was deliberately sent on a tour of the Scandinavian countries, but in vain: the Nobel Prize was awarded to Pasternak. In order to provide Sholokhov with publicity, Khrushchev had himself visited the Cossack village of Veshenskaya where he lived in September 1959 and invited the writer to accompany him on his tour of the United States. For two weeks *Literaturnaya gazeta* recited all the compliments paid Sholokhov by Khrushchev and even printed a long lead article entitled "An Artist Who Has Enriched the World."[29]

Yet the novel *They Fought for the Fatherland* in no way enhanced the reputation of this undoubtedly gifted writer. Despite its protracted gestation period, it made a very poor impression. There is no justification for example, for the opening which deals with an agronomist whose family life is unhappy. The author then jumps from the spring of 1941 to August 1942 and shows the agronomist as an ordinary soldier in a defeated regiment. The theme of the book as a whole is the story of the remnant of this regiment whose numbers are reduced during a fighting retreat in the Don steppes from 170 to 27 men. Battle episodes are described in order to illustrate the valor of Soviet officers and enlisted men, their devotion to their country, etc. A novel can, of course, be built out of such material, but the trouble is that the battle episodes are only incidental. Far more space is devoted to humorous little scenes and inconsequential stories. There are jokes, anecdotes, humorous situations and deliberate caricatures, but there is hardly a page on which the author does not lower the artistry of his work by overloading it with clumsy and crude witticisms. A soldier, for instance, speaks of his wife who is somewhere in the country:

Woman is an awfully cunning animal, I know them, old boy. See the scar on my upper lip? That happened last year. On the First of May my fellow combine operators and I decided to have a binge . . . But my wife is like a German tommy-gunner: if she loads — she doesn't stop shooting till all the belts are empty, and what's more she tends to use brute force.

---

[29] *Literaturnaya gazeta*, September 5, 1959.

Nine pages are devoted to the rather nasty story of how the wife flung a plate at her husband and bloodied his face. Sholokhov depicts the comradely feelings of these doomed warriors thus:

> If need be, I can give you a pair of shiners, but for now don't you cuddle up too close to me; I'm not your cow and you're not my calf, get it?

Throughout the book deliberate emphasis is laid on the boorish, leg-pulling relations between one man and another, despite the fact that this little group of men is closely bound by front-line experience, a feeling of solidarity and, may be, sacrifice. Of course it is not difficult to guess that it was the author's intention that the outward boorishness should serve as evidence of an underlying warmth, but he has lost his sense of proportion.

Sholokhov's literary decline was also evident in the second volume of his novel *Virgin Soil Upturned*, although this work was awarded a Lenin Prize.[30] This novel, on which the author worked for some 30 years, cannot be compared with his first great, original and talented *And Quiet Flows the Don*. Perhaps the main fault of the new book is that the author conceived the idea of portraying a Party leader resembling Khrushchev and as a result produced a stilted image of the local Party committee secretary Nesterenko. Before sunrise one day this secretary turns up at the tractor driver's field shelter where he kindles a fire for the collective farm cook, helps her peel the potatoes and makes a lot of meaningless conversation interlaced with salty jokes. Later Nesterenko cuts an even stranger figure. While walking around a ploughed field with the collective farm chairman he suddenly cries out eagerly and thumps the latter on the shoulder.

> The latter reeled and did not at first realize that he was being challenged to a wrestle, but when the laughing Nesterenko pushed him again hard Davydov planted his feet wide apart and leant slightly forward.
>
> They wrestled, seeking to grip one another by the belt.
>
> "By the belts or how?" asked Nesterenko, restraining his breathing.

For ten minutes on end these two adults, occupying responsible posts, wrestle with one another in front of the cook like ten-year olds. One can only wonder why the author could not have found some other way to portray these officials. Moreover he seems to have forgotten that this episode is supposed to take place at the beginning of the thirties when officials of the Stalin school, including minor ones, were doing everything in their power to give an impression of dignity. Thus in one absurd and

---

[30] *Oktyabr*, 1960, Nos. 2, 3 and 4.

contrived scene the author twice defies reality merely in order to endow
his new leader with some of Khrushchev's attributes.

There is also an absurdly simplified portrayal of an open Party meeting
at which old man Shchukar challenges collective farmer Kondrat who has
made an application for Party membership. Shchukar's speech begins
like this:

> Dear citizens and old women! I am going to give Kondrat a good
> thrashing! I am not like the others: with me friendship is friendship,
> but business is something quite different.

The old man's nonsensical speech goes on for nearly ten pages and
ends with the proposal that Kondrat be admitted to the Party. All this is
done to demonstrate the democratic nature of the Communist system and
the close links between Communists and the people. The deaths of the two
collective farm leaders are presented as being highly heroic and it is
concluded that their job, that is forcible collectivization, by reason of
their deaths, assumes great vitality and that the people are imbued with
love of Communists. In the last chapter of the book the same Shchukar
is sentimentally pictured thus:

> The graves of Davydov and Nagulny, enclosed by a low fence,
> were not far away, opposite the village store, and on the following
> day, equipped with an axe and saw, old man Shchukar fitted up a
> little bench beside the fence round the graves. There he began to sit
> through the nights.

This line is far too obviously rammed home in the novel, but far from
being a disadvantage it helped the book to gain very favorable reviews in
the Soviet Union.

These last works of Sholokhov have been dealt with at length only in
order to show more clearly the rift that took place at the beginning of the
sixties between those writers who saw in Khrushchev's leadership a final
rational starting point, an outlet onto an open road, and those who at that
same juncture launched the campaign for creative freedom.

This division into two camps was particularly marked at the time of
the Third Congress of Soviet Writers which outwardly went off very well.
Yet this congress coincided with a number of events which far from
corresponded with the official Party line of the congress. K. Paustovsky,
who did not speak at the congress, published an article in *Literaturnaya
gazeta* in which he spoke of the alternative paths the congress might
follow:

> The writers' congress is in session. Will it endorse for writers that
> free and manly creative drive which alone can create the greatest

of the literatures of our century — Soviet literature. Or will the congress engage in petty tutelage over writers and old conflicts. If the latter, it will do no good. It is necessary once and for all to stop calling friends enemies solely because they speak unpleasant truths, refuse to be hypocrites and, being supremely devoted to their people and country, do not demand a monopoly on this devotion and ask no regard for this.[31]

Paustovsky went on to speak of the abnormalities and sickness in literature:

It is impossible for those who attempt to combine service to half truths and half lies with service to their own welfare to exist in literature. Perhaps we shout so often and so loudly about truth in literature precisely because we do not have enough of it.[32]

With bitterness and puzzlement he asked:

Why are people permitted into literature and even admitted to the Union of Writers who do not know the Russian language and are quite indifferent to it? Why do we put up with the barrenness of bureaucratic and philistine language with its poverty and phonetic ugliness? By what right do we throw out into the backyard the classical and powerful speech created by generations of our great predecessors?[33]

This is an SOS, an appeal to save the Russian language, put forward as the next question on the agenda for artists.

Paustovsky also expressed his personal views on writers of the younger generation. It may be remembered that, as a penalty for disobedience in the form of "seditious" works, young writers were hardly represented at the congress: of 497 delegates only three were under 30 years of age. The dissatisfaction of the young writers had been emphasized frequently in the press before the congress, but Paustovsky found sufficient courage to state in his article:

There is a new generation. And a fine new generation... There are Yuri Kazakov, Sergei Nikitin, Nataliya Tarasenkova, Vladimir Tendrya-kov, Yury Trifonov, Richi Dostyan, Yuri Bondarev, Iosif Dyk, and a long list of other young writers.[34]

Not content with mentioning many names, he went on to stress that there was no need to panic because of the militant fervor of the young masters — this youthful fervor was useful.

---

[31] *Literaturnaya gazeta*, May 20, 1959.
[32] *Ibid.*
[33] *Ibid.*
[34] *Ibid.*

Another unscheduled contribution hardly in line with the spirit of the congress was an article by Ilya Ehrenburg entitled "Rereading Chekhov."[35] Referring to the basic principles of art, Ehrenburg stressed that it was possible to observe in contemporary works a "painstaking of colors, a diversity of nuances. The word 'realism' means nothing in itself..."

A critical article by V. Nekrasov, which appeared while the congress was in session, also had a direct bearing on the established image of Soviet literature. True the article was written about the film *Poem of the Sea* by A. Dovzhenko who was posthumously awarded a Lenin Prize three weeks before the opening of the congress, but nevertheless Nekrasov's remarks may perhaps be said to be even more pertinent to literature

> ... against the background of a mighty construction project move conventional people, symbolizing a specific idea, not doing very much but talking a lot, or to be more exact, thinking aloud in conventional journalistic language... [36]

The Soviet leaders quickly reacted to these views expressed behind the scenes and outside the congress. The official press charged that Nekrasov's inability to believe in the sincerity of romantic enthusiasm was a result of spiritual limitations and the blunting of his emotions.

A. Dymshits, one of the most ardent champions of socialist realism, assailed Ehrenburg on the following counts: he took too narrow a view of the aims of literature: he said nothing of the positive aspects of Soviet literature objectively; and, finally, he regretted that the word "inspiration" had been buried to no avail.

V. Kochetov countered Paustovsky's article with a lengthy one of his own in which he indignantly stated:

> So, we have not enough truth. This thesis will be forty-two years old in the fall. Earlier we used to get very incensed when our literature was accused of untruths. In 1956—57 Soviet writers fought uncompromisingly against this continually recurring thesis — fought because international revisionism sought to use it as a weapon for sallies and attacks against us. [37]

Kochetov's entire article was an attempt to prove that Paustovsky's assertion regarding the untruths in the works of many Soviet writers was itself "a complete untruth." It was particularly notable that he applied to Paustovsky's speech that most vicious of contemporary labels — revisionism.

---

[35] *Novy mir*, 1959, Nos. 5 and 6.
[36] *Iskusstvo kino*, 1959, No. 5.
[37] *Literatura i zhizn*, June 19, 1959.

Despite the strictly Party character of the Third Congress of Writers and the dutiful resolutions it passed, there quickly appeared more and more works which earned severe censure from official critics. There was Grigori Baklanov's *An Inch of Land* which related how a small band of soldiers carried on when cut off from the main army.[38] A feature of this work was the absence of the heroic line. The characters are ordinary people who know what fear is and are not inspired by political slogans. Their main traits are an instinct for self-preservation and a desire to live and escape from their dire situation. Of course this was utterly at variance with the official image of Soviet patriotism and the loudly proclaimed valor of Soviet fighting men. At the time of its publication the story passed without comment, but much later both *Literaturnaya gazeta* and *Molodaya gvardiya* came down upon it in unison.[39]

In September 1959, the journal *Neva* published a short story by its chief editor Sergei Voronin, "In Native Parts." The story consists of just one episode: a former Red Army soldier, Ivan Kasimov, learns that a childhood friend, Vasili Nikitin, is working in a neighboring village as a brigade leader on a collective farm. The trouble is that Kasimov believes that while he was a prisoner of the Germans he had seen his former comrade in German uniform among the guards. The meeting of the two takes place on the edge of a forest and Kasimov's suspicions are confirmed: today's brigade leader on the collective farm had, in order to save his life, served with the Germans. The conversation was difficult for both of them, and when Kasimov was alone again he at first did not know what he should do: reveal the secret or remain silent. The writer describes this trying moment:

> Later, climbing up to the top of a small hill, he looked round. And froze. Before him, everywhere as far as his eyes could see, lay a land beautiful in its peacefulness, clad in green and bathed in sunlight with the blue water, the pensive forest and an endless road winding among the fields. And along this road, the reins loose in his hands and his back bent, Vasili slowly rode.

> "No, there is nothing to be done..." thought Ivan as he turned to make his way home. "It can't be easy for him. Every day must be a torture..."[40]

The story deals only with the human aspects, human feelings. It is not surprising that Kasinov's final decision not to interfere with another's life is linked with the natural beauty around him. This short tale provoked

---

[38] *Novy mir*, 1959, Nos. 5 and 6.
[39] *Literaturnaya gazeta*, March 26, 1960; *Molodaya gvardiya*, 1960, No. 3.
[40] *Neva*, Leningrad, 1959, No. 9.

several derogatory articles and a meeting of all the Communist writers in Leningrad was held at which Voronin was censured.

The beginning of the sixties was mainly notable for considerable activity on the part of younger writers. A. Kuznetsov's "Continuation of a Legend" appeared, Inna Gof published a story "A Poet You Need Not Be," and Nikolai Dementyev his "I Go into Life." In addition there were frequent verse contributions from Yevtushenko, Slutsky, Voznesensky and Rozhdestvensky. These works were published for the most part in *Yunost* which by this time had gained great popularity and had become a mouthpiece for the views of the younger generation. In most of the works the hero was a young person for whom truth comes first, who refuses to accept any, including Party, authorities and is unwilling to build his or her life according to any prescribed pattern.

At about this time much comment was aroused by V. Aksyonov's novel "A Ticket to the Stars" which portrayed a group of seventeen-year olds who had just left secondary school. Their disillusionment with life around them begins within their families. They reject the ideals by which their parents live, although the latter are irreproachable Soviet citizens. As the story proceeds, the scope of their protest becomes greater: the youngsters are unwilling to come to terms with the social standards which are prescribed in a Communist society. These "disturbers of the peace" reinforce their words with deeds: they leave home, refuse to conform to any regulations and stop at nothing to reach their goals. Their revolt derives not from childish enthusiasm but from the power of their organic strivings for independence. Here is part of a conversation they have on the eve of their leaving school:

> Galya: Just imagine, boys, mother told me: either medical school or into a factory.
>
> Alik: Parents cannot understand that their humdrum interests don't go down with us...
>
> Yurka: My old man has already thought it all out. He's little hope that I'll get in, so he's already found me a place for the production stage. Apprentice turner in some factory. Like hell I'm going there. What do you think of that — apprentice turner![41]

The most colorful member of the group is Dimka who has no desire to be "a kid carrying out someone else's decisions." It is very significant that Dimka's elder brother, a young scientist, practically shares his younger brother's aspirations, or at any rate takes a favorable view of them. These youngsters do have their faults: the illogicality of their behavior, their sometimes unconsidered actions and the fact that among themselves they

---

[41] *Yunost*, 1961, No. 6, p. 10.

use outlandish slang. However, it is clear from the novel that the latter is not due to their attraction to the underworld but is merely an expression of their rejection of all strict canons. In the end they use their modest savings to leave Moscow and go as far west as possible — to Tallinn. This move reflects their attraction to the West; it is no coincidence that, on the train journey to the Baltic coast, they buy not Soviet newspapers, but English, French, German and Italian ones. They use a great number of foreign colloquial expressions, mainly common American ones, and call themselves "Soviet supermen."

In the numerous condemnations of the novel all these seventeen-year olds are placed in the dock together with their creator. Their crime is formulated by the critic M. Gus as follows:

> The only thing we learn from the novel is of Dimka's aspiration "to live his own life." "It is better to be a vagabond and suffer failure than to spend one's whole life a child carrying out other people's decisions," declares Dimka... [42]

The critic preaches that "to live one's own life" is impermissible in the age of the construction of Communism. It is only necessary to carry out the orders issued by the infallible leaders. Heroes should go to the Virgin Lands, to work on the construction of the Bratsk Hydroelectric Station, to Siberia, Kamchatka or the Kulunda Steppe, not to the west where young people are never compulsorily sent.

Another hero of the same mold is to be found in V. Rozov's *A, B, C, D, E*, likewise a youngster just out of secondary school. This obstinate and tenacious young man is unwilling to accept any kind of authority and seeks to do everything his own way.

The hero of Vilyam Kozlov's story "An Awkward Fellow" is also a rebel and on leaving home, even changes his name because, as he says:

> I had an unusual name too: Kim (Communist Youth International). And what sort of International am I? [43]

The youngster christened himself Maksim, left his parents (his father was a Party member of many years standing), took a hard manual job and later began to study.

In Yu. Shevkunenko's play *Seryozhka from Malaya Bronnaya* the central figure is also a young man with an independent nature.

In another play, *The Adventures of Krosh*, A. Rybakov describes his hero thus:

---

[42] *Oktyabr*, 1961, No. 12.
[43] *Neva*, 1962, No. 7, p. 18.

An untiring defender of justice and a constant victim of inex-
perience of the world, he is for ever ending up in funny situations,
always with the same craving for justice and a desire to defend it.[44]

The list of such works is fairly long and in each of them the heroes —
young Soviet citizens — are portrayed to a greater or lesser degree as disturbers of the peace. The young writers have in general proved extremely
restless. They pay no heed to the strictures of their critics and even
ignore directives from the highest quarters. This independent attitude
was still quite clearly expressed by the young poet Boris Slutsky even after
numerous moral admonitions and harsh judgements of his work:

> We have been innovators since childhood,
> We look back but rarely.
> Ourselves founders,
> Ourselves forerunners.[45]

Young people in revolt are also to be found in works not entirely concerned with the problem of youth. A particularly notable example of this
is D. Granin's novel *I Go into the Storm*.[46] Apart from venerable academicians and officials the characters include young scientists who have just
graduated. The spirit of revolt is typified by one small episode which
centers around a young man, Richard:

> In the spring they went to an exhibition of Polish art. In front of the
> paintings by abstractionists, people were arguing noisily. Naturally
> Richard quickly intervened, arguing that realism was out of date, that
> the progressives were out of date. Of course the orthodox threw them-
> selves upon him, demanding that he explain what these circles and
> blots signified, and he of course answered that they signified nothing,
> that one must be mature in order to understand modern art, that it was
> impossible to translate music into words — try explaining to a blind
> man what color is. This painting reflects modern physics — for the atom
> there is no difference between a chair and a stool, the world has
> become richer, more complex. They yelled at him: And what about
> Repin? And he shouted back: Your Repin is an old hat!
>
> He happily began a row with these cave men.[47]

But the reason for this row and Richard's eager defense of abstract
art is explained a little later when, as they leave the museum, the girl with
him timidly admits that she had not understood anything.

---

[44] *Teatr*, 1961, No. 9.
[45] *Yunost*, 1962, No. 2.
[46] *Znamya*, 1962, Nos. 8, 9 and 10.
[47] *Ibid.*, 1962, No. 9, p. 90.

"Neither did I," said Richard.

"Then why did you defend them?"

"Revolt! And why should they suppress them? Let me make my own choice."[48]

The beginning of the sixties was marked by the reemergence of a literary phenomenon which, it was thought, had been stamped out thirty years before. This was *poputnichestvo* or fellow-travelling, which was a fundamental feature of literary life in the early days of the Soviet regime and whose exponents including the leading writers of the time. Indeed, the main literary organizations — The Serapion Brothers, The Circle (Krug), and The Pass (Pereval) — consisted for the most part of *poputchiki* (fellow travellers). The term originated with Trotsky who used it to describe writers who did not subscribe to Communist ideology and interpreted the revolution in their own way. The principal characteristics of the *poputchiki* were their independent views on social problems and their great ability. When they issued their decree demanding socialist realism in all forms of art the Party leaders outlawed *poputnichestvo*. Many of the *poputchiki* were physically eliminated, some of those who survived were deprived of any chance of appearing in print, and a third group were forced to change their ways and subordinate their art to Party requirements.

The reemergence of *poputnichestvo* has been most evident in "People, Years, Life" by Ilya Ehrenburg, one of the most prominent *poputchiki* of the twenties. This autobiographical epic was begun in 1960, the first chapter appearing in the August issue of *Novy mir* which has continued to publish subsequent installments over a period of nearly three years. The autobiography is interspersed with lengthy digressions on the fate of many of the author's contemporaries, on his views on art, political events and the West, which he probably knows better than any other Soviet writer. The spirit of *poputnichestvo* in the work is most evident in that Ehrenburg's views are in no way compatible with the demands of socialist realism and Party aims. His assessments of individuals bear no relation to those of the Party. He recalls Professor F. A. Stepun, for instance, in the most benevolent manner:

> Savinkov introduced me to F. A. Stepun. I knew that Stepun was a philosopher, that he had written an interesting book *Letters of an Ensign*, in which he described war without any of the customary embellishments. I just could not picture him carrying out the duties of the political administration of a war ministry. His face was more that of a dreamer or a parson.[49]

---

[48] *Ibid.*

[49] *Novy mir*, 1961, No. 1, p. 93.

This meeting took place in the middle of 1917 before the October Revolution. Later Stepun emigrated from the Soviet Union and his name could no longer be mentioned in the Soviet press.

Ignoring the views of the Party, Ehrenburg recalls, not merely sympathetically but even lovingly, Osip Mandelshtam, Boris Pilnyak, Aleksei Remizov, Sergei Efron, Maximilian Voloshin, V. F. Khodasevich, Nabokov-Sirin and, in particular, Boris Pasternak. His references to the latter relate to precisely that period when the author of *Doctor Zhivago* was being labeled by the highest authorities as a traitor and enemy of the Russian people. Ehrenburg, however, said of him:

> I loved him, I loved and still love his poetry: of all the poets whom I have met he was the most tongue-tripping, the closest to the musical element, the most attractive . . . [50]

Moreover it should be borne in mind that this declaration, which appeared in print in February 1961, must have been made considerably earlier since the preparation of material for an issue of a journal is carried out at least two months before publication. It is not so startling that Ehrenburg should have dealt with the horrors of the Stalin period — after all by this time de-Stalinization had been legalized. What is far more significant is that the author should have expressed his independent views on such subjects as abstract art and the work of many Western writers and artists who are officially regarded in the Soviet Union as "bourgeois," harmful and decadent. In this case he had directly defied the official Soviet standpoint. It is also significant that he should state he considered the best of his own works to be *Julio Jurenito*, the one which is most clearly representative of *poputnichestvo*.

The reemerging trend toward *poputnichestvo* is very evident in Paustovsky's autobiographical *Story of Life* which has appeared in separate volumes covering specific periods.

Among writers of the younger generation the traditions of *poputnichestvo* have been revived by Viktor Nekrasov, Vladimir Tendryakov, Aleksandr Yashin and Yuri Nagibin. In Nekrasov's *Kira Georgievna*,[51] the two central characters are a man, who has returned from many years confinement in a Soviet concentration camp, and his former wife, a gifted sculptress who sometimes behaves in a scatter-brained fashion and makes mistakes but is constantly guided by the inclinations of her heart. The story was published without arousing comment, but eighteen months later criticism was leveled against both the heroine and the author. Nekrasov expressed his independent views particularly boldly in his travel

---

[50] *Ibid.*, 1961, No. 2, p. 87.
[51] *Ibid.*, 1961, No. 6.

impressions *On Both Sides of the Ocean* which provided an objective portrayal of America and praised the art which Party critics label "bourgeois."[52]

V. Tendryakov's stories *An Extraordinary Event, The Trial* and *Short Circuit* also belong to the category of works not customarily printed in the Soviet Union. The first of these tells of a tenth grade schoolgirl Lobkova, the daughter of a Party committee official, who believes in God.[53] The mathematics teacher is also a believer and these two facts develop into a critical situation because both of them stand up for their convictions. At a most unusual debate held at the school two motions are put forward: one is advanced by the "physicists," those who have a materialistic outlook, the other by the "lyricists," who hold that the most important thing in man is his spiritual world. Teachers and pupils cast written votes for one or other of the motions. The "lyricists" win, from which it may be concluded that, given freedom of choice, the majority supports an idealistic outlook.

An equally controversial situation is the theme of *The Trial*. Three men, an experienced bear hunter, a high official and a country medical officer (*feldsher*), are engaged in a bear hunt at night when one of their shots accidentally kills a man who wanders into the forest. The old hunter determines from the bullet extracted from the bear's carcass that the official is responsible for the man's death and tells him so. Subsequently, however, the blame falls on the medical officer. Apart from the hunter nobody knows the truth and he can no longer prove it because he has melted down the bullet taken from the animal so it cannot be used as evidence. The plot of the story is built around the struggle taking place inside the hunter's mind: should he stick to the truth, which he could no longer prove, or should he give what he knows to be false evidence. After a long struggle he chooses the latter course, going against his conscience. The decision is forced upon him by fear of being himself charged with perjury as the examining magistrate tells him he might be.

In *Short Circuit* Tendryakov returns to a similar theme the story of a power station director who makes a scapegoat of a subordinate colleague with whom he had worked for many years in order to save his own reputation after an accident at the plant.

A further new departure in Soviet literature is the de-Stalinization theme which has emerged only since the Twenty-Second Party Congress. The January 1962 issue of *Znamya* published the first installment of M. Zhestev's "Tatyana Tarkhanova" which described for the first time forcible collectivization and the expropriation of independent peasants' property which was an essential adjunct of this "reform." The novel describes how

---

[52] *Ibid.*, 1962, Nos. 10 and 11.
[53] *Nauka i religiya*, 1961, Nos. 7, 9 and 10.

one night some of the peasants classified as kulaks were removed under guard from the hamlet of Pukhlyaka:

> Armed with carbines and clad in sheepskin coats, riders guarded the snake as it wound its way through the snow so that it did not slither off anywhere. How simply, how ordinarily these people left their homes and all their property for ever .... And in this ordinariness lay their whole tragedy. Not the slightest hope was left. The force which compelled them to cast off their native villages and take to the distant road was too strong. In the face of this force it was senseless to moan and weep, it was useless to oppose it, resistance to it only threatened destruction.[54]

The writer even permits doubts to assail those carrying out the deportations, the Communists guarding the hapless peasants. One of them is shown as asking himself:

> Perhaps it would have been warning enough to deport half a dozen of the rich ones.[55]

Throughout the novel there are two main themes: the expropriation of independent peasants' property and the natural yearning of the peasant for his land and his own farm.

Hard on the heels of "Tatyana Tarkhanova" came Yuri Bondarev's "Tishina."[56] This dealt with several thorny questions, but first and foremost the situation of millions of men who fought at the front, spilt their blood, sought and won victory, and then returned home to civilian life. The hero of the novel is one of these millions, a Captain Sergei Vekhmintsev who had been wounded three times, had received several decorations and returned to Moscow in the winter of 1945. By this time, however, those who had won the war were of no use to anyone, nobody worried about them, and the authorities were only interested in wearing down their independent spirit. Of the many episodes illustrating the lawlessness and injustice of the time the most vivid is the sudden arrest of Sergei's father, who has been denounced as a Trotskyite. This takes place in 1950 when the hero is about to graduate from a mining institute. The author convincingly strips the covers from Soviet reality, portrays the triumph of arbitrariness, the whole horror of which is expressed in one line from a letter written by Sergei's convicted father from prison: "Be strong and do not grieve. Death is not the most terrible thing."[57]

---

[54] *Zvezda*, 1962, No. 1, p. 14.
[55] *Ibid.*, p. 15.
[56] *Novy mir*, 1962, Nos. 3, 4 and 5.
[57] *Ibid.*, 1962, No. 5, p. 82.

However the tragedy is not at an end. Sergei is expelled from the Party and then from the mining institute. He is unable to get a job in Moscow and is forced to give up everything and go off to Karaganda in the hope of finding a laboring job there. The title of the novel has three meanings: first Tishina is the name of the Zamoskvorechye market where the heroes of yesterday acquire the means for subsistence; second, *tishina* means the peace of the postwar period; third and most important, it means the silence resulting from fear and solitude, when a man is abandoned by everyone and left defenseless.

A work linked with de-Stalinization of particular note is V. Tevekelyan's "Granite Does Not Melt."[58] This deals with the Chekists, the men who were the instruments of Stalin's maniacal malevolence. Without a thought for what they were doing, they arrested totally innocent people and unscrupulously sent them to their destruction. The thought occurs to the hero of the novel:

> Is it possible that these men . . . never experience pangs of conscience, or do they even have consciences? No here it is not just a matter of conscience! Power is a dangerous thing, especially if it is in the hands of a man who is not very clever and, as a result, conceited. Power turns the head. A person fond of power loses the capacity to think objectively and is all too willing to believe in his own infallibility.[59]

Overall, 1962 may go down in the history of Soviet literature as the year which was marked by a series of works on de-Stalinization. It would not be sufficient to attribute this solely to the effect of the resolutions passed at the Twenty-Second Party Congress. Although the public dethronement of Stalin undoubtedly increased legal opportunities for revealing the facts about the terror, another reason was certainly the spontaneous mass demand for truth which had manifested itself in the Soviet Union.

Without question the most exciting of these works was "One Day in the Life of Ivan Denisovich" by a new writer Aleksander Solzhenitsyn.[60] It skillfully describes life in a Soviet concentration camp, a subject with which no Soviet writer before Solzhenitsyn had dealt. The author had himself been one of the many million victims of Soviet lawlessness. Born in Rostov-on-Don, the son of a teacher, he entered Rostov University, but volunteered for the army at the beginning of the war. He served at the front as an artillery officer, being twice decorated, but even before the war was over in 1945 he was imprisoned in a special camp where he spent eight years. However the story is not autobiographical. Solzhenitsyn does not write about himself but portrays the camp through the eyes of his hero,

---

[58] *Moskva*, 1962, Nos. 2, 3 and 4.
[59] *Ibid.*, 1962, No. 4, p. 84.
[60] *Novy mir*, 1962, No. 11.

Ivan Denisovich Shukhov, an honest and hard-working peasant who in 1941 was convicted for reasons unknown as a traitor to his country. The story describes one day in January 1951 — fourteen or fifteen hours in the lives of people doomed to what is virtually a permanent fate. There are no shootings or torture but just the description of a long, dreary day filled with unforgettable episodes and details which show how the systematic, endless punishment of innocent people took place at every step. Most of the characters in the novel have not only committed no crime, but are patriots and in some cases loyal Communists.

It is a virtue of this story that the author does not descend into melodrama. There are no tears, no complaints, no appeals to anyone; with courage and sparing use of words he drily recounts the shocking truth, using a narrative form in which he achieves a high degree of skill . . .

De-Stalinization found its way into all *genres* of Soviet literature, including poetry where the most prominent example was Yevtushenko's "Heirs of Stalin," published on the first anniversary of the removal of Stalin's embalmed body from the mausoleum on Red Square.[61] The poem is remarkable for two reasons: first, it is imbued with a hatred of the dictator such as cannot be found in any other works and, second, it is addressed not only to the dead Stalin but to all living Stalinists now masquerading as democrats.

Among dramatic works S. Alyoshin's "The Ward" is significant.[62] The action takes place in the ward of a hospital where four men are lying. Even in this little group Stalin's legacy finds its reflection. An argument is going on between two of the patients — the official Prozorov and a writer Novikov. When Novikov reproaches him for being a conceited Communist, Prozorov shows his true face:

> Prozorov: But you, of course, have already forgotten what Stalin said.
>
> Novikov: Unfortunately, I remember only too well.
>
> Prozorov: Huh, you are most likely one of those . . . Aren't you one of those who were in prison?
>
> Novikov: And you are what?
>
> Prozorov: I am one of those who think that some people were let out by mistake. Particularly your sort, the writers. They pet you, they give you advice, they try to convince you, they listen to you. But you shoot your mouths off all the same. You argue, you debate, you leap in with advice. They would have shown you before '53. You would have been . . . (and he bent an imaginary rod double with his hands.)[63]

---

[61] *Pravda*, October 21, 1962.

[62] *Teatr*, 1962, No. 11.

[63] *Ibid.*, pp. 29—30.

The Stalinist is shown in the most loathsome light, even to the extent of his throwing at Novikov, who is about to undergo a serious operation, the heartless and cynical remark:

"You'll not get out of here. You'll die under the knife. I heard it in the dressing room. You'll croak!"[64]

Although none of these works was condemned (such a step would have been in violation of the decisions of the Twenty-Second Party Congress), de-Stalinization was far from encouraged by the Party leaders. This is evident from the fact that none of the novels mentioned, not one story, not one play was proposed for a 1962 state prize and only one "One Day in the Life of Ivan Denisovich," has been proposed for a 1963 prize.

Each of these works suggests parallels between the fictitious characters and real people in high positions who not so long ago were active participants in the arbitrary acts now condemned. The question arises as to whether one man alone could have committed so much evil without the cooperation of the Party. Furthermore, the Communist system has preserved and taken over everything that was inherited from the period of the personality cult, from collectivization to false enthusiasm, and in the field of art has restored the compulsory requirement of socialist realism. As a result a paradoxical situation has arisen in which literary works on the subject of de-Stalinization are boomeranging.

Thus the three most important developments in Soviet literature of late are the oppositional attitudes of the younger generation of writers, the reemergence of *poputnichestvo* and overt de-Stalinization. Each of them is unacceptable to the Party leaders and poses a threat to them. The most dangerous is the first, since it relates not to yesterday or even today, but tomorrow, the future which the Party has already strictly prescribed.

Together these developments have provoked a mass Party crusade against free thinking. However, rather than starting with a direct confrontation, this crusade began with a Judas' kiss. Last year, quite unexpectedly, a considerate attitude was adopted toward the exponents of freedom. Works by Yevtushenko, Voznesensky, Rozhdestvensky, Slutsky, and other intellectual leaders of progressive Soviet youth began to be printed in the central Party organ. Yevtushenko and Aksyonov were made members of the editorial board of the popular youth journal *Yunost*. Somewhat earlier "rebels" had joined the board of the Moscow writers' organization, despite the fact that the critics continued to censure them. The turn of the year was marked by a series of meetings between Party and government leaders and representatives of the art world. The object of this "carrot" policy was clear. It was hoped that a few sops from on high would persuade the rebels

---

[64] *Ibid.*

to come to terms, that the condescension of the Party leaders would transform them into active defenders of the regime. These hopes were not borne out and indeed there came a spate of works explosive in content, although of no great volume.

The December issue of *Novy mir* published Aleksandr Yashin's half-story, half-sketch "Wedding at Vologda" which portrayed the miserable life in rural areas today, the bankruptcy of the collective farm system, the strength of many traditions long considered outworn, and people of all stations as they really are, faults and all.

The January issue of *Neva* printed Fyodor Abramov's sketch "Around and About" which also showed a present-day collective farm

> . . . seventeen years since the war ended, but in agriculture we are still struggling. We have a battle to get every bushel of grain.[65]

In the story the chairman of the collective farm goes round the village and finds that only one person is reasonably well off — an old man retired on a pension who cultivates his private plot.

Aksyonov's new story "Oranges from Morocco,"[66] dealing with young prospectors, sailors, and construction workers in the Far East, was an ideological sequel to "A Ticket to the Stars." It likewise concerns a group of young people, who are a little older than the characters in the earlier work, but who express the same views as the seventeen-year olds who went off to the Baltic.

Two stories by Solzhenitsyn appeared in the January issue of *Novy mir*. The first, "Incident at Stantsiya Krechetovka," belongs to the de-Staliniza-tion category and shows how demands for vigilance can lead to victimization of innocent people. The second, "Matryona's Home," is of greater signifi-cance and describes a squalid collective village of the post-Stalin era. The main figure in the story, however, is a simple peasant woman, Matryona, who devotes her whole life to others, leaving almost nothing for herself. Even her tragic death is due to her desire to help her relatives. The closing lines of the story resound with condemnation of the tenor of life and the society of today:

> Misunderstood and cast off even by her husband, having buried six of her children but not her own amiable disposition, estranged from her sisters and sisters-in-law, comic and stupidly working for others for no reward, she accumulated no estate against her death. A dirty-white goat, a lame cat, rubber plants . . . . We all lived next door and

---

[65] *Neva*, 1963, No. 1, p. 132.
[66] *Yunost*, 1963, No. 1.

failed to realize that she was that sort of humble person without whom, to quote the proverb, a village cannot stand.

Nor a city.

Nor our whole land. [67]

A. Arbuzov, this year published his "tale for the theater" "Somewhere They Are Waiting for Us." The hero, Anatoli Lednev, is one of the maligned younger generation and when he arrives to work at a factory a woman worker asks him:

"Member of the Komsomol?"

"Certainly not."

"What are you then?"

"Yes, indeed, what am I? Have you read that novel 'A Ticket to the Stars' which was condemned by everyone?"

"They did pull it to pieces."

"Well, I am one of that lot. Don't fit in anywhere, as they say in the papers. They went off to Tallinn, I have come to you."

"To be reeducated, are you?"

"What do you mean? I have come to reeducate you." [68]

The play contains remarks which attest to the younger generation's reappraisal of the young Communists' romanticism of the nineteen-twenties. Tenth grade pupil Fedya, for instance, the son of a local executive committee chairman, explains why he, an excellent student, only got a failing mark for literature in an examination:

It was Pavel Korchagin's fault. I said that he could not be a model for modern Soviet young people to imitate. [69]

Once again we see the emergence of nihilistic views.

Two stories by Vladimir Voynovich published in the February 1963 number of Novy mir also failed to fulfill the demands of socialist realism. There was a particularly large amount of "seditious material" in the first, "I Want to Be Honest," which is narrated by construction works superintendent Samokhin, a man who has somewhat gone to seed but is devoted to his job—building living accommodations. He complains that construction work is in an appalling state: there is no drying oil to thin the paint, the parquet flooring falls apart as soon as it is laid, pipes are carelessly welded and, above all, the workers are totally indifferent to their work: "We are

---

[67] *Novy mir*, 1963, No. 1, p. 63.

[68] *Teatr*, 1963, No. 1, p. 135.

[69] *Ibid.*

sullen people, what we want is good money and grub."[70] The climax of
the story is the demand by the Party organization that the building be
handed over in time for the October anniversary. If this is done Samokhin
will be appointed chief construction engineer. But at the last moment
Samokhin refuses to sign the false acceptance document. This is the beginning of his downfall: his appointment is rescinded and he himself ends
up in hospital because he overstrained himself working the day before the
building should have been handed over. His efforts to be honest are in vain.
True a report appears in a newspaper praising the high principles of the
works superintendent, but this tailpiece does not alter the moral of
the story.

Leonid Syomin's story "One Against One" dealt with a controversial
subject. The first installment appeared in the March issue of *Neva*, but
despite the customary "end of part one," no further installment has yet
appeared. The story is reminiscent of Solzhenitsyn's first work, but is at
the same time quite new. It tells of the fate of Soviet officers and men
captured by the Germans. They include a Hero of the Soviet Union, men
who had performed courageous acts and even one officer who was only a
prisoner for fifteen minutes, having been captured in Berlin when he
broke into a house occupied by German troops. The story is narrated by
political affairs officer Aleksei Klochkov, a Leningrad student, who had
himself been a prisoner. He describes the repatriation camp where freed
prisoners were stripped not only of their ranks and decorations but also of
their human dignity; where they were turned into convicts over whom
Chekists, who had not spent a day at the front, were given unlimited
power. In this camp they were not treated as human beings, but were
made to perform arduous and senseless work, carrying heavy mud bricks,
irrespective of their state of health. One of the men, badly wounded and
completely broken by imprisonment addresses the officer in charge:

> "I am not up to dragging this thing. Look how I am . . . ." He pulled
> his undershirt from under his belt, baring his stomach and chest. His
> whole body was a mass of scars and marks. His ribs stuck out sharply,
> covered with flaccid skin.
>
> "I cannot let you off," frowned the lieutenant. "It was not me
> who thought up this work."[71]

The tragic fate of men who fought honorably and by luck survived the
life in German prison camps is well expressed in a stanza by Elli, a poet
who also finds himself in this camp:

---

[70] *Novy mir*, 1963, No. 2, p. 153.
[71] *Neva*, 1963, No. 3, p. 92.

> How many tracks passed over,
> How many sorrows endured,
> How much awaited, suffered and then:
> Back in the same old mess.[72]

This is by no means a complete list of the works in which literary developments contrary to the wishes of the Party leaders are to be encountered. Perhaps the most unexpected event on the Soviet literary scene has been the publication of Yevtushenko's autobiography. Although it was published not in the Soviet Union, but in the Paris *L'Express*, a considerable number of the more controversial passages have become accessible to Soviet readers thanks to the action of *Komsomolskaya pravda* in printing a critical article under the title "Where *Klestakovshchina* (Bragging) Leads To" which quoted extensively from it. These excerpts give some idea of the views not merely of the poet himself but of the entire generation whose mouthpiece he is. Describing the Communist Revolution, Yevtushenko speaks of its real significance:

> The revolution brought the Russian people many new burdens and many new tears. This is true.[73]

He goes on to develop this theme:

> Russia suffered for Marxist ideals not only in the tsarist epoch. It continued to pay the price of pain and mistakes in the epoch of the construction of the socialist society.[74]

The tragedy of the peoples of Russia is most convincingly expressed in the poet's following statement:

> The Russian people worked bitterly hard that the roar of machinery, tractors, and bulldozers might drown the groaning and lamentation which broke forth from behind the barbed wire of the Siberian concentration camps.[75]

The aphorism he lets fall by the way, that "justice is a train which is always late," infers the failure of attempts to restore the principles of justice and legality, particularly since these attempts have affected only certain facets of Soviet life and the people hardly at all.

It should be noted that the poet frequently and quite deliberately demonstrates his desire to be objective. Comparing the West with the Soviet Union, for instance, he says:

---

[72] *Ibid.*, p. 103.
[73] *Komsomolskaya pravda*, March 30, 1963.
[74] *Ibid.*
[75] *Ibid.*

·Both sides have their shady aspects and unhealthy phenomena. I can criticize the West on many counts, but the West can at the same time criticize the East with equal justification.[76]

Yevtushenko's statements constitute no accepted political formula but his own. The gist of it is that one must live in a spirit of "instinctive brotherhood which overcomes all differences." There is every reason to regard this formula as a slogan for ideological coexistence.

The campaign against manifestations of free thinking was led by Khrushchev himself, who made it clear how important it was to suppress independent views and judgements in literature which commands such a wide audience both within the Soviet Union and abroad. Here one may recall the principle on which the work of the Cheka was based from its inception: "Thought is more dangerous than deed." The Party sought to place thought under its strict control. It is no mere coincidence that in his speech of March 8, 1963 at the most important of the meetings between Party and government leaders and representatives of the world of art, Khrushchev emphatically stated:

> Just as in an orchestra the conductor seeks to make all the instruments coordinate harmoniously, so in social and political life the Party directs the efforts of all Soviet people to the achievement of a single goal.
>
> Socialist society through the Party, as its guiding force, removes obstacles hampering the normal life of people and created the necessary material, cultural and ideological prerequisites for the building of Communism.[77]

If Khrushchev may be regarded as the commander-in-chief in this campaign, the role of chief of staff was filled by Central Committee Secretary Iljichev who formulated the strategy and tactics. This allocation of functions served as a model for all Party organizations at lower levels — republic, kray, and oblast central committees. In this way the entire Party was mobilized to suppress free creative thought. Just as forty or more years before the entire Party was mobilized against the mutinous Kronstadt sailors, so once more the Party, now an army of many millions, was thrown into battle against those writers who dared to think independently.

The Party enlisted the services of venerable scientists, academicians, and prominent persons ranging from cosmonauts to groups of production workers supposedly representative of Soviet public opinion, a force surpassing in its complexity any previously mobilized in the Soviet Union to suppress a revolt.

---

[76] *Ibid.*

[77] *Pravda*, March 10, 1963.

The attack was launched under the slogan of "Loyalty to the Party and People is the Most Important Principle of Our Art." There were two particularly notable events which marked the course of the campaign. The first was the Fourth Plenary Session of the Board of the Union of Soviet Writers held at the end of March 1963. Apart from the customary resolution this gathering also adopted a declaration addressed to the Party Central Committee which was in fact an official declaration by its signatories that in the future they would be steadfastly guided by Party directives. Thus any writer violating this declaration may be regarded as violating a decision taken by his own professional body.

The second event was the Fourth All-Union Conference of Young Writers held on May 7—10. Carefully prepared in advance, this meeting was not allowed any policy-making functions or even opportunities for discussion. It was organized as an educational measure and for the most part took the form of a series of seminars at which the 170 delegates had to listen to lectures assessing their work and telling them how they should write. In other words, the entire younger generation of writers were sat down at desks and made to listen without any opportunity to reply.

In this way the suppression of the revolt was assured. Not without good reason did Iljichev speak at the June plenary session of the Party Central Committee of manifestations of free thinking in art as a thing of the past:

> At one time in literature, in the cinema, and on theater stages one could glimpse pitiable, spiritually impoverished people, characters with limited horizons, primitive feelings and experiences. Should we, however, disregard works which portray our life one-sidedly and tendentiously, works in which a petty little truth is described in profuse detail, but the great truth is ignored? Perhaps one should name certain works which have been printed in the literary journals — *Novy mir, Neva, Yunost* and others — that met with the disapproval of the Soviet public. But let the authors and editors themselves say what they think about this. [78]

This part of the speech contains a proclamation of victory over free thinking, the discrediting of those who had expressed independent views, and a demand that authors and editors should acknowledge their errors. Now that Stalin's repressive methods are proscribed, Khrushchev's demands constitute the extreme forms of censure and punishment.

Having triumphed for the time being, the Party has once more clamped art into a strict framework, This was reflected in works published between April and September 1963, which did not included a single example that

---

[78] *Izvestiya*, June 19, 1963.

could arouse the ire of the Party critics. Tvardovsky's latest poem "Terkin in the Other World"[79] is an allegory, overloaded with puns, popular anecdotes and witticisms with the single refrain: "big guns are hauled into battle backwards," which is the key to the whole thing.

Still more significant are works of this period dealing with the present younger generation. Two of the more notable are Nikolai Dubov's "Boy at the Seaside"[80] and Vladimir Krakovsky's "Return to the Horizon."[81] Their characters include adolescents who suffer from no ideological frustrations or dangerous tendencies. The result, however, is quite convincing — the young people are quite credible and lifelike. And perhaps their most convincing trait is their dominant craving for truth, their desire to find it on their own, instinctively, without any outside help. This is a very natural characteristic and in a veiled form may be much the same as that to be found among those heroes so recently condemned. If so, those heroes must inevitably reappear again both in life and in literature.

[79] *Ibid.*, August 18, 1963.
[80] *Novy mir*, 1963, No. 6.
[81] *Zvezda*, 1963, No. 7.

LEONID D. RZHEVSKY

The New Idiom

Is not the literary language of a given people at a given time the language of writer A, writer B and writer C who represent this literature in
the most vivid and gifted manner? In other words, should not the
researcher primarily speak of the individual features of the language and
style of these writers, rather than make generalized observations?

Very likely he should. "Very likely" because literary linguistics, the
study of the literary language, is a young science and its methodology
is still in the process of formulation.[1]

However, it would hardly be possible to imagine a study of the peculiarities of the language, style and poetic quality of a given writer (in this
case Soviet) while ignoring the features or the dominant literary form
(in this case socialist realism) and the vital changes and constructive
trends within this form (as, for example, the trends toward emancipatory
realism in post-"thaw" literature). It is also impossible to imagine any
such study which ignores the general literary language in its contemporary
development.

In any case, in this necessarily short paper, I am embarking on what
might be termed a composite treatment of the subject. I shall therefore
begin with certain phenomena characteristic of the Russian literary
language in general in the last few years.

I am of the opinion that these years, the end of the fifties and the
beginning of the sixties, have been marked to perhaps a greater degree
than those which preceded them by a relaxation of standard literary
linguistic usage. This phenomenon, which has been variously described
as a deterioration of linguistic culture, an "impoverishment" or "choking"
of the Russian literary language, has evoked a particularly loud response
in the Soviet press, not merely in the form of alarm signals set off by
writers and philologists, but for the most part in the flood of textbooks
calling for correctness and purity of language, for the maintenance and
consolidation of standards of pronunciation, use of words and elementary
grammatical style. I would mention, for example, A. Mirtov's essays on
the Russian verb *Govori pravilno* (Speak Correctly) and B. Timofeyev's
Pravilno li my govorim? (Do We Speak Correctly?). In 1960, the

---

[1] See V. Vinogradov, *O yazyke khudozhestvennoy literatury* (Literary Language),
Moscow, 1959, Chapters 1 and 2.

Central Committee Higher Party School published V. Kostomarov's
pamphlet *Kultura rechi i stil* (Speech Culture and Style), and in 1962
N. Listvinov's two-volume work *Voprosy stilistiki russkogo yazyka*
(Problems of Style in the Russian Language).

The nature and acuteness of this phenomenon is, I think, linked with
the fact that the last few years in particular have reflected the passing of
the last representatives of the high linguistic culture of the pre-Revolution-
ary Russian intelligentsia — writers, scholars, artists, teachers — particularly in the latter: at least two generations have received their education in an unusually expanded school system laboring under the handicap
of a shortage of linguistically educated teachers. The so-called cultural
revolution, with its immense scope and achievements in introducing the
once illiterate masses to books, science and art, has certainly extended
linguistic culture, but has been quite unable to maintain it at the former
high level achieved by a quite different social stratum.

The violation of standards in the language of the contemporary Soviet
intellectual, including the writer, varies according to the speaking customs
of the environment in which he received his education. Sometimes, this
is not strictly a violation but rather an attempt to consolidate a new
standard supported by mass usage. Thus, for example, in the field of
pronunciation standards, the Moscow pronunciation as a model has been
subjected to official revision in Textbooks; the new standards follow the
practice of sanctioning changes *post factum*, as for example in bringing
pronunciation closer to spelling. It is primarily the widespread use of
incorrect stress that causes alarm. It is interesting to note the prohibitions
contained in certain standard textbooks such as the academic manual
edited by Avanesov, in which we find *zvo-nish'*, not *zvo'-nish*, *po'-nyal*,
not *po-nyal'*, etc.

Examples of incorrect stress are frequent in the works of modern
Soviet poets.

In Viktor Bokov we encounter the peasant colloquial or regional
sy-ty' instead of *sy'-ty*:

> О чем ты, желтогрудая овсянка,
> Оповещаешь тихие кусты?
> Снега лежат, как скатерть-самобранка,
> И снегири поэтому сыты. [2]

In Margarita Agashina — *ban-ty'* instead of *ban'-ty*:

> Дочка на пол спрыгнула упрямо,
> На косичках дрогнули банты. [3]

---

[2] *Literaturnaya gazeta*, January 5, 1960.
[3] *Ibid.*, January 9, 1960.

In Boris Slutsky:

> И чихают от звездной пыли
> Удалые собаки земли. [4]

And so forth. But of course incorrect stress is not such a terrible sin, particularly since the variations of Russian stress are indeed great and such inaccuracies are even condoned by the compilers of standard textbooks. [5]

Lack of an ear for a word as a whole, its form, its stylistic coloring and its sound in the context is a more significant indication of a writer's linguistic deficiencies. Here is a random example of almost comic stylistic dissonance — random because I do not even know the identity of its author — which I jotted down from a Soviet song I chanced to hear on Moscow Radio on October 7, 1960:

> Я даю вам слово джентельмена,
> Что на это дело мне плевать!

Indifference to choice of words amounting to a violation of literary standards may be met even in *Literaturnaya gazeta*, which prints so many articles appealing for purity of language:

> В связи с тем, что **зачтение** докладов ... отнимает много времени ... [6]

Why *zachteniye?* Far better *zachityvaniye* bearing in mind the repetition of the action, if there be any need at all to form this new verbal noun.

> Искусство ... неизбежно превращается в ... **упадническое**. [7]

The form *upadnicheskoye* is found once in Lenin, but the standard dictionary gives only one grammatically correct form: *upadochnicheskoye*. What is the point of insisting on the distortion?

Another example, from L. Rybak's article "At the Desks of Adults":

> Мне думается, что к молодому рабочему, пришедшему в школу, **перво-наперво** надо отнестись как ко взрослому. [8]

---

[4] *Ibid.*, August 23, 1960.

[5] In Professor A. Mirtov's *Govori pravilno* (Speak Correctly), we find on page 99 under the heading "Obvious Mistakes" the example *pe-re-so'len-nyy* a form very common in educated speech which is even referred to as standard in the USSR Academy of Sciences' *Slovar russkogo yazyka* (Dictionary of the Russian Language), Vol. III, 1959.

[6] *Literaturnaya gazeta*, January 1, 1960.

[7] *Ibid.*, January 21, 1960.

[8] *Ibid.*, May 30, 1963.

Pervo-napervo is a non-literary colloquial parallel to the literary *prezhde vsego*. But whence and why this colloquialism in an article by the former director of a school?

I pose this rhetorical question in order to dwell further on that feature of the general Russian literary language of today which, in my opinion, is most noticeable when reading books by Soviet writers. I would call this phenomenon "democratization of the, language." By this non-philological term I denote the approximation of Standard literary usage to the level of pure colloquialism. This process has many stages and is very complex. Colloquial lexical and phraseological elements and forms, regional words, professional jargon and the slang expressions of certain social groups become, under the influence of very varied stimuli, firmly entrenched in the everyday conversational language of the masses who are not particularly fastidious about the precise forms of the words they use. They later penetrate into the speech of educated well-read people, i.e., into the educated colloquial language, and so into the dialogue of stories and novels. To some extent they even creep into monologue — the speech of authors themselves, both poets and prose writers, seeking thus to be confirmed as standard usage.

I would mention the widespread use of the word *mozhet* in the sense of *mozhet byt*, *byt mozhet* and *vozmozhno*. Before the Revolution, it was used only in colloquial styles, mainly in dialogue as a speech characteristic and in the earlier Russian classics it is difficult to find it at all. Canonized for the most part by poets and prose writers with a peasant background it is now a regular feature of educated speech.

Similarly in contexts where there is no dialogue:

И по имени-отчеству, **может**, впервые
Командиры полков называли начдива. [9]

Может быть, гигантские муравьи ворочают государственны-
ми делами, а **может**, обезьяны или бобры, обладающие там
высоким сознанием и овладевшие всеми формами труда. [10]

This latter example occurs in a passage where a geologist muses t himself.

The word *vrode* used in uneducated colloquial in the sense of *ka budto* is also quite common:

Наговориться **вроде** досыта,
А ляжешь — не смыкаешь глаз. [11]

---

[9] G. Goppe in *Den poezii* (Poetry Day), Moscow-Leningrad, 1962, p. 60.
[10] A. Koptyayeva, *Oktyabr*, No. 6, 1963, p. 8.
[11] Sergei Orlov, *Den poezii*, Moscow-Leningrad, 1962, p. 158.

> А мне вот с музой вкупе **вроде**
> И нет премудрости сложней. [12]

... каждому **вроде** чего-то не хватило. [13]

In the last example, taken from Fedin's novel "Camp Fire," the context deals with peasant affairs, but the words quoted are supposed to be the author's own. Another example from Panfyorov's novel "In the Name of the Young":

... **вроде** неожиданно заклокотало море. [14]

Here, perhaps, one should also note the colloquial and slightly un-educated use of *pokhozhe* with the same meaning:

Трубы упрямо садились... на какой-то уступ, и, **похоже,** уже прихватывала их размокшая красная глина. [15]

The uneducated colloquial *srodu* is to be found in Gleb Pagirov's poem "Ilich":

Он человек, он **сроду** не был Богом. [16]

Colloquial forms of the type *polpyatogo, polshestogo* for indicating the time of day, which for many speakers have a slightly vulgar flavor, also tend to be adopted as standard usage by some writers:

> И лишь полпятого вы вспомнили:
> Будильник на пять заведен. [17]

In order to save space, I shall here quote without comment some examples of the use of uneducated colloquial words and word forms which I have encountered in contexts where there is no dialogue: *vlazit* for *vlezit* in V. Lipatov's "Cherny yar":

Аленочкин боком **влазит** в дверь кабинета. [18]

The same writer uses the regional *vzgalnyy:*

На него наваливается тугой **взгальный** ветер.

In V. Shchukshin's story "Leader of the Class" we read:

В светлых лучах **закучерявились** синие облака. [19]

---

[12] V. Kazin, *Den poezii 1962* (Poetry Day 1962), Moscow, 1962, p. 31.

[13] Konstantin Fedin, *Novy mir*, No. 9, 1961, p. 38.

[14] *Oktyabr*, No. 7, 1960, p. 83.

[15] A. Koptyayeva, *Oktyabr*, No. 6, 1963, p. 11.

[16] *Den poezii*, Moscow-Leningrad, 1962, p. 161.

[17] S. Davydov in *Den poezii*, Moscow-Leningrad, 1962, p. 69.

[18] *Novy mir*, No. 3, 1963, p. 34.

[19] *Ibid.*, No. 2, 1963, p. 94.

In the same work, *vstryat* in the sense of *vmeshatsya:*

Волноваться вредно, — **встрял** Пашка.

We also find *vstrevat* in Bubyonnov's "Orlinaya Step":

Он... встревал не в свои дела. [20]

In the same work:

... не давал Дерябе куролесить на тракторе и **булгачить** народ. [21]

И **той же секундой** он летел птицей по лестнице. [22]

In the collection of short stories *selenga* (The River Selenga), Moscow, 1961, A. Kuznetsov has:

Мотор собирался **забарахлить**.

... поначалу **вызверился** на него шофер.

... детей и жены, чтобы ради них **гробиться**, Алексей не имел.

Подчиненные были правы, пользуясь всяким случаем **пофилонить, потуфтить,** закрыть завышенный наряд. Ребята **травили** разные истории.

The word *travit* has evidently become extremely widespread, being used polysemantically to express, as a rule, the intensity of an action, the nature of which is conveyed by its object or by the context. In V. Aksyonov's "Ticket to the Stars", the speakers use the expressions *travil anekdoty* and *travil za bort* (he vomited); Solzhenitsyn has *travyat bditelnost* while Aksyonov also used *travit* in the sense of "to lie, tell falsehoods."

In Y. German's novel "My Dear Man" we find:

Уходили они **спехом**. [23]

Володя хлебал из котелка лошадиный **супешник**. [24]

Но и на этом тяжком пути постепенно **пообвыкли,** многие разулись — так было **ловчее**. [25]

In B. Voinovich's short story "A Half Kilometer Away":

Вся деревня хохотала **впокатыши**. [26]

---

[20] *Oktyabr*, No. 7, 1959, p. 46.
[21] *Ibid.*, p. 47.
[22] *Ibid.*, p. 27.
[23] *Zvezda*, No. 10, 1961, p. 91.
[24] *Ibid.*, p. 72.
[25] *Ibid.*, p. 38.
[26] *Novy mir*, No. 2, 1963, p. 191.

In A. Koptyayeva's novel "Gift of the Land":

Странная хворь подкосила ее. [27]

Сестра Минсулу — лаборантка, все еще **невестится**. [28]

Chuyem occurs as the equivalent of *chuvstvuyem*, *oshchushchayem* in the verse of I. Avramenko:

Редко **чуем** плечо. [29]

The poet V. Dagurov has:

Мы учились и **озоровали**. [30]

Further we find *prostyn* in Babayevsky's "The Sons' Mutiny"[31] *tovarnyak* for *tovarnyy poyezd* in Rozov's screen-play;[32] *otryakhaya sneg* in M. Sazonov's verse;[33] and in L. Pervomaysky's "Wild Honey":

. . . она **обула** черные туфли на высоких каблуках. [34]

I do not regard all these colloquialisms as unintentional lapses on the authors' part: some of them, no doubt, have a special function which I, as a reader, failed to appreciate. In this connection mention must be made of a tendency which has become particularly noticeable among certain writers, namely, a tendency to introduce elements of uneducated speech in order to imbue the literary style with a popular character. Such experiments are not new in the history of Russian literature: one need only mention Leo Tolstoy's *Kavkazsky plennik* (Prisoner of the Caucasus) or his *Narodnye rasskazy* (Popular Tales) of the eighties. In these works, however, the language is stylistically uniform; the stylization is complete and consistent to the end. In contrast, let us glance at a poem by Yaroslav Smelyakov entitled "Comrade Returned" and published in the April 1962 issue of *Novy mir*. The comrade returns from Cuba, where he:

> . . . все обаянье Фиделя,
> Всю ту атмосферу впитал . . .

Further:

> Он стал как бы выше и шире,
> И даже **красивше**, чем был.

---

[27] *Oktyabr*, No. 6, 1963, p. 11.

[28] *Ibid.*, p. 42.

[29] *Den poezii*, Moscow-Leningrad, 1962, p. 8.

[30] *Den poezii 1962g.*, Moscow, 1962, p. 8.

[31] *Oktyabr*, Nos. 1—3, 1961.

[32] *Yunost*, No. 9, 1961, p. 13.

[33] *Den poezii*, Leningrad, 1962, p. 183.

[34] *Oktyabr*, No. 3, 1963, p. 11.

It is impossible to believe that the introduction of the non-literary form *krasivshe* and its virtual juxtaposition with *atmosferu vpital* are fortuitous. Lexical and stylistic contrasts as an artistic device have a long history extending from Avvakum to Pasternak, but in the example just quoted the ugly contrast between the literary and the uneducated colloquial must be due to the author's failure to hear it.

Further instances are not difficult to find. For example, from M. Krivitsky's poem "Spring":

> Я парень из Иванова,
> Я — **оторви да брось,**
> Похожий (врать не стану я)
> На длинный острый гвоздь. [35]

From V. Lazarev:

> Как тебя зовут, речушка? — Сежей.
> Сежа... А меня **Володькой звать.** [36]

And from the poem by V. Kazin:

> Кто с другом, как **с родною маткой**
> До самой **старости** дошел
>
> . . . .
>
> Такой удар за весь захват
> Готовим,
> Что, **мать честная,**
> Врагу стал гробом Ленинград. [37]

The examples which I have quoted so far are taken from contexts where there is no dialogue, where the language is that of the author. If we turn to passages of dialogue, to the speech of literary personages representing the contemporary Soviet intelligentsia, the democratization of language, the departure from standards of educated speech, becomes particularly noticeable.

Here is the language of a construction engineer who is the narrator in V. Voynovich's story "I Want to be Honest." His style may be regarded as identical with that of the author:

> — У вас высшее образование?
> — Да, **вроде бы** высшее, — сказал я.
> — **Может,** кто разогнет? — спросил я.

---

[35] *Den poezii*, Moscow-Leningrad, 1962, p. 117.
[36] *Den poezii 1962g.*, Moscow, 1962, p. 13.
[37] *Ibid.*, pp. 31—32.

Other instances:

Кончайте **перекур**!

Он **распылился** [= разгорячился, вышел из себя].

Коллектив участка, — **тарабанит** Ерошин, — включившийся в соревнование за достойную встречу сорок четвертой годовщины Октября, ...

Я знал его еще **пацаном**.

Но **через эту книгу** и только через нее Иван Адамович постигает всю мудрость и красоту нашей жизни.

... снимает койку **на частном секторе**.

Я ... говорю ему несколько слов **на родном языке**.

and concludes with a stream of unprintable expressions. A surgeon in Yuri German's "My Dear Man" says:

— **Трепаться**, коллега, лучше, нежели принимать валерьянку, а у вас между прочим такой **видок**, что с вами непременно и **вскорости** случится дамский обморок.

"*Ne Ozoruy!*" says another surgeon, Yelena Gruzdeva, in Koptyayava's "Gift of the Land." In Voynovich's "I Want to be Honest," a woman teacher writes in a letter:

«Боязно о них говорить».

A secretary of the all-Union Party Central Committee in Panfyorov's "In the Name of the Young" remarks:

«Я же не статуй». [38]

Some excerpts from the language of Pridorogin, chairman of the Tula Oblast Executive Committee in Fedin's "Camp Fire":

На **ихнюю** площадь переселили жильцов ... Этак ты все новостройки очередникам **разбазаришь**. ... этот самый Кирилл Николаевич ... **шибко** требовательный.

На кой он мне сдался.

Пес его знает, что у Извекова за спиной. [39]

Here is a specimen from the same novel of the language of some actors, painters, and writers at a party:

---

[38] *Oktyabr*, No. 7, 1960, p. 14.

[39] *Novy mir*, No. 8, 1961, p. 81 ff.

Ну что вы подняли хай? — спрашивает один из гостей. «Если нынче потребуется плакат, я брошу пейзаж и стану **рубать** плакаты», — говорит художник. [40]

Заткнись, — одернула Муза Ивановна. [41]

It is interesting to note the popular forms of Christian names current among the intelligentsia. Almost all of them seem to be Vaska's, Lenka's or Tanka's, just as they are often *"devchata"* and *"rebyata"* when addressed as a group. In German's novel the hero calls his girl friend "Varyukha." *"Derzhi, Katka!"* says the young engineer to his chief's wife in Aksyonov's story "Oranges from Morocco."

Vulgar abuse is common in the speech of characters representing the intelligentsia. *"Tetka byvayut zanudy!"* says a doctor in German's novel "Zamolchi, zanuda!" exclaims Leonid Bagryanov, a young engineer in Bubyonov's "Orlinaya Step." One of the heroines in Panfyorov's "In the Name of the Young," a zoologist, exclaims after her chief, whom she dislikes, has proposed to her:

Пошел к... — И Елена так грубо, по-чабаньи выругалась, что Любченко сначала опешил, затем попятился к оседланному коню, вцепился рукой в колок седла, вскинулся в седло и, удивленно-растерянно оглядываясь на Елену, поскакал прочь.

— **Пробрало**... Наконец-то! — сказала она. [42]

Elements of uneducated speech in the language of fictitious characters are sometimes meant to serve as a social indicator. The above-mentioned surgeon in German's novel is of peasant origin, a fact which is emphasized by the author when, for example, the surgeon talks of his mother (p. 62)

... мама никак не могла понять, что я у нее доктор, врач **форменный**. И когда она расхворалась и ее **дядья** привезли ко мне...

Panfyorov, in "In the Name of the Young," directly refers to this aspect of the speech of his characters (p. 20):

И тут Кирилл Ждаркин, как всегда в затруднительные моменты, вдруг прикинулся мужичком, начал «чайкать», «байкать», запускать глаза в потолок, а так как Аким Морев и сам вышел из крестьян, то он тоже намеренно стал окать

---

[40] *Ibid.*, p. 49.
[41] *Ibid.*, p. 56.
[42] *Oktyabr*, No. 7, 1960, pp. 23—24.

вворачивать местные словечки, вроде «намеднисть», «ужо»,
и, произнося такие словечки, прискукивал крупной рукой по
столу, как бы прицепляя их ... И вдруг оба расхохотались ...

In addition to the introduction of non-standard, uneducated colloquial
elements into the language of modern Russian literature, the nature and
various types of which I have just attempted to demonstrate, attention
should be given to the influence exerted on this language by journalisms
and its various lexical, phraseological, and stylistic clichés. This concerns
primarily the works of the "programmatic writers" (*programniki*), as
I term that group — centred for the most part in the journal *Oktyabr* —
which sees its artistic function in rendering practical literary assistance
to the Party. I shall deal with this group separately, but for the moment
I should like to say something about the journalistic influence in general.

Our people learn to speak from the language of newspapers: after
the teacher of Russian at school, our newspapers are the basic instructor
of their readers in language.

This observation, which names, not the books of Pushkin, Turgenev,
Chekhov or Gorky, but the newspaper as "the basic instructor" of those
learning Russian, comes from N. Listvinov, author of the textbook
Voprozy stilistiki russkogo yazyka (Problems of Style in the Russian
Language), issued by the Central Committee's Higher Party School
in 1962.

There follows a reservation:

Poor-quality newspaper language not only makes it more difficult
for Soviet journalists to bring the ideas of Marxism-Leninism to the
mind of every reader..., but also does great damage to the cultural
growth of Soviet people.

It is precisely the "poor quality" of the language used by organs of the
central and provincial press, its poverty, the ugliness of its stilted bureaucratic jargon, the monotony of its officialese and rigid clichés, that is directly
or indirectly attacked by the stylistic purists. In an article on "*officialitis*,"
K. Chukovsky cautiously confines himself to bureaucratic clichés in general
use, but proceeds to refer to "bureaucratic forms" of languages in general
and concludes:

"New achievements," "creative successes" are magnificent
combinations of precious words, but the trouble is that they have been
transformed into familiar, hackneyed bureaucratic formulas which
have been rendered lifeless by mechanical repetition in thousands of
congratulatory letters and anniversary speeches.[43]

---

[43] *Literaturnaya gazeta*, September 9, 1961.

If we add, "also lead articles, decrees and official reports," the idea is expressed in its entirety and becomes fully applicable to Soviet newspapers in general.

Innumerable clichés have found their way from the newspapers into the stories and novels of the programmatic writers, where they occur both in connecting narrative, and, preeminently, in dialogue. The following words, for example, are spoken by a construction supervisor in "In the Name of the Young" (p. 56—57):

Кажется мне, что у членов этой бригады . . . труд обрел первоначальное качество, данное человеку от природы, то есть стал творческим трудом, естественной потребностью . . . Конечно, помимо крепчайшей материальной базы, основой основ коммунистического общества будет творческий труд масс.

In "Gift of the Land" we read the following in the connecting narrative:

Танечка, **взявшая на себя шефство** над мужем подружки . . . [44]

In the same work one chapter opens with the words:

Первоочередные объекты химического комбината принимали законченный вид. [45]

An exhaustive list of such illustrations would fill volumes, so I shall confine myself to the observation that the currency of a cliché in modern Russian depends not only on the frequency with which it occurs but also, as is inevitable when speech is not free, on the degree of "authority" which the cliché enjoys. The "authoritativeness" of individual words and phrases manifests itself in the caution, the wariness with which the speaker or the writer chooses his expressions and in the inevitability of his choice.

In his novel "Camp Fire" Fedin describes the speech of one of his characters — Pridorogin — thus:

«Он . . . даже разговаривать начал на каком-то геометрически закругленном языке, так что и щекотливая тема, обработанная этим способом и преимущественно с помощью молчания, не давала собеседнику подцепить какие-нибудь определенные выводы. Конечно, с друзьями он говорил более

[44] *Oktyabr*, No. 6, 1963, p. 6.
[45] *Ibid.*, No. 7, 1963, p. 77.

откровенно, чем с малознакомыми, да и то, во-первых, лишь в том случае, если разговор происходил с глазу на глаз, а, во-вторых, и с друзьями, в силу привычки и ОСТОРОЖ-НОСТИ, пользовался отчасти мимикой и языком округлен-ности». [46]

Yet another example — this time from Dolinina's sketch "In Our Eleven-Year School." A schoolboy is writing a report on a memorial meeting held at school. He is a "cub reporter "and wants to become a journalist:

«Учащиеся школы №… собрались на вечер, посвященный творчеству корифея русской литературы Л. Н. Толстого, задолго до начала. Красочно оформленный зал был переполнен. С неослабеваемым интересом выслушали учащиеся замечательные строки гения русской литературы в исполнении учеников девятых и десятых классов»…

— Зачем же ты пишешь неправду? — спросила я Толика.
— Ведь народу сначала было немного, и в зале стоял шум. Толик промолчал.
— И потом… разве у тебя своих слов нету! Что это такое: «красочно оформленный зал», «с неослабеваемым интере-сом»?
— А как же еще? — спросил Толик презрительно. — За свои-то слова и по шапке могут дать… [47]

Somewhat schematically and on the basis of similarities and differences in the choice of vocabulary and use of images, I would distinguish *three* stylistic trends in present-day Soviet Russian literature.

With regard to vocabulary and imagery the *first* trend is closest to the classical literary tradition. It is embodied in the later works of such "older" writers as Fedin, Leonov, Paustovsky, Kaverin, Sholokhov (with certain reservations) and a few others. By lumping these names together I am not, of course, trying to reduce the creative individuality of these writers to a common denominator. I merely wish to say that close study of their language reveals certain common elements which indicate that, in the process of creation, these writers have come to view the writing of fiction as a linguistic activity which is an end in itself and in which the criterion of the creative method is the *word as a vehicle of expression*, the word chosen for its expressiveness, precision, sound, imagery and "uniqueness." The search for the poetically striking expression, the absence of verbiage,

---

[46] *Novy mir*, No. 8, 1961, p. 80.
[47] *Yunost*, No. 7, 1961, p. 98.

and affinity with the traditions of classical Russian writing — these are
the features which bind together the proponents of the first trend.

In search is, of course, in each case individual, the nature of each
writer's search and discoveries shaping his style. I would, for example,
mention the tendency to use folk-expressions to be observed in Fedin's
novel "Camp Fire":

Путань (= путаница) . . . с фамилиями. [48]

. . . пригладил **кудерчатую** свою голову . . . точно скидывая с
нее мешающую **тяжень**. [49]

Всей **костоватой** некрупной статью своей отец казался . . . не
похожим на самого себя. [50]

. . . **бедованье** без мужа напримаяло ее . . . [51]

Но слышалось ему не одно только **гуторенье** стариков. [52]

Утро **сеяло мжичкой**. [53]

Сквозь частый **ситник** теплого дождика . . . [54]

These examples are for the most part drawn from that section of the
book in which, since it deals with the countryside, the author apparently
considered the use of linguistic local color justified. But here is an example
in a far from rustic context:

Где-то прилежно урчал мотор, и, будто стараясь **перебрехать**
его, **ярилась** собаченка. [55]

Paustovsky's narrative style features another kind of search for, and
selection of, words as an end in themselves. Paustovsky belongs to the
southern group of writers, whose stylistic cynosure was, perhaps, Babel. This
group's style is distinguished by its literally colorful vocabulary. Color
is an essential component of Paustovsky's prose. Sometimes its use seems
even to be excessive, as in "Sprint to the South":

Сироп этого варенья напоминал кровь горного заката. [56]

---

[48] *Novy mir*, No. 9, 1961, p. 51.
[49] *Ibid.*, p. 53.
[50] *Ibid.*, p. 6.
[51] *Ibid.*, p. 8.
[52] *Ibid.*, p. 41.
[53] *Ibid.*, p. 61.
[54] *Ibid.*, p. 62.
[55] *Ibid.*, p. 25.
[56] *Oktyabr*, No. 10, 1960, p. 10.

Or:

Отсюда было видно все, что происходило в порту и на море: все входящие и уходящие корабли, все белые и тенистые шквалы, носившиеся между Батумом и Поти, все многоцветные закаты, похожие на выставку скульптурных облаков или на выставку сумрака и света, пламени и мглы, серебра и крови, жаркого золота и оперенья незнакомых птиц. [57]

The second trend in present-day Soviet literature is represented by the programmatic writers — notably by those who write for *Oktyabr* (e.g., Panfyorov, Koptyayeva, Babayevsky, Bubyonnov and Chakovsky) — and many others who in practice support the theory that their craft should be an "aide of the Party" and back this belief by adhering to the vocabulary and didactic principles of socialist realism.

The predominant trait of these authors (as opposed to those in the first group), is, I would say, virtual disregard of the word as a creative end in itself. Peshkovsky once maintained that "every word contributes to the imagery of the work" as a whole, but in the works of the programmatic writers the pictorial function of the word yields to what must be called the communicative function. Meaningful description is replaced by empty decoration, creative inventiveness and stylistic individuality by rhetoric and stiltedness.

Panfyorov is the most important representative of this trend, if only for the large amount of work he felt some inner urge to write. I have already spoken about his use of local color. Here, for example, are the opening words of "In the Name of the Young":

Кирилл Джаркин уже не молод. Да, немолод: **катило** за шестьдесят, точнее в прошлом году **стукнуло** шестьдесят два, и голова его еще **пуще** засеребрилась. [58]

But this is not what shapes his narrative style. The "formative" element of Panfyorov's style (and of that of the other writers in this group) is something negative — the distinct hiatus between the intended creative expression and its implementation, to be more precise, "non-implementation." What is expressed lacks a *creative* ring. The word is sought but not found. I refer here not to the failure to hit upon distinctive and "original" turns of phrase in "In the Name of the Young" such as:

«он снова **застесненно** смолк»; «вот на такого бы на него посмотрели бы его **восхитители**»; «. . . говорил с грустинкой в голосе»

---

[57] *Ibid.*, p. 52.
[58] *Oktyabr*, No. 7, 1960, p. 12.

but failure to find the graphic word in general. Every description, be it
of the emotional state of a character, a love scene, or any situation whatsoever, even a simple narrative statement, leaves an impression of in-
expressiveness, of failure to find the *mot juste*, even of sheer helplessness.
Here are a few more examples from Panfyorov's novel:

Кораблев **внутренне закричал.** [59]

Опьянение Кораблева вызвало в ней **отвратность** к нему, и
ей почему-то захотелось, чтобы **такая же отвратность** воз-
никла и у других гостей. [60]

... Кораблев отшатнулся: в глубоком кресле сидела Елена
Виницына. Около нее Аким Морев, и оба они — **в интимной
непринужденности,** что и заставило Николая Кораблева от-
шатнуться. [61]

А ведь до этого славный был генерал, но **вогнал в душу болт**
и этим болтом смертельно **сам ударил себя по затылку.** [62]

Here is a typical specimen of dialogue:

«Я хотела ... я уверена была, что встречу тебя вот так же
радостно, как сейчас освещает нас молодое солнце. Я берегла
себя для тебя ... И недавно потеряла».
«Что ты потеряла?» [63]

and of landscape:

Пронизанная изобилием солнечных лучей, степь постепенно
таяла, уступая место утренней розовости, и на все это на-
ступало солнце, выкатываясь из-за казахстанских равнин. [64]

Even greater inadequacy of expression is to be observed in the works
of Koptyayeva, whose language is marred by the frequent use of clichés
and standing epithets such as *rodnoy:*

Тоже **родной,** как Хаятик, показалась Ярулле дочка Юсу-
фа. [65]

[59] *Ibid.*, p. 67.
[60] *Ibid.*, p. 73.
[61] *Ibid.*, p. 35.
[62] *Ibid.*, p. 85.
[63] *Ibid.*, p. 18.
[64] *Ibid.*, p. 75.
[65] *Oktyabr*, No. 7, 1963, p. 58.

Молча прижал к лицу волнистую прядь волос, ощутил их **родной** запах. [66]
Она положила ладони на его плечи, тепло взглянула в глаза, и губы их встретились в первом робком прикосновении. [67]

To search for individual stylistic features among the writers of this group is a fruitless occupation. Here, for example, is the opening of Babayevsky's novel "The Sons' Mutiny." It bears the irrefutable hallmark of the imitator; it is an apprentice's crib from Gogol's *Taras Bulba:*

«Посмотрим, посмотрим, что оно такое — этот сыновний бунт», подумает иной читатель. «Как-то и на слух непривычно, да и вообще непонятно, о чем пойдет речь. Известно, что когда-то на Руси были бунты голодные, соленые, картофельные — это понятно. В старину бунтовали казаки на Дону, были на Кубани кулацкие бунты. Или у А. С. Пушкина: «Опять моя старуха бунтует...» Но почему бунт сыновний? Молодое, новое берет верх над старым? Сыновья восстают против своих родителей? Неумирающая тема отцов и детей?.. Любопытно!»... [68]

So much for the beginning. The rest of the novel is littered with well-worn clichés:

«удивительно синее и чистое небо»; «окутанный красноватой дымкой [горизонт]»; «ноющая боль, кольнувшая сердце»; «небо, унизанное звездами и поднимающееся высоким шатром»; «страдающе плачущий баян»; «длинные, как плети, черные косы»; «строгие и задумчивые глаза»;

Perhaps the only slightly original thing about M. Bubyonnov's novel "Orlinaya Step" is the title. Its imagery and vocabulary are pallid and stereotyped:

«С болью, с кровью отрывалось сердце Леонида от Москвы»; «безбрежная равнина»; «сказочные просторы»; «вольное и загадочное царство»; «бесконечно струящееся марево»; «душа, охваченная внезапной тревогой»; «минуты тягостного молчания»; «затуманенный взгляд». [69]

The reader soon begins to feel that originality of expression is vastly less important to the programmatic writer than the "communication"

[66] *Ibid.*, No. 6, 1963, p. 13.
[67] *Ibid.*, No. 7, 1963, p. 62.
[68] *Oktyabr*, No. 1, 1961, p. 9.
[69] *Oktyabr*, Nos. 7—10, 1959.

of his chosen theme, which may revolve around Party leaders (as in the case of Panfyorov), oil workers (as in the case of Koptyayeva) or tillers of the virgin lands (as in the case of Bubyonnov). The writer's sole concern seems to be to put over his point.

The novels of the programmatic writers abound in technical terms, as, for example, this description of a drilling operation in Koptyayeva's "Gift of the Land":

На буровой начинается **«нолевка». Квадрат** с навернутыми **шарошечным долотом** нацеливается на **стол ротора**, входит в **«пасть»** и опускается под пол буровой: Ярулла вместе с другими рабочими намертво зажимает **квадрат** двумя половинами тяжелой **«челюсти»**, потом стальными клиньями. Все готово, и Ярулла торопится спрыгнуть с подмостков, чтобы увидеть **шарошку**, опущенную на **забой**. [70]

Such passages, which are quite incomprehensible to the uninitiated layman, can scarcely lay claim to literary merit. The author, however, finds them important and necessary for the "communication" of his point. Generally speaking, the more the programmatic writer tries to instruct, the more banal and inadequate his language becomes. The quality of writing often drops to the level of rhetoric and hack journalism:

«Теперь, казалось, все трудности останутся позади. Но никогда нельзя сказать наперед, что преодоленные трудности были последними: обязательно возникают новые» (Коптяева),

«Николай Кораблев смотрел на все это величие, созданное советским человеком, и гордость за свой богатырский народ росла в его душе» (Панферов),

«А тут над Москвой взлетело и зазвенело, как жаворонок над степью, **чудодейственное** слово — целина»... (Бубеннов).

The same applies to dialogue, with its tendentious concentration on whatever happens to be the order of the day:

«Мы руководителями стали теперь, значит, надо нам по-хорошему использовать трудовую гордость людей» (Коптяева)

«У всех молодых такие души. Нас только кликни — возьмемся за любое дело» (Бубеннов).

«А что на вооружении? — Кукуруза. Как это мы раньше жили без нее, ума не приложу!» (Коптяева).

---

[70] *Oktyabr*, No. 6, 1963, p. 10.

Or, at the idea of a trip abroad:

«Хорошо бы теперь посмотреть, как умирает капитализм» (Панферов).

The banality and sheer naiveté of some of the arguments which the programmatic writers in all seriousness put into the mouths of their heroes is sometimes devastating.

Koptyayeva, for example, writes:

Не раз восхищаясь созданиями человеческого ума, Надя с особенной остротой ощущала силу горьковских слов: «Человек — это звучит гордо».
Наука у порога новых ошеломительных открытий. Но еще никто не раскрыл, что такое любовь. [71]

Incidentally, we scarcely ever find the precision and aphoristic quality of Gorky or the vividness of Sholokhov in the writings of the programmatic authors. Here, for example, are a few rhetorical truisms from an unspoken monologue of the hero in Chakovsky's short story "Light of a Distant Star":

Человеку не дано все понять сразу. Опыт других — великое дело. Но он еще никогда не научил до конца. Есть дороги, по которым ты должен пройти сам. Есть нечто, что должны увидеть только твои глаза. Их не заменят тысячи других . . . [72]

The didactic elements in the works of the programmatic writers are selected and evaluated with exceeding care. If only the same consideration were given to the elements of style! Incidentally, errors also occur in the didactic elements — at any rate when literature is concerned. Here is an example from Panfyorov's "In the Name of the Young":

«А помните, как Собакевич угощал Чичикова? —
—· Слышь, в церкви места не было, а появился городничий, и место нашлось».

As it happens, Gogol's Chichikov was entertained by, and heard the anecdote about the mayor from Petukh (not Sobakevich) in the second volume of *Myortvyye dushi* (Dead Souls). If a secondary-school pupil were to make such a blunder in an essay he would certainly be given a lower grade. For the same reason the contributors to *Oktyabr* where "downgraded" in the eyes of the Soviet reading public. Perhaps Tvardovsky

[71] *Oktyabr*, No. 8, 1963, p. 22.
[72] *Oktyabr*, No. 12, 1962, p. 30.

had just such adherents of socialist realism in mind when he said at a
European writers' forum:

> As a reader I am completely at variance with the author: if the
> author wants to move me, I laugh; if he tries occasionally to make
> me laugh, he leaves me cold...[73]

It may be thought that the lameness and insipidity of the programmatic
writers' language is due to mere lack of literary talent in those I have
discussed. I do not think that this is the real reason, for it is unjust to state
flatly that writers like Panfyorov or even Chakovsky are devoid of literary
ability. I believe that the reason for the sterility of their prose should be
sought in the esthetic principles which govern their writing. In an article
entitled "The Fate of the Novel," Fedin wrote:

> The novelist's attitude to form springs from his awareness that it is
> derived from the material chosen by the artist.[74]

Is it not possible that this basic tenet of "Marxist esthetics," which
so insistently stresses the subordination of form to content, has rooted
itself rather too deeply in the minds of some Soviet writers? — Not all,
however, for form, which is primarily the system of images as expressed
by language, is viewed by some as having a value and end in itself. It is
my opinion that to set oneself a pragmatic task in a literary work is bound
to restrict creative freedom and foredoom the author to linguistic sterility.
This, apparently, is what has happened to the programmatic writers. This
explains their lack of individuality and their drab and stereotyped language.

In his book *O yazyke khudozhestvennoy literatury* (Literary Language),
Academician V. Vinogradov quotes Emile Zola's still apt comment on
writers who are prone to use "commonplaces." These writers, said Zola,

> ...appropriate that style which is hanging in the air. They seize
> upon ready-made phrases which are hovering all round them. Their
> phrases never come from the personality, and they write as if they
> were taking dictation; probably they only have to open a tap in order
> to write...[75]

If we agree that, unlike the language of everyday conversation,
business, and science, the language of the short story or novel is governed
by its own immanent laws (in other words, its phonetic structure, vocabu-

[73] *Literaturnaya gazeta*, August 10, 1963.
[74] *Literaturnaya gazeta*, August 6, 1963.
[75] Translated from the Russian.

lary, syntax, expressiveness and imagery are conditioned by poetic considerations), it is at times difficult to call programmatic writing literature. If we did, we should have to revise the very concept of literature.

*

Despite its affinities to the first, traditional, trend, I feel justified in dealing separately with the literary stream which has emerged in recent years and which I call "emancipatory realism." The elements which link the representatives of this third group are their striving for the maximum "liberation" of their creative "egos" and their search for new linguistic and stylistic forms. The authors whom I have in mind are, primarily, Kazakov, Solzhenitsyn and Aksyonov — writers who are dissimilar in style but resemble one another in their unconditional and energetic rejection of the pragmatism and verbal poverty of the programmatic writers.

The greatest affinity to the first, or "classical," group of modern Soviet writers is displayed by Kazakov. The precision, polish and forcefulness of his vocabulary are reminiscent of Bunin, as is the plastic quality of his characterization. The short story "Manka," which appeared in the anthology *Na polustanke* (At the Half-Way Point) in 1959, is a case in point. This does not, however, make Kazakov an imitator, for his works contain an incontestably individual element, something intrinsic to the very nature of his esthetic approach which is reflected in his ability to reveal the finest emotional nuances of his heroes. This he achieves by methods of implication or suggestion which are entirely his own. The following lines from the short story "Tralivali," which tells of the buoy-keeper Yegor, a dissipated drunkard and talented singer, illustrate this:

И, волоча полушубок, идет он в сторожку, ложится к Аленке, будит ее и жалко и жадно приникает, прижимается к ней, чувствует только ее, как ребенок, готовый заплакать. Зажмурившись, трется он лицом о ее плечо, целует ее в шею, слабея от радости, от горячей любви и нежности к ней, чувствуя на лице ответные, быстрые и нежные ее поцелуи, уже не думая ни о чем и ничего не желая, а желая только, чтобы так продолжалось всегда. [76]

Kazakov's handling of peasant speech is magnificently fresh, and enables him to achieve the "ornamental effect" of a *skaz* (tale) as the following quotations from the short story "Nikishka's Secrets" demonstrate:

Конь издали еще заметит, **насторчит** уши. [77]

---

[76] *Po doroge* (Along the Road), Moscow, 1961.
[77] *Na polustanke* (At the Half-Way Point), Moscow, 1959, p. 113.

Видит, что отец в шторм на льдине качается, **ревит**; еще видит, семга огромная сердитая **бережает**, по дну плывет. [78]

Likewise the line of dialogue from the short story "Old Men":

«Я тебя переживу! Моя кровь **неумирущая!**» [79]

Kazakov does not use popular speech in his connecting narrative.

Solzhenitsyn's emergence in Soviet literature was an event of immense importance. I believe that it is no exaggeration to say that, with regard to language and style "One Day in the Life of Ivan Denisovich" is a milestone in the history of Russian literature. The very structural principles on which this *skaz* is built are remarkable and out of the ordinary. It combines in a strange and productive, that is, striking, amalgam ordinary first-person narrative with a peculiar form of indirect speech in which the personality of the narrator intrudes, speaking of himself as if in the third person (and sometimes in the first person as well) as in:

«А миг — наш! Пока начальство разберется — приткнись, где потеплее, **сядь, сиди,** еще наломаешь спину».

The imagery, use of words and phrases, rhythm, and flux of this story are all drawn from the depths of the language of the people, a language which, particularly in the last few decades, seemed to have been drubbed to death by other writers and stylists. In Solzhenitsyn's hands, however, it is alive and genuine; for which reason it is unjust, as certain critics have done, to number Solzhenitsyn among the disciples of such an artificial stylist as Remizov:

И все равно не **слышит,** обалдуй, спина еловая, на тебе, толкнул поднос! Плесь, плесь! Рукой его свободной — по шее, по шее!..

The new sounds, forms, shades of meaning, neologisms, and sayings with which "One Day in the Life of Ivan Denisovich" abounds are so real and convincing that it is difficult to decide what the author has borrowed from life and what he has invented:

«**Прокликаться** через толпу»; «**разморчивая** минутка»; «**недокурок**»; «**терпельник**»; «**дежурняк**»; «валянок **горетый**»; «не **пролья**»; «обычай знает **напрожег**»; «снег **мелочкий-мелочкий**»; «**ни укрыва ни грева**»; «теплый зяблого разве когда поймет».

[78] *Ibid.*, p. 123.
[79] *Ibid.*, p. 163.

At the European writers' forum Tvardovsky said of Solzhenitsyn:

> I'd like to hear anyone say that this writer is weighed down by the narrow precepts of socialist realism, that he is not free in his discourse with the reader, that his hands are in any way tied... [80]

This is a prime example of word-juggling. If we leave aside the consideration that his choice of political prisoners as characters may have been dictated by extraneous circumstances, then the author was indeed free, and the very fact of freedom enabled him to create a genuine masterpiece untrammelled by the limitations of the officially-prescribed literary method.

The last of the writers of whom I wish to speak as literary innovators against the background of traditional as well as "socialist realist" prose is Aksyonov. With regard to language, he is extremely gifted and original, although here, as in other respects, he cannot yet, perhaps, be considered as having attained complete mastery of his craft: his choice of words and phrases is sometimes a little haphazard; certain stylistic mannerisms are sometimes overdone, and on occasion his style is simply slipshod. In "Oranges from Morocco," for example, as a result of insufficient individuality of style, the identity of the various narrators sometimes becomes confused in the reader's mind.

Viewed as a whole, however, his work displays freshness and talent. Both Aksyonov and his characters are young, and their language is the language of a generation *in statu nascendi.* The last important feature of this language is its slanginess, the use of such expressions as: *chuvak* (boy), *chuvika* (girl), *rubat* (to eat); *nakiryatsya* (to get drunk); *razognut* (to stop lying) an antonymic formation from *zagibat; zasmuret* (to grow sad); *skazat dlya ponta* (to say for fun); *podkleit kadrishku* (to "pick-up" a girl).

What is important is the extraordinary, almost unprecedentedly intense expressiveness of the spoken and written word. One cannot help interpreting this feature of his work as a protest against the drab jargon of the newspapers and officialdom, which has taken root in the language of daily intercourse. What a contrast between *blesk!* or *zhelezno!* and the deadly dull, bureaucratic *neplokho!* How vivid are such compounds as *paren-gvozd!* or *molotki rebyata!* A certain striving towards self-assertion and independence is to be detected in the dynamic expressions of this generation:

«схвачено?»; «тягомотина!»; «кончай рязину тянуть!»; «Фидель толкнул речугу»; «закапать мозги»; «здесь нам не обломиться»; «надоел ты мне по зеленые лампочки», и т. д.

[80] *Literaturnaya gazeta,* August 10, 1963.

From this viewpoint of linguistic purity, vulgarisms such as the diminutives *privetki*, *perepasovochka*, *otgazovochka*, *kadrishki*, are, of course, unacceptable, but this is only a minor consideration in relation to the essence of the phenomenon as a whole.

I should like to note a few of Aksyonov's stylistic peculiarities, his monologue structure, for example. Here is the scene in "Ticket to the Stars" in which the brothers take leave of each other:

«Скажи там папе и маме» . . . говорю я.

«Скажу», говорит он.

«Пиши им, старик», говорит он.

«Обязательно», говорю я.

«Вот и отдохнул», говорит он.

«Жаль, что так получилось», говорит он.

«Ладно, старик», говорит он.

«Держи хвост пистолетом», говорит он.

«Пока!» говорит он. [81]

or the unusual style of "Oranges from Morocco":

«А мы стоим в очереди за апельсинами. Да, мы стоим в очереди за апельсинами! Да, кретины-мозговики, и вы, мальчики-умники. Я Колька Калчанов, хочу поесть апельсинчиков, и в моей руке холодные пальцы Кати! Да, я строю дома! Да, я мечтаю построить собственный город! Фиг вам! Вот мы перед вами все, мы строим дома, и ловим рыбу, и бурим скважины, и мы стоим в очереди за апельсинами!» [82]

The method of achieving effect by repetition and cumulation is also to be found in the poetry of the younger generation.

In the poem "A Window Overlooking White Trees," for example, Yevtushenko writes:

В костюме и не модном и не новом,
Как и всегда, не модном и не новом,
Да, как всегда, не модном и не новом,
Спускается профессор в гардероб.
«Ну что такое, — где же этот номер?
А может быть, не брал у вас я номер?
Куда он делся?» — Трет рукою лоб.

---

[81] *Yunost*, No. 7, 1961, p. 57.
[82] *Yunost*, No. 1, 1963, p. 36.

In conclusion, I should like to make a few observations about the effect of Western influences on the language of Soviet literature, particularly on that of its younger representatives. I shall draw most of my examples from Aksyonov.

The "pernicious" aspects of Western culture — "pop" music, for example — exert a powerful attraction on Soviet youth. Two *stilyagi*, in Aksyonov's "Ticket to the Stars" put a tape recorder on a window-sill and flood the whole courtyard with jazz music:

«Герка! Герка! — кричит дворник. — Кончай **тлетворную!**»

But:

«Я все что угодно могу танцевать . . . И **липси**, и вальс-гавот, и даже», — она шепнула мне на ухо, «**рок-н-ролл**». [83]

Почему он не может послать ее подальше и уйти, насвистывая **рок-н-ролл**? [84]

Буги-вуги [записанные] на рентгеновских пленках. [85]

Разрешите пригласить вас, **миледи**, на один фокстрот . . . наверно научился в каком=нибудь **дансинге**. И сделав пробор, напялив лакирки . . . : «**О, май дир!**» [86]

Двубортная рубашка «демократка» ему бы даже не пошла, а уж расписная **голивудка** — тем более. [87]

Как это в столицах называется — **бармен**, что ли? [88]

The names of Western filmstars and other celebrities are in frequent usage:

Расскажи ему про **Брижитт Бардо!** [89]

. . . смугляночка. Тип **Сильваны Пампанини.** [90]

. . . играть так, как играет всемирноизвестный негр **Уилт Чемберлен.** [91]

In connection with the film "Mother Johana":

[83] "Oranges From Morocco," *Yunost*, No. 1, 1963.
[84] "Ticket to the Stars," *Yunost*, Nos. 6—7, 1961.
[85] *Ibid.*
[86] German, "My Dear Man," *Zvezda*, Nos. 10—12, 1961.
[87] Chakovsky, "Light of a Distant Star," *Oktyabr*, No. 12, 1962.
[88] Fedin, "Camp Fire," *Novy mir*, No. 8, 1961.
[89] "Oranges From Morocco," *op. cit.*
[90] "Oranges From Morocco," *op. cit.*
[91] "Ticket to the Stars," *op. cit.*

«Помнишь колокола? Беззвучно . . .»
«И женский плач . . .»
«Масса находок . . .»
«Неореализм трещит по всем швам . . .»
«Но итальянцы . . .»
«Если вспомнить 'Сладкую жизнь' . . .» [92]

. . . знаешь, что такое супрематизм, ташизм, экзистенциализм, а не можешь отличить Рубенса от Рембрандта. [93]

Foreign expressions are also fairly common in colloquial speech:

«**Киндер**», сказал Фрам. [94]
«Все будет **тип-топ**». [95]
Ну, пошли! . . **Аривидерчирома**. [96]

The most frequent loans are made from American words and expressions. These are by no means limited to the numerous transliterated sporting terms which have found their way into Russian of late such as: signer, liner, sprinter, sparring partner, hook (to the jaw):

«У **миледи** новое платье?» [97]
«Наш простой советский **супермен**». [98]
Я пошел в сторону фосфаторского **Бродвея**. [99]
«**Сэр**, я предлагаю провести . . .» [100]
«**Гуд бай**, пожиратели». [101]
«И вообще все — **о'кэй!**» [102]

Or, finally, school slang:

«Держи гуся [= пожми руку]!»
«**Гуд монинг, леди!**» [103]

[92] "Oranges From Morocco," *op. cit.*
[93] "Ticket to the Stars," *op. cit.*
[94] *Ibid.*
[95] *Ibid.*
[96] "Oranges From Morocco," *op. cit.*
[97] "Ticket to the Stars," *op. cit.*
[98] *Ibid.*
[99] "Oranges From Morocco," *op. cit.*
[100] "Ticket to the Stars," *op. cit.*
[101] *Ibid.*
[102] *Ibid.*
[103] Dolinina, "In Our Eleven-Year School," *Yunost*, No. 7, 1961, p. 95.

BURTON RUBIN

Highlights of the 1962–1963 Thaw

The first definite signs of the "thaw" in the fall of 1962 began to appear in September and the most decisive one was the Plenary Board Meeting of the Moscow Organization of the RSFSR Union of Writers. It took place at a time when the news from the Soviet Union had been almost uniformly discouraging. In other areas of Soviet life there had been a marked tendency during the preceding months toward a greater harshness of controls as well as toward increased hardships for the population. One might have expected that the discontent and popular resentment engendered by these national misfortunes would have issued in a tightening of controls in cultural life. This, as the results of the plenary meeting showed, did not happen. In fact, the meeting, which was called to discuss the work of young Moscow writers, turned out rather well for the young writers and the forces of liberalism they represent. It would have been rash to say that the meeting heralded any final resolution of the war that had been raging for several years in the Soviet literary world between the defenders of old-style orthodoxy and the liberals. But it clearly promised a somewhat less harassed development for the literary tendencies that the liberal writers, both young and old, had been fostering.

The meeting lasted two days, September 28–29, and was attended by some three hundred writers, editors and journalists. It signaled the opening round of a discussion of the work of young Soviet writers that was to have culminated with two further meetings at the end of the year: the Fourth All-Union Meeting of Young Writers, scheduled for December, 1962, and the Plenary Meeting of the Board of the USSR Union of Writers the exact date of which had not been announced.

On the very eve of the meeting, Stepan Shchipachev, the chairman of the board of the Moscow organization, addressed himself in an interview in *Literatura i Zhizn* to the question of why such a great fuss was being made about the young. Didn't it serve to point up a division between the generations which was in fact doubtful, and, in effect, harmful? Shchipachev implied that some anxious thought had been given to this question, but that nevertheless "the necessity for a serious discussion of the work of the young has grown ripe and it will not do to shy away from such a discussion."[1]

---

[1] *Literatura i Zhizn*, September 28, 1962

The need for a "direct, comradely and sincere discussion" of the literature of the young had become, he stressed the point once more, "all too apparent." Shchipachev's words were portentous, and a measure of the importance that was being attributed to the discussion. What reason did Shchipachev cite to justify this special attention to young writers? Only that growing numbers of them had appeared in Soviet literature in recent years and had made their presence felt with a surge of talent that could not be ignored. He did not, however, adduce another fact which had much more to do with the initiation of the discussion than did the numerical strength of the young writers. That is, the special character of the literature they had produced, and the embittered polemics, just a step this side of being internecine, that had broken out around it. Shchipachev did point out, without directly naming it as the underlying reason for the meeting, that too frequently in the past the works of young writers had become an occasion for critical excesses on the part of certain unnamed critics, and complained that such excessiveness could lead to no good. Instead, he advocated for the forthcoming meeting a "calm, reasonable and objective discussion." As it turned out, the most notable feature of the meeting was precisely the establishment of a "calm and reasonable" tone with respect to the young writers. The attempt to normalize relations to initiate a domestic literary policy of peaceful co-existence by seeking to convince its enemies that they had nothing to fear of distrust in the young—these were the key notes that were struck in the two reports read at the meeting by A. Borshchagovsky and Ya. Smelyakov.

Borshchagovsky reported on the prose of Moscow's young writers, and at the very outset announced his theme:

> I want to say at once that the young literature of recent years — and I will try to prove this with examples — naturally and correctly evaluates the past, deeply and sincerely believes in the great feats of the Communists of our country, and precisely in these feats sees its own moral ideal. [2]

In other words, we were left to conclude that the accusations of nihilism, cynicism, of the rejection of Russia's revolutionary past and the acceptance of bourgeois ideological influences, accusations which Kochetov and critics of his persuasion had been bringing against the young for several years, were completely unfounded. This, in precisely these words, is what Borshchagovsky said. His main point was that the appearance of a young generation of Soviet writers had not been marked by any break in the ideological traditions of Soviet prose; that the fictional heroes of the young writers, their hopes, political outlook and ambitions for Soviet society were identical with those of the earlier heroes of Soviet literature

---

[2] *Literaturnaya Gazeta*, September 29, 1962

And who is Alexander Kashurnikov, the hero of Chivilekhin's *Silver Rails*? A Communist, a fighter, the spiritual brother and inheritor of Pavel Korchagin, a paver of new roads, a man who has given his life for his motherland and the future victory of Communism.[3]

It is with such arguments that Borshchagovsky sought to provide a framework in which the literature of the young would appear as orthodox as that of their literary predecessors. He detailed the character traits of several contemporary literary heroes from the works of such writers as Julian Semyonov, Yuri Kazakov, and Vasili Aksyonov, and concluded:

We are obliged to say with all directness and sharpness that these figures have not only not allowed themselves to be subjected to bourgeois and modernist influence, but, on the contrary, are polemically and passionately opposed to bourgeois ideology and the fashionable literary and philosophical theories of the West.[4]

Borshchagovsky's conclusions had to be honored in their intention. They were aimed at disarming the Kochetovs. Nevertheless, it was impossible not to resist his effort to deny that there are any differences in principle between the literature of the Stalin era and the mentality it reflected and the literature and mentality of today's young writers. Neither could Borshchagovsky's all too transparent strategem fool the proponents of the Stalinist literary orthodoxies. They were right, after all, in detecting in the work of the young a freedom from ideological dogmatism which leaves them ready to accept new artistic methods and social truths from wherever they may come. They were equally correct in seeing that the young do reject crucial aspects of the past and wish to have done with more of them that have continued to exist into the present. Borshchagovsky did not exaggerate when he said that the young are, for the most part, loyal Communists and patriotic Soviet citizens. But the orthodox critics are again right in understanding that patriotism and Communism have meanings for the young that are completely at variance with the ones they give to these ideas; and that the Communist society the young envisage, one in which Yevtushenko wants "Truth to be President," will do without the services of the defenders of orthodoxy, just as it will do without the services of the Communist Party as it is presently constituted.

How much better it would have been if Borshchagovsky had been able to admit all this openly, without disguising his purpose. In any case, Borshchagovsky's own attitudes towards the prose of the young Muscovites he discussed clearly showed where he stands on these issues. He spoke out in favor of many of the demands the young have advanced: for a more

---

[3] *Ibid.*
[4] *Ibid.*

complex, non-dogmatic view of life — "I don't much like people for whom everything is simple," says one of Gladilin's heroes; for the right of young writers like Aksyonov to portray their "confused" young heroes who are skeptical of all the truths of the past and given to reflecting out loud on all kinds of forbidden questions. Borshchagovsky comforted the opposition with assurances that these young skeptics are at bottom decent Soviet patriots who will eventually take their places as workers for the cause of Communism. His final appeal was to an open mind, to the avoidance of judging dogmatically by the various norms "which so hindered us, the writers of an older generation . . .[5]"

Ya. Smelyakov, who spoke about the poetry of young Muscovites, was somewhat less tolerant in his approach than was Borshchagovsky. But even he supported the central thesis put forward by the latter:

> From whence have our present day young poets appeared? They have emerged from the people, and the peculiarities of their work are explained by the present atmosphere of the life of the country. They do not stand opposed to the Soviet poetry of the older generations, but represent, so to speak, new branches in the eternally green tree of Soviet Russian poetry.[6]

Smelyakov placed great emphasis upon certain critical standards that were largely ignored by Borshchagovsky. Civic-mindedness (*grazhdanst-vennost*), commitment to [Communist] ideas (*ideinost*), and publicism (*publitsichnost*) are the virtues he singled out as constituting the highest measure of talent in poetry. He found many of the young poets lacking in these respects. The tone of his criticism was restrained. He had nothing but the highest praise for the artistic skill of such poets as Vosnesensky and Akhmadullina, but he found their talents too personal and exotic, too removed from the general life of the nation and the everyday concerns of the Soviet working men.

> The young poets of the present time have been in the [Soviet] Far East, in Siberia, in Paris, in Prague, in New York and even in distant splendid Cuba. But they have left almost untouched the life of our working class. It seems to me that the young poets not only simply ought to, but are obliged to devote lyrical and epic works to the working class.[7]

Robert Rozhdestvensky, on the other hand, is a young poet who earned Smelyakov's unqualified admiration. Rozhdestvensky "likes t conduct sharp polemics with our ideological opponents." Rozhdestvensky'

---

[5] *Ibid.*

[6] *Ibid.*

[7] *Ibid.*

polemical verse, Smelyakov declared, "seems to me important, and more-over, essential. It would be very fine if poems like these were in every book of every young poet."

Such admonitions to convert themselves into political propagandists could not be any more palatable to the young now that people like Smelya-kov were making them in a spirit of "comradely" criticism than they were in the form in which they were previously put. They do not wish to be gently coaxed into embarking on discredited artistic roads any more than they wished to be intimidated into doing so. Smelyakov's report indicated that the young will, if ever, gain recognition of their independence only after a hard fight which still lies in the future.

Smelyakov's report was a good example of the conservatives' "new look" last fall. Both its tone and its slogans were destined to be imitated by those who were unhappy about what the young stand for. This was made clear by the character of the summary of the plenary proceedings that appeared in *Literatura i Zhizn*. The summary carried the significant title "From Positions of Civic-mindedness." In keeping with the "new look" the conservative newspaper's summary was moderate in tone; its criticism of the young, as was stressed in several places, was motivated by the purest "friendliness." But a comparison of the summary in *Literatura i Zhizn* with that in *Literaturnaya Gazeta* was instructive.

Literatura i Zhizn was careful to select more passages in the reports which drew attention to the ideological lapses of the young. Especially in Smelyakov could the newspaper find support for contending that the young literary generation frequently failed to perform its civic duties as Soviet writers. Still, there was something unmistakeably new afoot when this newspaper, striking a self-critical pose, admitted that in the attitudes of many writers of the older generation toward the young "one can often notice excesses: some encounter the pleads of new names with disapproval and irritation."[8]

Hardly a word was said at the meeting about the death-dealing Stalinist literary dogmas, socialist realism and *partiinost*. This silence was welcome. But it could not be taken as an occasion for true rejoicing as long as the defenders of orthodoxy kept trying to force the same old ideological traitjacket upon the young under cover of a new slogan. The literary tradition of "civic-mindedness" is an honorable one in Russia. In the 19th century it had no other meaning than that writers should stand in an antagonistic relation to reality, that they should consider it their duty as men to criticize the evils and shortcomings of their society as they, and not any supposedly omniscient political authority, understood them. This

[8] *Literatura i Zhizn*, October 5, 1962

is the way the young wish to understand their own duty to Soviet society. The change in terminology from *partiinost* to *grazhdanstvennost* could only be as significant as the Party would permit it to be. And there was very little likelihood that the Party was prepared to understand *grazhdanstvennost* as the young wished it to be. This again meant that the young would continue to have a fight on their hands.

The young writer who benefited most conspicuously from this new, tolerant attitude toward his generation was Yevgeni Yevtushenko. Critics formerly antagonistic toward him, now became friendly. But, they still had reservations; and, these reservations made it clear why their sympathy for the poet was bound to vanish as soon as the Party's support for him did.

In October 1962, *Nezhnost* (Tenderness), a book of poetry by Yevtushenko which had just been published, was reviewed in *Izvestia* by Stepan Lesnevsky.[9] As the reviewer pointed out, *Nezhnost* was the twenty-nine-year old poet's ninth book of poetry.

At that time, a new attitude toward Yevtushenko had developed among critics who had formerly been unfriendly toward him. He was no longer the bad boy of Soviet poetry. Almost with a single voice, critics had begun to talk of him as having grown "more serious." One did not have to go far to find the reason for this. Yevtushenko had been writing poems about the Cuban revolution in such a way as to win the praise of all right-minded Soviet critics. It was not that Yevtushenko had "sold out" and deliberately sought the praise of men for whom the faithful reflection of official ideology is all that matters in literature. Yevtushenko felt no closer to those people than he did when he was their favorite whipping boy. The fact is that politically he has more in common with the young Western radicals of the "New Left" than he does with these self-styled "Communist" critics; he simply believes that popular socialist revolutions are to be welcomed, and he finds them especially exhilarating in their heady initial stages when they are still free of grosser degenerative phenomena. So, Yevtushenko has written verse celebrating Revolution — "The Queen of Beauty," — particularly the Cuban revolution and the self-sacrificing revolutionaries he met during his sojourn in Cuba as *Pravda* correspondent. All this gave Lesnevsky grounds to assert that the essential quality of Yevtushenko's latest collection of poetry consisted in it *grazhdanstvennost* (civic-mindedness), which means, in the Soviet critical vocabulary, its fidelity to the ideological tradition of Soviet literature.

Yevtushenko has a poem in *Nezhnost* in which he says that the step of the Havana sentries sounded in his "soul as once (oh, time — you are no

---

[9] *Izvestia*, October 3, 1962

barrier!) did the steps of the Red Guard patrols on the streets of pitch-black Leningrad." Lesnevsky commented: "No, these are not merely the echoes of sublime memories, but the lofty standard by which the poet seeks to measure his contemporaries." Lesnevsky's observation is correct. Yevtushenko does indeed seek to measure his contemporaries by the standards of pure idealism he sees in the early years of the Russian Revolution; but, he finds most of them sorely lacking. It is at this point that Lesnevsky runs out of praise for Yevtushenko. There is the following stanza in one of Yevtushenko's poems:

> Let us think about the great and the small,
> So as to live deeply, to live not just any old way.
> What is great cannot be a betrayal;
> But it can be betrayed by men.

"Isn't this said too hastily?" Lesnevsky asks. "The haste is not a matter of sloppiness; it is not that the poet worked too little over his form. It consists in a kind of light-headedness with which Yevtushenko rushes to pronounce words whose cost was suffering and heroism."

One has to be initiated into the polemics that have raged around the issue of the attitudes of writers like Yevtushenko toward the Soviet past in order to appreciate what this skirmish is all about. Lesnevsky is quick to take personal offense at the accusatory tone of Yevtushenko's words. The past, according to him, is not correctly described in terms of men who betrayed a great ideal, but rather of men who, at the cost of great personal suffering, did Stalin's bidding because of their heroic devotion to an ideal which they knew his wickedness could not prevent from being realized. This is one of the characteristic defenses of the Stalin generation, as it is of the present Party leadership. Lesnevsky is willing to go along with Yevtushenko's declaration that "the revolution" needs "soldiers and not lackeys." As long, that is, as Yevtushenko's belligerence is directed against approved targets like the bureaucrat, "Chairman Pankratov," in one of his poems, or, in another, the time-serving, cynical professor. But he is angered by hints that there are other foes besides the approved ones against whom Yevtushenko is waging a war. Yevtushenko has given a definition of poetry in *Nezhnost:*

> Poetry is not a peaceful chapel
> Poetry is a cruel war
> It contains its own deceptive maneuvers.
> When there's war, then war is what poetry must be.

Lesnevsky's irritated response to this is amusing in its fidgety suspiciousness: "Now look here," he writes, "we don't need any deceptive maneuvers in poetry. Let's have it so that not only Yevtushenko, but also we who love his youth, shall possess the firm knowledge that 'since dawn awaiting the trumpets call, the cavalry stands ready for battle . . .' And then we will be able to predict with certainty from what flank and in what direction the cavalry of verse will set out.''

During the "thaw" in the fall of 1962 there were several revealing items in the Press which contained vivid descriptions of how the Soviet literary process makes certain that the "cavalry of verse," and of prose as well, sets out from the right direction. In November, two young writers from Rostov-on-the-Don had a letter published in *Literaturnaya Gazeta*.[10] They complained that of the fifteen newest members of the Rostov writer's organization, the youngest was just under forty, the rest ranged in age from old to ancient. Young writers were being barred from the Rostov organization, and the letter explained how. First of all, they have difficulty getting their first books published and, thus, of meeting one of the pre-requisites of membership. But even when they finally do come out with their first books, there is no guarantee of automatic membership.[11] Before the Rostov literary officials will accept the membership application of a young writer he has to demonstrate that he has become sufficiently "kneaded" (*obkatyvat*) — an interesting professional colloquialism used in the letter.

> Not all of them become "kneaded" even with their fifth book. Some lose their peculiarities too slowly, others acquire them too slowly . .
> How many times have the young poets Skoryatin, Vegin and Primerov been treated to the edification: — this isn't your Moscow here! We've got enough Yevtushenkos and Voznesenskys.

> What are these "edifiers" afraid of more than anything else. The possibility of mistakes. Their own, of course. But they pretend that they themselves are infallible, that only the young can make errors. Out of "love for humanity" the demand arises that the young poets travel along only well-beaten paths, and not turn off into treacherous, unexplored . . . virgin fields.

> And so a flood of mediocre, but, on the other hand, "errorless" poems and stories begin to inundate the champions of the golden (but, in reality — grey) mean.

Apart from the obvious, there is an additional point worth taking note of here. Very often it is not because the men who pass judgment on the

---

[10] Daniil Dolinsky and Veniamin Zhak, "A gody prokhodyat," *Literaturnay Gazeta*, November 24, 1962.

[11] Nor are these first books quite the ones their young authors had originall written: "Usually the life and breath is cut and compressed out of it. You see 'brevity is the sister of talent.' But, wherever you look, this sister turns out to be th murderer of her brother."

work of young writers are die-hard obscurantists of the Kochetov camp that they exert their conservative influence, but because they belong to the class of people called the "scared ones," men who were broken by the trials of the past and who, last fall, were too timid to take advantage of the newly legitimatized opportunities for freer artistic expression.

The principal complaint of the two Rostov letter-writers is one that was heard from young writers with increasing frequency last year. Their older colleagues positively "distrust" them. The result is that some of them find it advantageous to adapt to the requirements of the people who stand above them, thus destroying whatever talent and originality they happen to possess. Egor Isayev, a poet just under forty who himself is usually numbered among the younger generation of writers, gave a particularly unpleasant illustration of this human and artistic misfortune. Shortly after Leonid Ilyichev, the chief of the Central Committee's "Ideological Commission," had initiated last winter's ideological campaign with a speech he delivered on December 26 before a delegation of the young artistic intelligentsia, Isayev met a friend who inquired about what had been said by Ilyichev. Isayev's friend had a book of poetry about to be published, and, Isayev reported, it contained several "formalistic" poems which its author had refused to exclude from it. Isayev described Ilyichev's harsh words about formalism and reminded his friend of the poems which he had insisted upon including in his forthcoming book. His friend's response is instructive and sad: "He smiled and said: Well, you see, afterwards . . . I took them out . . ."

In November 1962, an exciting new talent emerged in Soviet literature. Alexander Solzhenitsyn, whose story, "One Day in the Life of Ivan Denisovich," marked the high-point of the wave of "anti-Stalin" literary protest at this period. The critical reception this story and his subsequent ones received provides a perfect reflection of the course of the "thaw."

When Alexander Solzhenitsyn's unprecedented account of life in a former Soviet concentration camp appeared in *Novy mir* it was accorded what can only be described as an ecstatic reception. The verdict of the critics was unanimous: "One Day in the Life of Ivan Denisovich" was hailed as a sublime new work of Soviet literature, one whose superlative qualities derived not only from its uncompromised portrayal of a bitter and important truth about the past, but also from the talent with which it was written. The critics were clearly overwhelmed. Tolstoy's and Dostoevsky's names came to the lips of one trying to measure Solzhenitsyn's magnitude; several found an authentic epic quality in his story; all of them would at least have agreed with Konstantin Simonov's appraisal — "a powerful talent has arrived in our literature." This was a rare phenomenon, the sudden emergence of a forty-four-year old Ryazan mathematics teacher, formerly

a complete unknown, with not a single published work behind him, into
the company of Russia's finest prose masters.

"One Day in the Life of Ivan Denisovich" possesses a peculiar power
It is not written in the offended tone of "About This I Cannot Keep Silent.'
It is contained by a detached, workmanlike narrative manner that come
from the concentration of its energy on the most meticulously minute
description of the details involved in getting through the single day o
prison life, from reveille to lights-out, it covers. In places it reads almos
like a kind of manual, a book of instructions on how to survive hunger and
cold and the sadistic ferocity of the guards — the three elements agains
which Ivan Denisovich and his mates must wage their daily battle in
order, literally, to live another day. Ivan Denisovich has wet his felt boot
while washing the floor in the guard-house: "It wasn't a good idea to ge
your felt boots wet first thing in the morning. You didn't have anything
extra to change into, even if you could run back to the barracks. During
his eight years inside, Shukov had seen all kinds of ups and downs in the
footwear situation . . ." Now, a tip on how to get most out of a meal
"Shukov ate his ration nearly to the end, but he saved a bare crust, a
round piece from the top, because you couldn't clean out the mush in you
bowl with a spoon like you could with bread."

"One Day in the Life of Ivan Denisovich" is not a cry of pain; it doe
not pile on horrors. The shattering impact of this story is produced precisely
by its restrained, objective manner; the suppressed force of that matter
of-fact appraisal of a bread crust's superiority over a spoon is sprung by th
reader's imagination, and how slight a movement of it is needed to under
stand how hungry a man can be. Solzhenitsyn's prose style contribute
powerfully to the story's effect. In keeping with Shukov's village speech
it is frequently ungrammatical, composed in rich variety of the colloquial
isms of the uneducated folk and the semi-obscene, harsh argot of the camp
It has a jagged texture. Frequent ellipsis and the staccato brevity o
thoughts and observations reported on the run, broken down into th
most simple primitive statements. It is a coarse style, completely adequat
to the unbeautiful material it governs, capable of striking with a kineti
immediacy at the reader's perception.

Solzhenitsyn's laconicism frequently moves into aphorism — a specia
macabre variety of aphorism, again, appropriate to his material. Th
prisoners waited in the freezing cold while they were counted a half-doze
times on their way to work and back; counting was an important ceremon
at the camp, and Solzhenitsyn gives whole pages to describing how th
guards repeated the same process several times, until they came out wit
the right number of prisoners. For the guards, counting was especiall

important: — "The men meant more to a guard than gold. If there was one man missing on the other side of the wire — he'd soon be taking his place.

The prisoners worked in gangs, and whether they got their 550 grams of bread for the day depended upon how well they fulfilled their work norm. Shukhov's gang chief was a severe guardian of the brigade's interests; if he hadn't been feared by his men, some of them would have made off to a warm spot somewhere and ruined the day's work and the day's ration for the whole gang: — "Beat a dog once and you only have to show him the whip. The cold was vicious, but it had nothing on the gang boss. They all went back to work."

Nothing is more horrible in the story than the intolerable mutual dependence of one prisoner upon the other: if one shirks work, the others starve, if one is caught at the search with concealed chips of wood he had gathered during the day and was supposed to give up to the guards for their own stove, then even those who that evening would have had the right to add what they had gathered to the under-fed stove in their freezing barrack would have to give it up. — "Who is a prisoner's worst enemy? The guy next to him." — The pint-sized Moldavian, for example, who fell asleep in the construction shed, keeping several hundred prisoners waiting for an hour in the frozen, wind-torn steppe while the guard worried over the after-work count: — "If the escorts had handed him over to the crowd, they'd tear the goddam bastard to pieces."

It is with such aphoristic soundings of the depths of camp life that Solzhenitsyn punctuates his story. The prevailing prisoner ethic sums up the relationship into which hunger and cold had set these men, as beasts, against one another: — "You croak today, and me tomorrow."

From a purely artistic point of view, in its language, style and in the nobility of its author's vision, "One Day in the Life of Ivan Denisovich" was the most excitingly fresh work to have appeared in Soviet literature in many years; Solzhenitsyn earned the praise he received. But, of course, there was at least an equal measure of politics in the enthusiasm of Solzhenitsyn's reviewers, and this, at the time, was its most significant aspect.

The circumstances surrounding the publication of Solzhenitsyn's story were so extraordinary as to invite almost limitless speculations as to just what was going on in the Soviet Union at that moment. On November 23, 1962, in yet another secret speech (this time delivered at the final session of a plenary meeting of the Communist Party's Central Committee), Khrushchev was reported to have said that the story had been read by the Party leadership before it was published, and that he, Khrushchev, had personally authorized its appearance in its full, uncensored text. Moreover, he claimed to have done so against the opposition of other top Party leaders who had wanted various sections cut.[12]

Whatever Khrushchev's purposes were in undertaking last fall's vigorous resumption of de-Stalinization — it would be out of place here to speculate about them — its effects in Soviet literature were quite startling.

One of Solzhenitsyn's earliest reviewers[13] was Al. Dymshits, a critic whose relative intellectual sophistication has made him one of the chief theoreticians of the so-called "conservative" or Kochetov camp of Soviet writers.

The choice of the term "conservative" to describe these writers is not altogether satisfactory. But in one respect at least, in the position they took toward the Stalin era, they did adopt the posture of a classic conservatism. Ever since 1956, they had been insisting that the past had to be regarded as constituting a harmonious whole with the present, its achievements as representing an organic link with the well-being of Soviet society today. Any work of literature which described the grim truths of the "thirties" and "forties" uncompromisingly, unsweetened by a proper mixture with the achievements of those years, was aesthetically defective: disfigured by a "distorted perspective" on the past, and consequently, unacceptable by the standards of artistic truth applicable to realistic fiction. Under ordinary circumstances, this was the response one would have expected from Dymshits to so merciless an "anti-Stalin" work as Solzhenitsyn's story. That he did not respond to it this way, but, instead, added his voice to the unbroken chorus of praise Solzhenitsyn was receiving, was no small matter. The surrender it signalled seemed to mean that the Party had unfrozen a piece of artistic territory, located in the past, in which at last genuine standards of artistic truth could be applied. This is what, for the moment, it did mean. And what it implied, in the way of questions it would raise about the present as well as the past, was indeed startling. Dymshits' surrender was one of the more important promises that filled the air in Moscow in November 1962 with the excited expectation of a "new era"; an excitement best typified by the flurry of poetry evenings it engendered, including the huge evening of "young poetry" on November 30 in Moscow's Luzhniki sports stadium, where Robert Rozhdestvensky expressed his own and his audience's exhilarating confidence that "We will no longer say someone is thinking for us."

---

[12] The reports that "One Day in the Life of Ivan Denisovich" had been read and approved for publication by the highest Party authorities were later confirmed by L. F. Ilichev. About the resistance Khrushchev allegedly had to overcome in getting it approved, Ilichev had nothing to say. (*Pravda*, December 22, 1963.) That Khrushchev undoubtedly was resisted, however, and successfully so after December 1, 1962, was made quite clear by subsequent developments.

[13] *Literatura i Zhizn*, November 28, 1962

Unfortunately, this confidence was as short-lived as Dymshits' surrender. We now know that it was precisely because of the questions writers were raising about the Soviet past and present that Khrushchev was forced by the men they menaced to put a temporary end to the new wave of liberalism which he had sanctioned. By January 1962, the atmosphere had changed sufficiently for a discordant note to be sounded in the chorus of Solzhenitsyn's critics. In the third issue of *Literaturnaya Rossiya*, Lidia Fomenko had an article reviewing the imaginative prose of 1962. Among other things, she had this to say of Solzhenitsyn:

> Solzhenitsyn's tale, with all its artistic refinement and its cruel and bitter truth, nevertheless does not reveal the entire dialectic of that time. In it a passionate "No!" is said to the Stalin order . . . But the tale does not rise to a philosophical perception of that time, to a broad generalization capable of embracing within itself the conflicting phenomena of that epoch . . .
>
> "One Day in the Life of Ivan Denisovich" only approaches a tragic work of complete and all-embracing truth.[14]

Why this sudden reservation about Solzhenitsyn? Where does Fomenko see his failure to tell the whole truth about the Stalin era? She pin points it in the following words:

> One must not see in the past only monstrous evil-doings. The fortunate fact is that the cult was not as all-powerful as Stalin himself thought, as almost everybody thought then. The mighty power of the people was ascribed to one man. But that inexhaustible creative force carried on its great historical task.

Fomenko's criticism of Solzhenitsyn represented a reversion to the standard "conservative" manner of resisting works of literature about the Stalin era whose general approach to it was regarded as being too "gloomy," too "negative." The author, it would be pointed out, had forgotten that, despite Stalin, the Party had continued to pursue a correct line — the construction of Socialism. Despite Stalin, the people's life was based on heroism and fidelity to its Communist ideals. And, in order to represent a true perspective of the past, an author must allow the accents of his work to fall at least as heavily on its positive aspests as on its negative ones. He must, as Fomenko says, be able to show the *"creativity as well as the lawlessness of that time."* Fomenko carries her insistence on accenting the positive to absurd lengths. In "exposing the evils of the past," she writes, it is essential not only to counter-balance it with the good contained in the past; a writer "should also not lose sight of what is most important and new in the present." The logic here is elusive. Apparently,

---

[14] L. Fomenko, *Literaturnaya Rossiya*, No. 3, 1963.

if things are better today, this serves as proof that they could not have
been so bad yesterday. The logic of this argument may escape one, but its
intention is perfectly clear! "If we are unable to see the joy of our own
day, we will turn into professional dirge singers."

This, of course was the danger. In his speech to the artistic youth on
December 26, 1962, Leonid Ilyichev complanied that writers were swamp-
ing the literary journals with manuscripts on the "camp theme" and
stated that this was impermissible: it threatened to "push out the portrayal
of other aspects of our past and present" and to "impoverish the life of
the Soviet people, its history, its great achievements and splendid aspirations."[15] Fomenko's reservations about "One Day in the Life of Ivan
Denisovich" were an echo of this anxiety. Their aim was not only to prevent any truthful portrayal of the past, but also to suppress questions
about the personal and political responsibility for it of men and institutions still flourishing today.

In January the cultural situation in the Soviet Union was still unclear.
Fomenko was even rebuked for her temerity in criticizing "One Day in the
Life of Ivan Denisovich," and although since then several critics have
raised similar objections to the story, it continues, for obvious reasons, to
enjoy a peculiar immunity from official criticism. Two months later, however, when the critics got around to reviewing Solzhenitsyn's next story
"Matryona's Home," the terms of Fomenko's argument had been belliger-
ently fixed in the official position on literature. The position was stated by
Vadim Kozhevnikov, the editor of Znamya. Kozhevnikov's criticism of
"Matryona's Home," is worth quoting in full, for with it we have an interesting statement of the basic principle of socialist realism.

The science of joy is an inseparable quality of our literature, an
expression of its deepest optimism. It is true, it seems to me, that
recently there have been appearing on the pages of our journals too
many "querulous" stories and tales ... I must confess that I experienced a feeling of deep spiritual pain when I read in Novy mi
the story "Matryona's Home" by A. Solzhenitsyn, who has written such
a remarkable work as "One Day in the Life of Ivan Denisovich."
It seems to me that "Matryona's Home" was written by its author when
he was still in a state of mind in which he could not with any depth
understand the life of the people, the movement and real perspective
of that life. In the first post-war years, such people as Matryona really
did harness the plough to themselves in villages desolated by the
Germans. The Soviet peasantry performed a great feat in those circumstances and gave bread to the people, fed the country. This alone must
evoke a feeling of reverence and delight. To draw the Soviet village a

---

[15] *Literaturnaya Gazeta*, January 10, 1963.

Bunin's village of our day is historically incorrect. Solzhenitsyn's story convinces one over and over again: without a vision of historical truth, of its essence, there can be no full truth, no matter what the talent.[16]

This was not the first time that a Soviet writer had been told that he was lacking in that peculiar "vision of historical truth," or, rather, of its "essence," which is alleged to be the natural property of any artist who has mastered the philosophy of Marxism-Leninism and the "method" of Socialist Realism. The mystique of "historical truth" is the central doctrine of Socialist Realism and it has been used with unholy effect ever since the Charter of the First Congress of Soviet Writers in 1934 defined Socialist Realism as a method which demands of the artist an "historically concrete portrayal of reality in its revolutionary development." According to this formula in its customary interpretation, the ability of the writer to tell the truth about Soviet society depends upon his ability to grasp those essentially "progressive" elements in it which are illustrative of the major directions it is holding toward the future (its "revolutionary development.") He must know how to highlight the general and the typical in social development at the same time that he exposes the individual and aberrant for what they are. Lastly, he must be able to clearly announce his own sympathies for the "progressive" processes, thus aiding them along.

Since the mystique holds that the "essential" historical processes of Soviet society are moving unalterably toward the creation of a glorious new historical phenomenon — Communist society — any Soviet writer who understands this is bound to look upon his society with joyful optimism. If he should happen to notice, as Solzhenitsyn did in the post-war Russian village, some untoward aspect of Soviet reality, he will, nevertheless, also turn this to good account. He will view such aspects as "typical," inessential disharmonies in the overall historical process, and if he deals with them at all, it will only be in order to look behind them to the "essential" and to soften their features by placing his emphasis upon the latter. Thus, if Solzhenitsyn had grasped "the movement and real perspectives" of peasant life in 1953, he would have placed his portrait of the thoroughly forsaken, half-starved and overworked old peasant woman Matryona into the gilded frame of a eulogy for the "great feat" of the Soviet peasantry which did, in fact, feed the country after the war under impossible conditions. How much sense so happy a tale would have made to Matryona, and how just a story by Solzhenitsyn so conceived would have been to her life, is a question to which the sense of reality that underlies Socialist Realism is not particularly alert.

The argument of the Kozhevikovs is as old as philosophical rationalism, and owes much, in particular to Hegel in whose system the harmonious,

---

[16] *Literaturnaya Gazeta*, March 2, 1963.

rational development of reality took a peculiar vengeance on individual incongruities. Soren Kierkegaard in Denmark, and Vissarion Belinsky in Russia, raised a revolt against the Hegelian system in which the pain of individual human beings who somehow stood outside the "essential" development of reality was nullified by reality's overall harmoniousness and rationality. We recognize Hegel in modern dress in the Soviet critic who described a visit to an ancient burial mound, the scene of a bloody battle in which thousands had perished. He wrote that he was seized by horror at the thought of the suffering, death and grief that the ancient battle had brought. And then, not far from its site, he visited the Volgograd Hydro-Electric Station: " . . . the stunning spiritual experience was even doubled in force. Such a blinding force of truth opened up to us as alone could justify the whole enormity of the sacrifices."

What does one say to such a man? Do we remind him of Ivan Karamazov's refusal to accept God's entrance ticket to the eternal harmony as long as that harmony had been bought at the price of the tears of a single child who had suffered innocently? Or do we take a less uncompromising position, recognizing that future goods sometimes demand present sacrifices, but preserving at the same time enough moral fastidiousness to regard these sacrifices as desperately lamentable, in no easy way "justified"?

Viewed philosophically, the concept of history that lies at the center of Socialist Realism is a particularly pernicious example of the "tyranny of abstractions." Viewed politically, it represents a maneuver by an arbitrary political power to defend its authority from the challenge of the critical artistic imagination.

*

By early summer 1963, the fury of the official campaign against artistic dissidence had spent itself. In August, there were fresh signs of what for the moment appeared to be the onset of a new "thaw." Once again, Khrushchev had taken a direct hand in promoting it, and in doing so raised some unavoidable question about the future of Soviet literature and art and about himself as well.

The best literary news to have come out of the Soviet Union in many months was the publication in *Literaturnaya Gazeta* (August 13, 1963) of the speech which Ilya Ehrenburg delivered at the meeting in Leningrad of the European Association of Writers. The announcement on the eve of the four-day meeting (August 5—8) that Ehrenburg had been named as one of its participants seemed, in itself, a hopeful sign. But it was difficult to know at the time how exactly to evaluate it: was Ehrenburg's presence at this prestigious gathering with prominent Western writers merely a false show of official liberalism, or did it actually have some bearing on the internal cultural situation? When, however, the contents of Ehrenburg's speech became known, the answer to this question appeared to be less in doubt: the *Le Monde* correspondent reported that Ehrenburg's renewed advocacy, despite all the criticism of the previous nine months, of artistic experimentation had "excited lively interest among the young Soviet intelligentsia."[17] And, when this speech was published in *Literaturnaya Gazeta*, a newspaper in which Ehrenburg and his views have been anathema since Alexander Chakovsky became its editor in December 1962, it became even more difficult to doubt that official cultural policy was about to take a more liberal turn.

For several weeks, rumors of a new "thaw" had been current in Moscow. Max Frankel, who covered the signing of the nuclear test ban treaty for the *New York Times*, wrote of the conviction of Soviet artists and intellectuals that the easing of tensions with the West would result in a new period of internal relaxation as well. They were looking forward to regaining some of the ground they lost after Khrushchev's December 1 visit to the Manezh art exhibition. It is perfectly reasonable that the signing of the test ban pact and a new "thaw" should be tied together. The men who brought Khrushchev to the Manège and who stand for a "hard line" in domestic policy are, generally speaking, the same men who stand for a "hard line" in international politics. The signing of the treaty is a token of Khrushchev's strength and their weakness. And, when it is remembered that the thing they liked least about the artistic developments of last fall was not their "formalistic excesses," but the inexorable way in which writers were asking the questions Khrushchev's renewed de-Stalinization campaign raised, this fact takes on special importance. The de-Stalinization campaign of 1962 was clearly Khrushchev's own personal project; it is equally clear that it was designed to have concrete political results. Whatever Khrushchev's purposes were in undertaking the campaign, he had to lay them aside when the men it menaced forced him to bring it to an end: and it could have been expected that as soon as his position allowed he would take them up again. This seemed to be precisely what he was doing. The publication of Alexander Tvardovsky's "Tyorkin in the Other World," over two full pages of *Izvestia* on August 18, 1963, and the announcement that a new "anti-Stalin" story by Alexander Solzhenitsyn would appear in a future issue of *Novy mir*[18] were events which paralleled the publication of "Stalin's Heirs" and "One Day in the Life of Ivan Denisovich" in October and November 1962. The publication of these new writings raises a number of intriguing questions: who and what was

---

[17] *Literaturnaya Gazeta*, August 12, 1963.

[18] It did indeed appear in the July 1963 issue under the title "For the Good of the Cause" and proved to be an attack on the "heirs of Stalin" every bit as fierce and telling as Yevtushenko's poem on this theme.

Khrushchev after in his resumption of the attack on "Stalin's Heirs?" What assurance did he have that Soviet writers and artists would not again interpret it as an invitation to "anarchy" and demand freedom from Party control over the arts — a charge he repeatedly made against them in his speeches the previous winter. Or, now that he presumably had a freer hand, was he prepared to make concessions to this demand?

As for Ehrenburg's speech at the Leningrad meeting, it was remarkable on several counts. He was not reluctant in front of foreign guests to dispute Konstantin Fedin who, in describing the work of Joyce, Proust and Kafka as a mere "variety of decadence," took it upon himself to speak for Soviet writers: "We decline [their] banner." Ehrenburg's reply is not a defense of the "ideology" of these writers; he has reservations about the social and political mood out of which their work grew. It is a plea, first of all, that they be recognized as great talents who have made decisive contributions to the growth of modern literary art, and, secondly, that a reasonable, not stereotyped, approach be taken toward them:

> Is it possible to reject Joyce and Kafka, two great writers who are dissimilar from one another? For me, this is the past, they are historical phenomena. I do not make a banner of them, but neither do I make of them a target to be shot at.[19]

It is at this point that Ehrenburg renews his advocacy of literary experimentation, and he made it obvious that, at least as far as Soviet literature is concerned, Joyce, Kafka and Proust have still some valuable contributions to make. He spoke about Vladimir Khlebnikov:

> This is a very difficult poet; I am able to read in one sitting no more than a page or two of Khlebnikov. But Mayakovsky, Pasternak, Asayev have told me that without Khlebnikov, they themselves would not have existed. Many of our young poets who have never read Khlebnikov have inherited many of his poetic discoveries from Mayakovsky, Pasternak or Zabolotsky. Joyce ferreted out the tiniest psychological details, discovered the mastery of inner dialogue; but an essence is not drunk in pure form, it is diluted with water. Joyce is a writers' writer.[20]

Ehrenburg is not troubled by the official concern, and, it should be said, the genuine concern of some of his fellow writers, with the problem of a democratic art. What he wants is to see art develop freely, even if this has to happen at the cost of excluding the masses from access to it in the higher reaches:

---

[19] *Pravda*, August 6, 1963
[20] *Literaturnaya Gazeta*, August 13, 1963

It seems to me that it is unnecessary to fear experiments. In my book, I cited the words of Jean-Richard Bloch at the First Congress of Soviet Writers. He said that there should be writers for the millions and writers for five thousand readers, just as there should be pilots' "who work on already tested models" as well as test pilots. One can and ought to reject charlatanism, but one ought not to reject the right of experiment to exist in literature.[21]

Only a few months ago, young writers who argued this way were denounced by Khrushchev, Ilyichev and the whole army of "official" critics as "snobs and aristocrats" who set themselves above "the people," who accepted its "bread" but disdained to create for it. Ehrenburg's words are a bold challenge to this position and there is special reason for wondering about the liberty he took in making it. Several days before the conference Khrushchev invited him to an interview. Presumably, he acquainted Khrushchev with the contents of his speech and received approval for it. Once again, we must ask ourselves questions about Khrushchev. How are we to square his approval of Ehrenburg's speech with the bitter things he said about Ehrenburg's defense of modernism in his own speech on March 8, 1963? How much of what he said then was said under pressure and how far is he prepared to allow the Soviet arts to depart from Socialist Realist orthodoxy?

---

[21] *Ibid.*

ANTHONY ADAMOVICH

The Non-Russians

When, under Stalin, the concept of a "single, multi-national Soviet literature" was implemented in the USSR — a concept supported by the authority of Gorky — the effect was to deprive all the non-Russian literatures, then and now known as "national" literatures, of their national status and to reduce them to the status of provincial literatures. Not only the central but also the centralizing position in the complex of the "multinational literature" was given to Soviet Russian literature, still referred to both in the West and in the USSR by the genuine name of Soviet literature.[1]

Beginning in 1956, I have more than once had occasion to express and to enlarge upon this statement concerning the result of what I have described as the "all-Union unification of literature" in the USSR under Stalin.[2] Evidently statements of this kind have been viewed as a challenge by a number of Soviet critics, one of whom found it necessary to argue to his colleagues that:

---

[1] In Soviet practice all the non-Russian literatures of the USSR are referred to often simply as the "national literatures," more rarely as the "literatures of the peoples of the USSR" (although neither term is applied to Russian literature); sometimes more accurately as "national Soviet literatures" (though the adjective "Soviet" is often omitted, as if it were self-evident). But Russian Soviet literature is most often described simply as "Soviet literature" in the West as in the USSR, the adjective "Russian" being omitted as self-evident. But the same expression "Soviet literature" is sometimes, although much more rarely, used instead of the term "multi-national Soviet literature," with the qualification "multi-national" similarly omitted as self-evident, and as a result the whole expression acquires a broad general sense covering all Soviet literatures, Russian and non-Russian (the "national literatures") i.e., a collective meaning in which the singular ("Soviet literature") completely coincides, in the scope of the concept it expresses, with the plural ("Soviet literatures"), as in such expressions as "West European literature" and "West European literatures." This confusing use of words reflects the indubitable fact that Russian Soviet literature, historically and practically, is generally taken to be the same as "Soviet literature."

[2] A. Adamovich, "Socialist Realism and Its Current Aspects," *Report on the Soviet Union in 1956* (A Symposium of the Institute for the Study of the USSR), Munich, 1956, p. 117; "Soviet Literature and Art," *Forty Years of the Soviet Regime*, Munich, 1957, p. 113.

We can and must make a convincing reply to various nationalists and caluminiators abroad who shout about the "unification" of our literatures and say that there is apparently no opportunity for their free development under the conditions of the Soviet system and that they are being "suppressed" by Russian literature.[3]

In the meantime, while waiting for both studies to appear, the best we can do is to support once again the proposition advanced as a starting-point for the present review, especially since the essentials of the proposition are gradually being confirmed by Soviet critics themselves. For instance, the writer quoted above, although he does not "shout," nevertheless emphasizes — and not without vigor — that "it is precisely the unity of multi-national Soviet literature which is its distinguishing feature as a new phenomenon in the artistic life of humanity"[4] and considers it a "correct idea" that "all our literatures are united not only by a common artistic method, the principle of Party-mindedness." "They are," he declares, "the literatures of a single state,[5] and he remarks in a later passage that "each of these literatures is an inalienable part of a single Soviet literature."[6] He repeats, then, everything I have said about a "single Soviet literature" and its "integral parts," while avoiding only my general term, "unification."[7] The same article speaks of "the role of Russian classical and Soviet literature in cementing brotherly unity,"[8] while another Soviet critic maintains that "Russian Soviet literature is the soul of the all-Union literary process"[9] and that "in the entire epoch of socialism there has been a *rapprochement* of the peoples of the Soviet Union and a fusion of their interests. And Soviet Russian literature has played the part of teacher in the whole of this historic process."[10] This again is substantially but in the more emotional tone customary for Soviet writers[11] what I myself have said about the central and centralising position of this literature.

---

[3] A. Dmitrieva, "Single and Multi-National" (Dispute on the History of Soviet Literature), *Voprosy literatury*, 1962, No. 5, p. 64.

[4] *Ibid.*, p. 65.

[5] *Ibid.*, p. 66.

[6] *Ibid.*, p. 72.

[7] As far as I know, this term has been used by no-one but myself in this connection, so that I have to assume responsibility for it and for the whole Soviet challenge.

[8] *Ibid.*, p. 85.

[9] A. Petrosyan, "Multi-National Unity," *Oktyabr*, 1962, No. 2, p. 190.

[10] *Ibid.*, p. 191.

[11] The statement about the "suppression" by Russian literature of other literatures, is in spite of the inverted commas attributed to us only by virtue of the emotional overstatement which is customary for Soviet writers and according to which any normal conversation which may be unpleasant for them is described as "shouting," "shrieking," "slander," etc.

It is. on the other hand true that some Soviet critics have expressed dissatisfaction that the prospectus for the projected *History of Soviet Literature* gave them

> . . . the impression that processes in Soviet Russian literature are the main subject, while mere illustrations of them are taken from the other literatures. On reading the propectus, you cannot imagine precisely what any one literature has contributed to the common store, what novelty it has produced and what developed from the traditions. The aspect of each literature is blurred, pale and indistinct . . .[12]

and complained that the prospectus failed to name "many writers without whom it is impossible to present the development of the individual literatures: M. Dzhavakhishvili (Georgia), A. Bakunts (Armenia), H. Taktash (Tataria) and others." They even call for "real courage to introduce many undeservedly forgotten names into the *History*.[13] The reason why they have to call for courage in this respect is, however, because the names they mention as missing from the prospectus have been forgotten because their owners were removed from the official history of literature during the Stalin terror, so that even in 1962, when the above quotation was written, people were still afraid to speak of them, and real courage was needed to do so. The critics proceed to express their dissatisfaction with what they call, in their customary euphemistic fashion, "the consequences of the personality cult . . . which are making themselves especially strongly felt in the study of the history of the literatures of the peoples of the USSR," since "the undeserved repression to which outstanding Soviet writers were subjected, the subjectivism and vulgarization of theory, influenced literary life in our republics."[14] All this confirms indirectly, but quite sufficiently, my picture of the reduction of non-Russian literature to a provincial status, not rising above "illustrations of the processes in Russian Soviet literature" and with the representatives of their traditions removed from both literature and life.

*

The unequal status under Stalin of Russian literature as the centralizing center and the non-Russian literatures as its provincial branches determined the fact that the literary process did not develop identically for both in the post-Stalin epoch. As early as 1957 I had occasion to observe that:

> By dint of strong hierarchical ties between the center and the provinces, a new movement can arise only in the center, from which

---

[12] Dmitrieva, *op. cit.*, p. 73.

[13] *Ibid.*, p. 68.

[14] *Ibid.*, p. 63.

it may or may not spread into the provinces. The short-lived "literary thaw," for instance, did not spread. There were transfers, but to a limited degree in the cases of the "rehabilitations."[15]

This observation is still basically true. The short-lived literary thaw had as perhaps its only reflection in the non-Russian literatures the last writings of Alexander Dovzhenko, a Ukrainian author who died in 1956, but they did not represent a movement as did the first thaw in Russian Soviet literature. But in the case of the non-Russian literatures the rehabilitations which started somewhat later than in the case of Russian literature — in the summer of 1957, when I had occasion to refer to them in the words just quoted, they were still on a very limited scale — progressed in the following years to such an extent and became so typical of these literatures that these years may well be regarded as a period of rehabilitation which has still not come to an end. (Sometimes aptly called the "Rehabilitance Period" by analogy with the Renaissance Period, which does not quite fit this case.)

The term "rehabilitation" in Soviet usage designates any restoration of rights, non-legal as well as legal. Such usage sometimes causes objections, especially on the part of Russian critics, one of whom, charged with being guilty of a "rehabilitation of decadence," replied that "the history of literature is not jurisprudence."[16] But such objections are isolated cases. Reference is still made to the rehabilitation not only of dead or living personalities, but also of literary works and movements. And behind the rehabilitation of personalities and writings in the non-Russian literatures of the USSR can be sensed a general movement for the rehabilitation of the national status of each literature which has been reduced to a provincial status. This is the basic meaning of the rehabilitation now being experienced by the non-Russian literatures.

The first instance of literary rehabilitation, if certain cases during the war, when Stalin was still alive, are discounted,[17] was probably that in Armenia in 1954 when Mikoyan, who had gone to the capital, Yerevan, in connection with elections to the Supreme Soviet, spoke out for rehabilitation of the writings of the classical Armenian authors Raffi (Akop Melik-Akopian, 1835—88), a novelist, and Rafael Patkanian (1830—92), a poet, shortly after which both were rehabilitated.[18] Both of these classics had been expelled from Armenian literature under Stalin — posthumously

[15] Adamovich, "Soviet Literature and Art," *op. cit.*, p. 114.

[16] T. Motyleva, "On the Discussion of Realism of the Twentieth Century," *Voprosy literatury*, 1962, No. 10, p. 144.

[17] Adamovich, "Soviet Literature and Art," *op. cit.*, p. 87.

[18] S. Torossian, "Developments in Armenian Literature," *Studies on the Soviet Union*, Institute for the Study of the USSR, Munich, Vol. II, No. 3, 1963, p. 112.

suppressed, so to speak (like the posthumous rehabilitations now, there were posthumous repressions then) — for their "bourgeois nationalism," and their expulsion had constituted one of the heaviest blows at the national status of Armenian literature, perhaps more serious than that suffered by any other literature of the USSR; as to the other literatures, writers "repressed" in the same manner but not yet rehabilitated include the Ukrainian Panteleimon Kulish, a contemporary of Taras Shevchenko, and the Belorussian Ales Harun, a contemporary of Janka Kupala and Jakub Kolas, although Kulish and Harun are less outstanding figures; as to Russian literature, there has, of course, never been any suggestion of suppressing the works of Gogol or Lermontov, for instance, who may be considered the Russian equivalents of the above-mentioned Armenian classics). Therefore this first rehabilitation itself implied the restoration of national status to a literature which had been degraded to provincial status.

But effective pre-conditions for the further development of this trend were brought on only by the tide of rehabilitation of literary personalities which took place in all the literatures of the peoples of the USSR in 1956—58, following the "ideological revolution," as it was called by a leading personality in Soviet literature, initiated by the Twentieth Party Congress. Most of the writers whose names had been struck out under Stalin were rehabilitated at this time, including those who represented the national status of these literatures and, as the critic cited above has said, "without whom it is impossible to present the development of the individual literatures." A few names connected with some of the national literatures may be mentioned as examples: Egishe Charents, Vahan Totovents and Aksel Bakunts in Armenia; Paolo Yashvili, Titsian Tabidze and Michael Dzhavakhishvili in Georgia; Ahmed Dzhevad, Husein Dzhavid and Michael Mushfik in Azerbaidzhan; Sibgat Sunchalay, Zaki Derdmend and Galimdzhan Ibrahimov in Tataria; Abdulrauf Fitrat Abdulhamid Chulpan and Mahmud Batu in Uzbekistan; Maksim Harecki Uladzimir Dubouka and Jazep Pusca in Belorussia; and Mykola Zerov and Mykola Kulish in the Ukraine. These names give to anyone acquainted with these literatures a sufficient idea of the importance of their rehabilitation for the restoration of the national status of these literatures; for those who are acquainted only with Russian literature, it should be said that the Russian writers who more or less correspond to the above as far as the importance of their work and place in the literary process are concerned are Blok, Yesenin, Mayakovsky and Gorky, who, by the way need no rehabilitation as they were never suppressed even under Stalin although their deaths may be attributed to his régime.

Even after this wave of rehabilitations some names still remaine unmentioned, such as those of the Ukrainian writers Volodymyr Vynny

chenko and Mykola Khvylyovy (as well as Panteleimon Kulish); and the
Belorussians Franicisak Alachnovic, Adrejy Mryj and Lukas Kaluha (as
well as Ales Harun) but, in the first place, these are isolated cases, and in
the second, the period of rehabilitation cannot be considered to have come
to an end (in Belorussian literature, for example, the poet Uladzimier
Zylka was quietly rehabilitated in 1961; the question of rehabilitating the
outstanding critic Adam Babareka was raised in the press at the beginning
of 1963, so that at least his name may be considered to have been rehabilitated; and in April 1963 Larysa Henijus, a Belorussian poetess who grew
up in the anti-Soviet emigration, was rehabilitated). It is accordingly too
early to emphasize that the delay in the rehabilitation of the actual
writings, as opposed to that of the names of the authors, has lessened the
actual volume of rehabilitations. The number of unrehabilitated writings,
i.e., writings which have not yet been re-published or objectively criticized —
by authors whose names have been rehabilitated (and by authors who never
suffered personal repression, but only had some of their writings suppressed,
such as the Ukrainian Pavlo Tychyna and the Belorussian Janka Kupala)
is still considerable, but is decreasing more perceptibly than the number of
unrehabilitated names. In order to exhaust in the present article the
question of the rehabilitation of individual writings, it is necessary to note
the fact, important for literatures which have not left their folklore
traditions far behind, that such large-scale popular epics as the Kirgizian
"Manas", the Uzbek "Alpamysh" and the Buryat "Gaser," have been
rehabilitated, (although, on the other hand, the Tatar epic "Edige" has not).

The most important consequence of this entire process of rehabilitation
of names and writings has been a general revival of the traditions of the
non-Russian literatures as the starting point for their further development.
I have had occasion earlier to note the decisive influence on the de-
nationalization and provincialization of the non-Russian literatures of
"the concept of following the example of Russian literature and art . . .
as the 'classical' patterns for all others, a concept finally canonised in the
Stalinist neo-pseudoclassicism of socialist realism."[19] After the rehabilitations, the orientation of the non-Russian literatures towards their own
traditions became possible: for instance, one of the oldest Turkmenian
writers, Berdy Kerbabayev, is already courageously speaking of "the fine
examples which the budding author can follow" in his native Turkmenian
literature and recommending that he "learn from the works of Russian
literature"[20] only after he has studied these native models. But even
before Kerbabayev had offered this advice, the orientation towards native

---

[19] Adamovich, "Soviet Literature and Art," *op. cit.*, p. 113.
[20] B. Kerbabayev, "For A Good Harvest," *Literaturnaya gazeta*, May 7, 1963,
p. 3.

traditions in Turkmenian and other non-Russian literatures had begun to
manifest itself as a natural consequence of the wave of rehabilitations.
In Armenian literature, for example, the very first instance of rehabilitation, that of Raffi noted above, immediately "influenced such contemporary Armenian poets as Shiraz, Sevak, Silva Kaputikyan and the prose-
writers Zoryan, Dashtents and Matevosyan among others."[21]

The impact of Russian literature was also reduced in another way.
Under Stalin, Soviet Russian literature had become the sole intermediary
in contacts between non-Russian and other literatures, including non-
Soviet literatures, even to the point where translations from these literatures were allowed to be made only from Russian translations, and not
direct from the originals. With the weakening of the centralising position
of this literature in the process of rehabilitation, the non-Russian literatures began to bypass the Russian literature as an intermediary and thus
another sort of rehabilitation began to take place quietly — the restoration
of the right of the non-Russian literatures to maintain direct contact with
other, particularly non-Soviet, literatures. In some cases, as in Kazakh
literature, the question was raised as a matter of principle, but although
the "center" described it as a "stupid onlaught against the great Russian
language" it adduced no arguments against the principle of direct contact
as far as translation was concerned.[22] The restoration of this right was
especially important for the Turkic literatures of the USSR, which were
now able to resume contact with related literatures of the East — contact
which had been completely broken off by the compulsory mediation
through Russian literature, for which such contact had never been
important.

But here we are dealing with the rehabilitation, not of names and
writings, but of literary-artistic features which were excluded or restricted
in literary practice under Stalin. The rehabilitation of these features took
place on all-Union scale: for example, such ideologically neutral genres
and genre elements as lyricism and landscape were revived in both Russian and non-Russian literatures, as already noted.[23] Experimental art
and genuine literary criticism and discussion also became acceptable.[24]
But in the non-Russian literatures certain features re-appeared which
were of primary significance for it alone and of small account in Russian
literature. For instance, the free expression of the national *eros*, the love

21 Torossian, *op. cit.*

22 "On the Responsibility of the Editor," *Izvestia*, December 28, 1962, p. 6

23 Adamovich, "Soviet Literature and Art," *op. cit.*, p. 114.

24 The times of such "discussions," when the outcome was predetermine
and everyone came to a "unanimous opinion" and when if there were some wh
thought differently they were often declared "on the other side of the barricade,
have passed. (Dmitrieva, *op. cit.*, p. 61).

of one's native land, was revived. It had been suppressed under Zhdanov, among whose victims was the Ukrainian poet Sosyura with his poem "Love the Ukraine" and the Belorussian writers Maksim Tank, Maksim Luzanin, Kanstancyja Bujla, Anton Bialevic, P. Hlebka and P. Brouka, who expressed similar feelings. The most important feature of the whole period of rehabilitation, however, has been the movement towards the rehabilitation of national character, the very nationality of literature in general.

According to Stalin's well-known formula of 1925, an obligatory maxim until the present, the form alone of the culture, and therefore of the literature, was to be national. I have illuminated sufficiently on another occasion the history of Stalin's formula borrowed from non-Marxist socialists, and in particular the fact of its non-Marxist, non-dialectical character. Certain Soviet investigators began to come to the same conclusion at almost the same time. According to an article by G. Kuklis in *Literaturnaya Rossiya*, the late Petr Georgievich Skosyrev, who had become acclimatized and almost completely assimilated in Turkmenia,

> . . . devoted many years to the study of fraternal literatures and promoted their development. After the Twentieth Congress of the CPSU he came to the mistaken conclusion that the well-known formula "Soviet culture — socialist in content and national *in form*" was not Marxist, but had been invented by Stalin and could not be regarded as an esthetic category.[25]

Skosyrev's book *Listya i tsvety* (1957) does not criticise Stalin's formula so severely, but does remark that "art, which is a special form of cognition of life and particularly of the life of man in society, cannot help being national. We use the conventional designation of national form for the specific national features of art. It is a working term, no more."[26]

In 1958 the publication in Armenia of an article by Robert Karapetyan, "On the National Content of Literature," raised a storm in the Soviet press. Approaching the problem from another angle, the author maintained that:

> The change undergone by Armenian literature found expression not only in the fact that it became socialist in content and national in form, but also that by virtue of its content it became a literature expressing the organic unity created by national development between social aspects of life and national features. In content, Armenian literature, now as always, remains national.[27]

[25] G. Kuklis, "Holy Truth and Nuances," *Literaturnaya Rossiya*, April 5, 1963, p. 18. For the history of the Stalin formula see Adamovich, "Soviet Literature and Art," *op. cit.*, pp. 111—13.

[26] P. Skosyrev, *Listya i tsvety* (Leaves and Flowers), Moscow, 1957, p. 10—11.

[27] Torossian, *op. cit.*, p. 113.

In 1962, the Ossetin writer Nafi Dzhusoity, speaking to an all-Union audience through the journal *Voprosy literatury*, asked a rhetorical question: "And why should the form alone be called national, do we not call literature as a whole national?"[28] and at the beginning of 1963 the Tatar writer R. Bikmuhametov supported him by an article in the same journal:

It has now become clear that the development of the fraternal literatures cannot be reduced to the mere possession of a national form. P. Skosyrev observed that "recently the expression *national form*, as applied to literary phenomena, has been more seldom used and people prefer to speak of national specifics."[29]

And only after Khrushchev's speech in March, and obviously in the course of working it over, did *Literaturnaya Rossiya*, in the article by G. Kuklis, quoted above, attack these critics of Stalin's formula with the statement that "Petr Skosyrev, who did not live to see the new CPSU Program, may be forgiven, but N. Dzhusoity and R. Bikmuhametov may not because they know that the CPSU Program accepts this formula as a Party weapon in the field of esthetics as elsewhere." Kuklis went on to demand the observation of "the golden rule: if the editors of a journal make a mistake it is better to admit it than to make it worse." Nevertheless, not only did no-one admit to any mistakes, but a month and a half later *Literaturnaya gazeta* defended Dzhusoity and Bikmuhametov in an editorial, with only the mild rebuke that their fears concerning the suppression of national characteristics in the literatures of the Soviet Union were exaggerated.[30] Moreover, the revival of national characteristics continues, if not in theoretical articles at least in practice in the non-Russian literatures, where, although it is not officially acknowledged, the demand for national characteristics in fact is on the same level as the main official requirements, of "people-mindedness" (*narodnost*) and even "Party-mindedness" (*partiinost*).

To conclude the account of the main background of the period of rehabilitation in the non-Russian literatures of the USSR, it behooves us to dwell on yet another factor which at first sight appears to be of a purely external nature. In 1957, speaking of the Union-wide organizational unification of literature in Stalin's unions of Soviet writers. I had occasion to draw attention to the circumstance that:

---

[28] N. Dzhusoity, "The Unity of Peoples, the Unity of Literatures," *Voprosy literatury*, 1962, No. 19, p. 74.

[29] R. Bikmukhametov, "The Renovation of Perspective," *Voprosy literatury*, 1963, No. 1, p. 56.

[30] "On Certain 'Nuances' in Polemics," *Literaturnaya gazeta*, May 21, 1963, p. 3.

. . . In this last form unification achieved full identity of structure with the structure of the Party itself. Whereas VOAPP (All-Union Organization of Associations of Proletarian Writers) included RAPP (Russian Association of Proletarian Writers) as a special organization for the RSFSR, in the Stalinist unions as in the Party there were no longer any such organizations and there are still none, and it is only now that voices can be heard calling attention to the necessity of creating them.[31]

As we know, after these "voices" (at the time a speech by the Belorussian poet Brouka, who was the first to raise this question was noteworthy) a separate Union of Writers of the RSFSR was formed in December 1958 and Russian literature thus lost something of its centralizing position, if only outwardly and in regard to organization, and was to a certain degree placed in a status of equality with the non-Russian literatures. On the other hand, as Max Hayward and others have correctly noted, another purpose of creating the Union was "to reduce the cohesiveness of the rebellious writers concentrated in the metropolitan centers of Moscow and Leningrad by diluting them with a mass of tractable provincials," and accordingly in regard to the central Russian literature as well as in regard to the provincial national literatures reliance was placed on the "province," which "is by nature, and should be, more reactionary; it should appear in the role of a bastion of reaction" — as I once noted in defining the status of the non-Russian literatures after their reduction to a provincial level[32] — and the implementation of this purpose also had the effect of equalizing the status of Russian and non-Russian literatures.

*

Most of the more prominent among the rehabilitated non-Russian writers, such as those listed above, had no opportunity to return to literary activity — their rehabilitations were posthumous. Only Belorussian literature seems to have been relatively fortunate in this respect, Uladzimier Dubouka and Jazep Pushcha having returned after twenty-seven years. For them, as for all rehabilitated writers returning to literary activity, rehabilitation did not end with the re-establishment of their literary names and a greater or lesser number of writings attributed to these names: to be successful in their literary activity or even merely in order to support it they had to continue the rehabilitation themselves,

[31] Adamovich, "Soviet Literature and Art," *op. cit.*, p. 113.
[32] M. Hayward, "Conflict and Change in Literature," *Survey*, London, No. 46, 1963, p. 11 (cf. also p. 6); Adamovich, "Soviet Literature and Art," *op. cit.*, p. 114.

not only by resuming their former lines of development, but also by aligning it more or less with the current literary trends, which had to be taken into account somehow and which, of course, necessarily differed from the line and the general atmosphere of the time when they had been compelled to break off their literary activity. Dubouka without loss to his dignity or to the value of his work, was so successful in this self-rehabilitation that he was the first to receive the newly founded republic literary prize, named after Janka Kupala (the establishment of literary prizes in non-Russian republics named after Kupala and Kolas in Belorussia and Shevchenko in the Ukraine, may, incidentally, also be regarded as a part of the restoration of the national status of the non-Russian literatures of these republics).

On the other hand, a sort of self-rehabilitation, only in the reverse direction, may also be observed in the case of writers who survived in literature under Stalin (some of whom, as I have remarked earlier, were rehabilitated while he was still in power) but who were constrained, or constrained themselves ("took their own song by the throat," as Mayakovsky said) or felt under artistic constraint, but who in the new circumstance of the period of rehabilitation gained the opportunity of rehabilitating their artistic being and of trying to return to the line of work which they had once followed but have been compelled to abandon. The first instance of such self-rehabilitation was that of Ilya Ehrenburg with his epoch-making novel *The Thaw*, which constituted a sort of return, even in essential details, to the line taken in his novel *The Second Day*, in 1932—33, but which it was impossible to follow under the conditions of growing Stalinization.[33] This line, however, was, in terms of the history of Soviet literature, only one of the several variants of the general line known as that of the "fellow-travellers," which had been taken up by a whole "camp," as it was called at the time, of writers in the period of the Sovietization of literature in the USSR (1917—32) and which was outlawed and had no "raison d'être" in the following period of literary Stalinization (1932—53). With his *Thaw* Ehrenburg began his own rehabilitation as a fellow-traveller and thereby introduced a revival of the whole fellow traveller position, a move in which he was followed, or accompanied by several of the other surviving former fellow-travellers, for instance Paustovsky.

But the movement set in motion by Ehrenburg's literary thaw, as I have observed on a previous occasion and have repeated above, did not extend to the non-Russian literatures of the USSR. The main internal reason was that in these literatures the fellow-traveller movement had always been rooted in a rather different soil than in Russian literature

---

[33] Adamovich, "Socialist Realism and its Current Aspects," *op cit.*, p. 107.

being concerned as it was first and foremost with the development of the national cultures, or, on a wider scale, of the nations themselves (even if these were "socialist" by Stalin's definition, this was at first of no practical significance), a path along which the non-Russian fellow-travelling writers and the Party could "travel" as "fellows." In this instance, therefore, the rehabilitation of the fellow-traveller movement practically coincided with the rehabilitation of the national status of the literature discussed above, pushing into the background what was of primary importance to Ehrenburg — the rehabilitation of the status of the artist as a free fellow-traveller of the Party and not merely as a rigidly disciplined Party "soldier," as Khrushchev recently put it.

Nevertheless, self-rehabilitation in the sense of attempts to restore their own artistic integrity on the part of writers who had suffered constraint under Stalin also made its appearance in the non-Russian literatures, although not on the same scale as the rehabilitation of fellow-travellerism. Such, for instance, was the return of the Ukrainian poet Mykola Bazhan to his former baroque manner in his *Poems of Italy*, a fact noted by the critic Bohdan Kravtsiv.[34] Similar cases may be found in other literatures. In some, self-rehabilitation of this type was accompanied by repentance for the weakness of spirit shown under the pressure of the "cult of the personality." One such repentant self-rehabilitator, a "repentant cultist," so to say (like the "repentant noblemen" in Russian literature) was the well-known "order-bearer," winner of the Stalin Prize and of the new state prize when it was last awarded, the Avar poet Rasul Gamzatov. There were similar cases in Armenian literature.[35]

Finally, alongside the writings of the self-rehabilitators (both in fellow-travellerism and in general), there began to appear the writings of authors who had only begun their literary careers in Stalin's time and had therefore never been fellow-travellers nor had suffered any particular constraint, but who had nevertheless begun to try — not without the influence and example of the self-rehabilitators and especially under the impact of the general "ideological revolution" — to display independence and even a certain degree of courage in their unorthodox judgements and attitudes to the reflection of reality, thus taking steps in the direction

---

[34] B. Kravtsiv, "The Birth of the New," *Slovo*, New York, No. 1, 1962, p. 356.

[35] R. Gamzatov, "My Heart in the Mountains" Section III (a poem translated from Avar into Russian), *Ogonek*, August 10, 1958. The author regrets and "seeks forgiveness" for the fact that, in the condemnation of the national hero of the Caucasus, Shamil, on Stalin's orders, his own "hasty song" had sounded "in the discreditable choir." In Armenia much discussion was aroused by the poem "Repentance" by the poet Sarmen, in which the author condemas himself for having written in favour of the "cult of the personality" (although he wrote much less than others who did not "repent").

of a sort of new fellow-travellerism. Writings of this type appeared not only in Russian (the most famous of these was Dudintsev's *Not By Bread Alone*) but also, even after the pogrom-like reaction against such works by Russian writers, in other languages (the story "The Suffering Soul" by Isa Huseinov and the novel *Sincere Friends* by Ali Valiev in Azerbaidzan; the story *Dabrasieltsy* by Alaksiej Kulakouski and the play *So That People Should Not Be Sad* by Andrej Makajonak in Belorussia; and the novels *May* by Zarzand Daryan and *Ashkhen Satyan* by M. Aslanyan in Armenia).

But from the middle of the fifties and especially in the sixties writers of the younger generation began to appear. We shall have to call them "neo-fellow-travellers," a term which, in the context of the history of Soviet literature is far more exact than labels largely accidental, vague, or transplanted from other periods, such as *shestidesyatniki* (men of the sixties), "angry young men" or "innovators." These neo-fellow-travellers differ from the historical fellow-travellers in that their path does not lead from the bowels of non-Soviet to Soviet literature nor from the former in the direction of the latter, as in the case of the historical fellow-travellers, but the other way round, from Soviet literature, upon the bosom of which they appeared in the world, and indeed from its historical, traditional bosom. For this reason their path sometimes leads them in a direction making them literary contemporaries of the non-Soviet or even the non-Communist world, so that they occasionally display a tendency to become fellow-travellers of this other world and its literature. Long before Khrushchev's speech in March a Soviet critic had pointed out the "peculiar aping of foreign writers" on the part of representatives of this trend:

> In some literatures, for instance the Georgian and Lithuanian, a good many young epigones of E. Hemingway, H. Richter and I. Reding have multiplied; the Belorussian B. Sacanka and the Russian Yu. Kazakov seem to compete in imitating the late I. Bunin. This is a peculiar, sporadic literary cosmopolitanism of styles, manners, a competition of epigonism.[36]

Leaving aside the exaggerated expression ("aping," "epigonism," "cosmopolitanism") customary among Soviet critics, this charge is essentially true. The path for this movement, whose slogan, according to the same critic is "Import! Before everything else! Indiscriminately!"[37] was cleared by the restoration of direct contact with other literatures, especially the non-Soviet. The tendency to imitate the literatures of the non-Soviet, even the non-Communist, world, and therefore this world itself, could

---

[36] V. Chalmayev, "The Most Vital Concerns," *Druzhba narodov*, 1962, No. 9 p. 273.

[37] *Ibid.*, p. 262.

not but alarm the leaders of the Communist Party to such an extent that they began to apply all possible means to put a stop to this neo-fellow-travellerism which was so harmful from their point of view.

Thanks in large measure to such efforts the name of the colorful neo-fellow-traveller Yevgeny Yevtushenko, a "real Russian," as he calls himself, although his name is typically Ukrainian, has achieved world-wide renown, but the non-Russian literatures have their own Yevtushenkos and large cohorts of neo-fellow-travellers of their own. None of them has become widely known abroad because the Party has avoided sending young non-Russian writers abroad after the suicide of the Belorussian writer Usievalod Kraucanka during a visit to France in 1961. Furthermore, these writers avoid the political sensationalism which attracts attention abroad, because of circumstances which non-Russian writers have to take into account. Among the most outstanding such writers are Ivan Drach, Mykola Vinhranovsky, Vitaly Korotych and Even Hutsalo in the Ukraine; Uladzimier Karatkievic, Ales Naurocki, Ryhor Baradulin and Barys Sacanka in Belorussia; Ojar Vacietis, Jeronims Stulpan, Arvid Skalbe and Janis Lusis in Latvia; Paul-Eerik Rummo and M. Rauda in Estonia; Algimantas Baltakis, Justinas Marcinkiavicius, R. Lankauskas and M. Sluckis in Lithuania; Archil Sulakaurim, Otiya Ioseliani, Otar Chiladze and Shota Nishnianidze in Georgia; Nansen Mikaelyan, Hrant Matevosyan and Aramais Saakyan in Armenia; Yusif Samedoglu and Halil Riza in Azerbaidzhan; Ildar Yuzeyev, Afzul Gamils and Shauket Galiev in Tataria; Ramis Ryskulov in Kirgizia; and Olzhas Suleimenov in Kazakhstan. This list could, of course, be extended considerably, but I shall add only the names of a few young poetesses who are playing a fertile part in this movement: Lina Kostenko, chronologically the first and artistically the most mature, Svitlana Yovenko and Irene Zhilenko in the Ukraine; Jeudakija Los, Viera Viarba, Danuta Bicel and Sviatlana Marcanka in Belorussia; H. Jurisson, Milvi Seping and V. Verev in Estonia; E. Muklinova and S. Suleimanova in Tataria; Marlene Shabanian in Armenia; and Anna Kalandadze in Georgia.

The Soviet critic quoted above gave a correct description of the basic difference between the young Russian and non-Russian neo-fellow-travellers in his comment that, among the young Ukrainian writers:

. . . Neither I. Drach nor M. Vinhranovsky nor V. Symonenko can be considered a Ukrainian variant of Ye. Yevtushenko or A. Voznesensky. They are much more people-minded in language and in the meaning of their work in poetry. They are all inspired by a sincere, perhaps sometimes naive inclination towards a generalizing view in respect of the people, the working Ukraine, they have very little interest in the trivial.[38]

[38] *Ibid.*, p. 261.

This comment also applies to the neo-fellow-travellers in the other non-Russian literatures. Not long ago there was an interesting piece of evidence that some of the young non-Russian neo-fellow-traveller poets regard themselves as members of a world literary movement, not confined to the Soviet Union, a movement in which they include certain of the less well known Russian neo-fellow-travellers. The source of the evidence was the above-mentioned young Belorussian poet Uladzimier Karatkievic, who was expressing his satisfaction that

> . . . so many good youngsters (with the same holy sincerity of line . . .) have appeared recently. Strong ties bind these people in whatever country they live. The brotherhood of nations, the brotherhood of sincerity, the brotherhood of poetry. And here already on the face of the Earth is a network of diamonds — from heart to heart. These are only the ones I know: Znamensky, Nishnianidze, Astafiev, Boriskov, Ioseliani — there are hundreds and hundreds of others. And how many of them there are in Belorussia, and how many elsewhere! Over rivers, seas, oceans — thousands of strong ties, a brotherhood of hearts.

Karatkievic even includes in the brotherhood his Latvian friends Stulpan, Vacietis, Skalbe and Lusis.[39]

The neo-fellow-traveller movement brought the freshness of youth into literature and in many ways stimulated self-rehabilitation and a fresh approach to their work on the part of the older writers. Bohdan Kravtsiv regards the advance in the poetry of Mykola Bazhan, referred to above as an example of self-rehabilitation, in precisely this way and mentions in the same connection the poets Andriy Malyshko (who published a volume of verse, *Transparency*, in 1962), Stepan Kryzhanivski (*Not Yet Evening*, in 1961) and other Ukrainians.[40] Among Belorussians he could have named Maksim Tank, Maksim Luzanin, Arkadz Kulasou, Pimien Pancanka, Anatol Vialuhin and, as a particularly vivid example, a poet who by virtue of his chairmanship of the Union of Soviet Writers of Belorussia should have been the incarnation of orthodoxy in literature — Piatrus Brouka.

It should be noted in the same connection that in some non-Russian literatures, for instance Armenian, Azerbaidzhani and Belorussian, the rupture, not to speak of the conflict, between writers of the younger and older generations becomes less and less marked as time goes on. Rather there can be felt on both sides an urge towards a "united front" of the generations in literature as in life in general. In a certain respect this is a

---

[39] U. Karatkievic, "Fairy Tales of the Amber Land," *Polymia*, 1963, No. 2, p. 108.

[40] Kravtsiv, *op. cit.*, p. 356; Chalmayev, *op. cit.*, p. 261.

sort of "united national front" resting, on the one hand, on the same basis as fellow-travellerism in the non-Russian literatures, as noted earlier, and, on the other hand, on the danger threatening the very existence of the non-Russian languages and literatures and the nations themselves, to be dealt with in greater detail below. To no less extent, it is a united literary and artistic front. The young Belorussian poet Vladimir Pavlov (who, by the way, took part in the last all-Union conference of young writers) questioned the division of writers into "detachments of young and old" as if "on military maneuvers" and declared quite sincerely, "we have no disagreement anywhere: we have one home-land and one watershed," a watershed which does not follow a line dividing the different generations, but is formulated in the expressive slogan: "Away with the time-server and the hack from the flinty road!"[41]

One can, in fact, observe such a watershed with its hacks, i.e., strictly speaking, graphomaniacs (the term preferred by Maksim Tank, one of Pavlov's senior literary countrymen) and time-servers in all non-Russian Soviet literatures. An even more expressive term for "time-serving" has appeared in Tatar literature, that of "Kushtanism," from the word *Kushtan*, meaning "devoted," but not "devoted without flattery," as the saying goes, but precisely the opposite, "with flattery," or, to use a more modern term which is especially current in Soviet life, with toadyism.

But on the same side of the watershed and, so to speak, on its very crest, is yet another phenomenon, although it is not equally pronounced in the various Soviet literatures. In some cases rehabilitation, especially the appearance of the first works of the self-rehabilitators and newly designated fellow-travellers, has evoked a negative reaction on the part of writers who remained unshaken in their orthodox positions under the banner of socialist realism, still enforced officially. This reaction has followed the pattern of historical anti-fellow-traveller "on-guardism" completely and may therefore, following the same system of terminology for the history of Soviet literature, be spoken of here as "neo-on-guardism," which differs from the old on-guardism by being less aggressive, more protective and even defensive, by virtue of the new circumstances. Although such an outstanding representative of this neo-on-guardism as Vsevolod Kochetov has not appeared in the non-Russian literatures, orthodox writers of the same type, such as Lyubomyr Dmiterko, Mykola Sheremet and Platon Voronko in the Ukraine, have revealed themselves sufficiently.[42] This neo-on-guardism is seeking and finding its basic support in the literary province to which reference has been made above and which forms the best

---

[41] U. Paulau, "We Have the Only Watershed," *Cyrvonaja zmiena* (Red Shift), May 7, 1963.

[42] Kravtsiv, *op. cit.*, p. 356.

breeding-ground for the time-serving kushtanists and the graphomaniac
water-carriers.

The neo-on-guardists, on the one hand, relying on the province,
and the neo-fellow-travellers and their brothers-in-arms the self-rehabilitators on the other, represent in general the two extreme flanks of the
modern Soviet literary front. Their positions represent in respect of
principle two poles of an axis around which Soviet literature has revolved
over the whole duration of its existence, with ideologism, i.e., the emphasis
on ideology, on political awareness — the position of the "neo-on-guardists"
— as one pole and formalism, i.e., emphasis on expression in an artistic
form, on artistic quality,[43] as the other. That ideology and artistic expression are the two poles is clearly demonstrated by the fact that the
organic merger, the mutual penetration, in theory not only desirable
but necessary, has in practice never occurred in Soviet literature as a
whole, nor in the writings of authors who are held up as models, nor even
in individual writings, and the relationship between them does not extend
beyond co-existence, the most usual and the only inevitable relationship
between poles of one axis.

The co-existence of ideology and artistry now represents one of the
most general characteristic positions, if not the most general characteristic
position, for each of the Soviet literatures, especially the non-Russian,
and indeed for the literary front as a whole. Although this co-existence
may not always be peaceful, it is unavoidable co-existence, involuntary
but protected and even guaranteed in a way by the Party leadership, which
has the power of life and death over Soviet literature and which permits
neither the complete victory nor the complete defeat of either flank in
spite of obvious favoritism for one of them. For those writers, however,
whose opposition in the literary front is not on the flanks but somewhere
between them, more often closer to the center (and if they are not in the
majority they are in any case an impressive and qualified quorum which
is more often than not increased by addition of the new arrivals in
literature), this co-existence, which is moreover completely peaceful,
becomes a sort of internal condition within the entire scope of their work
and often within the framework of their individual writings.

Thus between neo-on-guardism and neo-fellow-travellerism there
arises a third broad position, "coexistentialism," so to speak, to which the
neo-fellow-travellers themselves have recourse when they, and literature
in general, are subjected to ideological pressure. In certain non-Russian
literary circles this position finds a sort of theoretical basis in the Biblical
formula for co-existence: "Render unto Caesar the things that are Caesar's

---

[43] This is the meaning attached to "formalism" in orthodox Soviet criticism
(cf. Adamovich, "Soviet Literature and Art," *op. cit.*, p. 88).

and to God the things that are God's," so that ideology and political awareness are regarded as a tribute which the writer cannot avoid paying to the Caesar of Soviet life — the Party — in order to enable him to serve his own God — literature — with genuine artistic creativity. The attitude to the "ideological preparation" of the writer in the spirit of this formula particularly disturbed the Latvian writer Jan Niedre, who recently wrote an article in the Moscow *Literaturnaya gazeta* based on Khrushchev's speech in March,[44] but the same formula had been played upon in other non-Russian literatures as much as a year before in poems expressing such a thesis. In the living practice of these literatures obedience to this formula may be observed with the naked eye. In poetry it takes the form of two sharply separate poles — an outward ideological rhetoric and fervor, intended as tribute to Caesar, and a genuine, sometimes really "God-like," poetry of thought and feeling. In prose it takes the form of the co-existence of equally separate poles — instructional, pedagogic or even demagogic (as a non-Russian writer described one of his products which had especially pleased orthodox critics) pseudo-literature, demanded by the same Caesar, and *belles lettres* of great esthetic and informational value. It is also characteristic that, with this division, the tributes to Caesar have, in the same literary circles, become technically known as "locomotives," since it is their task to pull God's tribute through the censorship, which it would be difficult to do without them.[45]

This kind of coexistence has been skillfully and thoroughly examined by a Ukrainian critic abroad, Vasyl I. Hryshko. In his view the point of departure is "the contradiction between 'socialist realism' as a creative method of Soviet literature and . . . 'realist socialism' as the life material for creativity by Soviet writers." As a result of the resolution of this contradiction, "living life, as it actually is in the reality of 'realist socialism,' is mortified in the artificial forms of 'socialist realism.' But sometimes the reverse occurs, depending on the writer's talent, which can breathe life into even a dead pattern or at least combine both that they can exist side by side in the work without excluding each other."[46] To illustrate this co-existence of socialist realism and realist socialism the critic thoroughly and convincingly analyses a number of writings by Soviet Ukrainian authors ("Poem on the Sea," by Alexander Dovzhenko; stories by Ivan

----

[44] Jan Niedre, "The Weapons of the Artist," *Literaturnaya gazeta*, May 11, 1963, p. 1.

[45] "Without any ceremony at all or clumsiness some poets use a poetical new term in literary circles: 'locomotive' (this is what they call one or two verses on a 'political theme' to which are 'attached' lyrical verses)." — D. Starikov, "Times Change," *Literatura i zhizn*, September 12, 1962, p. 3.

[46] V. I. Hryshko, "The Living and the Dead in Ukrainian Soviet Prose," *Slovo*, No. 1, 1962, p. 401.

Senchenko; and the novel *Man and Weapons* by Oles Honchar). Similar writings may be found in other non-Russian literatures: for instance, the novels *The Golden Valley* by Christopher Tapaltsyan and *All Life Under Fire* and *Not To Forget* by Mkrtich Sarkisyan in Armenia; the play *Lavonicha in Orbit* by Andrej Makajonak, which won the Janka Kupala Literary Prize in Belorussia; and the novel *A Village Without Men* by Lilli Promet in Estonia.

In the writings analysed by Hryshko, and in most cases of this sort in general, the leading position, even in purely quantitative terms, continues to be held by socialist realism, but he also notes the appearance of writings, such as the novel *The Whirlpool* by the late young Ukrainian writer Hryhory Tyutyunnik, in which realist socialism predominates — "genuine realistic works in the proper, traditional meaning of the concept of realism, with no additional qualification."[47] Nevertheless, these are as yet isolated instances: hardly more than one or two large works of this kind are to be found in each literature (for instance, the novels *Urtsi Meran* by Khachik Rachiyan and *The Sowers Did Not Return* by Bagish Ovsepyan in Armenia; the novel *On Alazan* by Tina Donzhashvili in Georgia; the novel *In the Middle of a Big Field* by R. Lankauskas in Lithuania; the story *Captivity* by Barys Sacanka and the novel *People on the Bog* by Ivan Mielez, if one can judge by the first part of the trilogy in Belorussia, which has won the Jakub Kolas Prize while in some literatures not even a single one will be found, it being almost impossible for such a work to pass the censors and editorial boards, especially in the watchful provinces. We know how difficult it was for Solzhenitsyn's "One Day in the Life of Ivan Denisovich" to be approved by the Presidium of the Party Central Committee, and then only after repeated votes. To this day it continues to be unique in Soviet literature; in the non-Russian literatures only small fragments of a similar nature have appeared on a subject which is so delicate for the régime and is depicted with such genuine realism.[48]

On the other hand, the attraction of genuine realism for the writer and the reader is now very strong. Official slogans on "socialist realism" and "humanism" with their hidden temptation to put the logical emphasis

---

[47] *Ibid.*, p. 402.

[48] Torossian, *op. cit.*, p. 116, speaks of Mikirtich Armen apparently with reference to his published stories "My Letter" and "The Bird" from the unpublished collection "I Was Told To Say," which has been discussed in public, and the novel "A Place in the Sun" which has also been discussed, but not published. Reference is also made to the extract from the story "Mother and Son" by Anatol Dimarov which was published in *Literaturna Ukrayina*, November 27, 1962, and to the story "Mikitka," the only story from the cycle *From the Recent Past* by the Belorussian Ales Palceuski to appear (cf. *Litaratura i mastactva*, January 8, 1963, pp. 2—4).

on the grammatically basic nouns "realism" and "humanism" (whereas in the official concept it should be put on the "additional qualification," the adjective "socialist") and the voices of authority of Ilyichev and Khrushchev himself calling for "truthfulness" and "truth" (although Stalin also hypocritically ordered: "Write the truth!") cannot discourage them but can on the contrary only stimulate them. Young writers with tendencies to neo-fellow-travellerism permit themselves to attack those who "under the label of socialist realism have created social illusionism." They are beginning to arrive at "a realism which is as close as possible to life," a single, indivisible truth, and are ready to declare that the Party is dear to them but to paraphrase Aristotle, that truth is dearer still.[49] Orthodox official criticism reacts sharply to such statements and to attempts to embody them in works of art which somehow or other are passed by the censors. Only a sort of "Hottentot realism" and "humanism" are sanctioned.[50] As a result, the same attraction of genuine realism finds an outlet in a revival of a cryptographic approach to literature — the insertion of the truth between the lines, and artistic cryptography, which has come to life after Stalin's death, as I have noted on a previous occasion,[51] continues to live in co-existence with well-meant ideologism. But to refer to instances of such cryptography here would be unfair to the authors who resort to this device.

Genuine realism is not the only artistic "ism" which co-exists with socialist realism. Tendencies and elements of a long series of other literary "isms" such as romanticism, a certain degree of co-existence with which is even permitted by socialist realism, and such seemingly incompatible if not downright contradictory movements as sentimentalism, symbolism, even surrealism and other recent variants of modernism which are sometimes noted by Western observers in recent Soviet Russian literature are not alien to the non-Russian literatures either; in some of them, attempts at a theoretical rehabilitation of some of these "isms" have been observed,

---

[49] The term "social illusionism" was invented by the young Georgian critic Guram Asatiani (cf. the article "The Great People's Cause Must Be Advanced Together," by Revaz Dzhaparidze in the Georgian literary paper *Literaturuli Sakartvelo*, April 12, 1963, p. 3). The expressions "realism which is as close as possible to practice" and "single, indivisible truth" come from the pen of a young non-Russian writer who has already been slightly involved in the process of "working over" Khrushchev's March speech.

[50] Hryshko, *op. cit.*, p. 400, very neatly characterises "the well-known 'Soviet humanism' which, like 'Hottentot morals,' is guided by the principle that any crime against mankind is branded as an atrocity if it is committed by fascism or any other system, but immediately becomes the height of humaneness if it is committed by our government."

[51] Adamovich, "Soviet Literature and Art," *op. cit.*, p. 110.

such as romanticism and symbolism in Armenian literature.[52] Under the same heading come attempts to continue the search for a "style of the epoch," i.e., for new "isms" which were alive in the 1920's but were buried with the proclamation of socialist realism, while they are now coming to the surface again in connection with the rehabilitation of the literary names of the time and with them and behind them the rehabilitation of the phenomena and currents which they represented; the search for a "new style" on the part of the neo-fellow-travelling flanks of all Soviet literatures is part of the same process and is reflected chiefly in the discussion of tradition and innovation which occupied all literary circles before Khrushchev's speech in March.

Of course, all this co-existentialism of "isms" great and small, which leads in the final count to the co-existence of the two principal positions — the two basic "isms" of ideologism and formalism — must seem in the eyes of the Party to be a co-existence of ideologies because, in Lenin's words, any dismissal of ideology (i.e., that which gives rise to formalism) and even the mere absence of ideology are in themselves also ideology and moreover hostile, bourgeois, ideology. In so far as the line of ideological coexistence is now rejected by the Party the whole position of co-existentialism in literature is now under attack. It is true that the blow which first fell with Khrushchev's speech in March at first concentrated on aspects where the undermining of the Party princple or the concrete fact that the line of co-existence pointed towards the West bore an obvious, if not simply an openly challenging, character. It is difficult to say whether this attack will in the end be extended further and deeper along the whole front or whether it will become systematic; it is hazardous to make any forecast concerning the present post-Stalin period, the basic characteristic of which remains "an uneasy balance between the tendencies of de-Stalinization and re-Stalinization" as I have observed elsewhere or, in the language of imagery, of "thaw" and "freeze-ups."[53]

*

The suppression of inter-literary coexistence would mean, of course, the return of literature to its state under Stalin, whereas if co-existence is allowed to continue, the non-Russian Soviet literatures may eventually enjoy a real renaissance and not merely a rehabilitation. Nevertheless, notwithstanding the importance of co-existence for the non-Russian literatures of the USSR, an even more important problem has been impending in

---

[52] Torossian, *op. cit.*, p. 114; cf. L. Massissyan, "The Development of Critical Tendencies in Soviet Armenia," *Caucasian Review*, Institute for the Study of the USSR, Munich, 1957, pp. 60—64.

[53] Adamovich, "Soviet Literature and Art," *op. cit.*, p. 81.

recent years — their national existence itself. It represents the reverse side of the problem of the amalgamation of nations, their cultures and even their languages under Communism. This problem was first considered by Lenin, then exploited by Stalin and his successors (their approach was not perceptibly different, which is characteristic and symptomatic) and was included in the new program of the CPSU, approved by the Twenty-Second Party Congress in 1961, in the form of a definite decision that "the nations will draw still closer together until complete unity is achieved." Likewise, the statement that "the obliteration of national distinctions, and especially of language distinctions, is a considerably longer process"[54] does little to alter the first unfavorable impression, since obliteration and achievement of complete unity continue to be only a question of time, not of principle. Accordingly the existence of the individual "national" non-Russian literatures is acknowledged to be only provisional, and the cessation of their existence — their death — an inevitability to which they are irrevocably doomed.

Thus, these literatures, as represented by their poets and other writers who are constantly being called upon to fight for Communism, to praise it and to welcome its rapid advance — the same Communism which in the end will bring them death — are in a tragic situation comparable to that of the Roman gladiators with their cry: "Ave, Caesar, morituri te salutamus!" The situation is so clear that it would be difficult to imagine that the modern gladiators of the Soviet Caesar themselves are unaware of it, the more so since they are poets and writers; in some cases, distinct proof of such awareness may be found as, for instance, in Alexander Dovzhenko's "Poem of the Sea," which I have mentioned earlier.[55] But this position, since they are aware of it, is compelling them to seek a way out by means of self-preservation, whether of the nation or the individual, although at present the latter is not so important as the former.

---

[54] *Programma Kommunisticheskoi partii Sovetskogo Soyuza, prinyataya XXII syezdom 31 oktyabrya 1961 g.* (Program of the Communist Party of the Soviet Union Adopted by the Twenty-Second Congress on October 31, 1961), Part II, Section IV.

[55] Hryshko, *op. cit.*, pp. 359—60, 366, has convincingly revealed the allegory contained in the "artificial future the name of which is 'Communism' in the main image of the given work by Dovzhenko—the image of an artificially created sea In the name of which . . . native settlements have to be destroyed, sites of past glory have to be drowned forever and those who are creating this artificial sea have to part with everything which is so dear to their souls,' i.e., the foundations of their own nationality; moreover, 'the builders themselves . . . personify in their heroic labour rather the sacrifice to the force of necessity than enthusiasm for the idea and faith in it,' although the author, as we can see, is sincerely attracted by the idea."

As a result of all this, every non-Russian Soviet literature is now becoming more and more an arena for the struggle for national self-preservation, justifying more and more expressively its everyday name of "national literature," which at first sight may seem accidental but under present circumstances expresses its original mission and highest calling. The entire movement for the rehabilitation of the national status of literature, upon which I have had occasion to dwell here in all possible detail, finds its ultimate meaning on this plane. Here the importance of the revival of the direct expression of the national eros becomes clear. Every non-Russian Soviet literature is now filled with the warmest and most varied expressions of this feeling on the part of prose writers and poets, especially the younger ones, who are taking up literature in unprecedented numbers, as if following a secret but real national mobilisation caused by a state of national emergency. Here also (taking precedence over the "all-Union" land) are endless confessions of love for their national motherland and everything related to it, oaths of fidelity to it and to them, and insistent calls not to leave their native hearths and homes and to work selflessly under their roofs and for them, before all else (sometimes even contrary to the official demand for "exchange of trained personnel between nations").[56] This unprecedented intensification of national feeling in Soviet literature speaks for itself. No less eloquent is the turning to "national self-awareness" (even though it may be "socialist" in the "style of the epoch") and "national thought," which is particularly characteristic of some Turkic literatures, and to heroic deeds in the struggle for national self-preservation in the historic past, especially in the Turkic, Armenian, and occasionally in Belorussian literatures. The conscious, sincere affirmations of national pride are part of the same process.[57]

---

[56] *Programma Kommunisticheskoi partii . . .*, *op. cit.* The story by the Belorussian Mikola Tkacou, "In Search of Treasure" (*Polymia*, 1962, No. 12) is especially interesting in this respect. Also in the Belorussian literature the poem "An Oath" by Siarhiej Novik-Piajun is the climax of modern poetry of the national eros, where the author takes an oath of fidelity to "Belorussia, his own mother" and indirectly to his native language and his "native school," which is especially symptomatic in the circumstances of Khrushchev's school reform (*Cyrvonaja zmiena*, May 29, 1963, p. 3). Foreign and even Soviet critics note the very strong current of the national eros, "patriotism," in the work of the young Ukrainian poet Mykola Vinhranovsky the Armenian Ovanes Shiraz and the Tatar poets F. Hasanov, R. Safetdinov N. Asanov and Sh. Satretdinov.

[57] "I am an Azerbaidzhani and proud of it. The traditions and character traits of my people, their literature and art are dear to me" — this statement by Yusif Samedoglu seems to express a mood which is typical of young non-Russian writers (*Voprosy literatury*, 1962, No. 9, p. 152). After Khrushchev's speech in March the expression of national pride was again condemned as "national conceit" and even all poetry of the national eros was dubbed "national narrow-mindedness."

The sector of language is becoming a particularly important and animated part of the arena of the struggle for national self-preservation in literature. The preservation of the language is of exclusive importance for the existence and development of the national literature and of the particular nationality in general and it is for this reason that the greatest pressure is being applied here, often in the form of extremely shrewd strategic maneuvers. In this connection I have had occasion to speak of Khrushchev's school reform of 1958, which was clearly aimed among other things at tearing the rising generation away from their native non-Russian languages, at destroying the tree of life of these languages by striking at its very roots, and at condemning to gradual withering all its leafage, however green and flourishing it may have seemed under the deceptive rays of various "rehabilitations" and "liberalisations." Policy regarding publication in non-Russian languages forms part of the same series of strategic maneuvers.[58] Finally, there is yet another move the aim of which is openly revealed (and which, therefore, has perhaps been less successful so far) in the discussion on the adoption by non-Russian writers of the Russian language; this discussion started in 1961 almost immediately after the adoption of the new program by the Twenty-second Party Congress and clearly in connection with the provision for "still closer drawing together" of nations contained in the program.

The discussion was started by the Dagestani writer Ahed Agayev, who attacked the "national egoism" of the non-Russian peoples of the USSR and called upon writers belonging to these nations to adopt Russian in their work as opening wider prospects to the "Highway of History" while not hindering the writer from retaining his national identity and even "national form." Nevertheless, in spite of support from *Pravda, Izvestia*, and *Literatura i zhizn*, the weekly organ of the Union of Soviet Writers of the RSFSR which was abolished and replaced by *Literaturnaya Rossiya*, Agayev was attacked by numerous non-Russian writers, including Dzhusity and Bikmuhametov, and even by the Russian poet Vladimir Soloukhin, so that even now Agayev remains in a minority. The support given to his thesis by Brezhnev who, a year after the initiation of the discussion, stated that "the process which is taking place in practice, in which in-

---

[58] A. Adamovich, "Towards a Single Socialist Nation," *Studies on the Soviet Union*, Institute for the Study of the USSR, Munich, Vol. I, No. 3, 1962, p. 37. Data relating to Belorussia show policy regarding publishing: in 1961 in Belorussia, where 81.1 per cent of the population are Belorussians, only 8,576,000 copies of books in the Belorussian language were published and 10,378,000 copies in Russian, although Russians form only 8.2 per cent of the population. When a collection of Byron's works in Belorussian translation was published in 1963, the entire edition of 1,200 copies was sold in a single day (*Literatury i mastactva*, May 21, 1963).

dividual national writers voluntarily choose the Russian language as their
literary language, has, objectively, a positive significance," leaves no doubt
as to the official attitude on the matter, but neither does it indicate a
victory for the thesis.[59]

The adoption of Russian as their literary language by non-Russian
writers is nothing new in Soviet literature and was not unknown even
before the Revolution. Under Stalin and after him it was consistently
encouraged, especially by means of special Russian-language journals and
publications of local writers which were introduced in every non-Russian
republic under Stalin. There are, however, no indications that this policy
has made perceptible progress after the adoption of the new Party program
and the discussion started by Agayev. The reverse, however, is also occur-
ring: some Russian writers have started using languages other than
Russian. The young poet Robert Tretyakov, for instance, writes in Ukrain
ian; another young poet, Vladimir Pavlev, writes in Belorussian; and
Nadezhda Lushnikova even writes in the Kazakh language,[60] all in spite
of Agayev and the new Party program. If the adoption of the Russian
language by non-Russian writers may suggest the practical purpose of
self-preservation, to the extent of careerism, the adoption of other langua
ges by Russian writers may be attributed to idealistic and romantic motives
and sentiments.

The same is true of Soloukhin's support of the non-Russian languages
In this respect attention should also be called to the attitude of the above
mentioned P. Skosyrev, who long before the discussion on the adoption
of Russian by non-Russian writers had said: "We call verses and poem
written in the Turkmenian language Turkmenian poetry. A Russian
writer who lives in Turkmenia remains a Russian writer, even if he writes
on Turkmenian subjects."[61] The position of Vladimir Karpov, who has
not only become acclimatised to Belorussia but has for a long time been

[59] A. Agayev, "On National Egoism and National Feelings," *Literatura i zhizn*
November 17, 1961, p. 1; "In a New, Free Family," *Izvestia*, December 5, 1961
p. 4; "The Highway of History and the Byways of Vladimir Soloukhin," *Literatura
zhizn*, March 2, 1962, p. 1; V. Soloukhin, "What Makes Us Related," *Literaturnay*
gazeta, February 6, 1962, pp. 1—3; L. Brezhnev, "The Triumph of Lenin'
National Policy," *Izvestia*, December 30, 1962, pp. 1—3; see also P. Fedenko, "The
Nationality Question," *Studies on the Soviet Union*, Munich, Vol. II, No. 3, 1963
pp. 110—11. The comment of the fairly orthodox but non-Russian critic Chalmaye
(*op. cit.*, p. 271): "Agayev's insistence on the adoption of Russian as the mai
language for creative work is quite annoying."

[60] For Tretyakov, see Kravtsiv, *op. cit.*, p. 533; for Lushnikova, see Zh. Mulda
galiev, "The Connection With Life is the Main Thing," *Literaturnaya gazet*
April 2, 1963, p. 1.

[61] Skosyrev, *op. cit.*, p. 11.

writing in Belorussian (although he is sometimes deservedly reproached
for insufficient knowledge of the language) is exactly similar: recently he
refused to acknowledge as a Belorussian writer a Belorussian author who
had published his work in Russian.[62] Further, some non-Russian poets,
particularly young ones, remember with gratitude the help they have
received from such Russian poets as Leonid Martynov and Yaroslav Smel-
akov (which may not be accidental, since these two had been in Stalin's
concentration camps, a school of real "friendship of the peoples").[63]

Some Russian writers, however, have met a different attitude in non-
Russian literary circles. During the discussion on Khrushchev's March
speech, Ukrainian writers reminded Viktor Nekrasov of the facts that he
had charged someone with "nationalism" and had uttered "destructive"
criticism of Dovzhenko and reminded Yevtushenko of his "nihilistic" and
scornful attitude toward Ukrainian poetry in general, extending even to
such poets as Ivan Drach who write in a vein similar to his own. During the
same period there were attempts in Belorussia to build up the poet Igor
Shklyarevsky, a Belorussian who writes in Russian, into a "local Yevtushenko" who would be guilty of the same "sins" a vivid illustration of the
attitude toward writers who do not write in their native language.[64]

While the thesis of the new Party program relating to the "obliteration of language differences" started discussion on the adoption of Russian,
it also caused numerous non-Russian poets to produce poems which were
deeply emotional and lyrical, full of expressions of love for and fidelity to
their native language and of disgust for the "renegades" who had abandoned it. In almost every non-Russian literature poems in this vein by
young poets appeared and continue to appear; the most vivid of them,
noted even in the foreign press, are those of the Azerbaidzhani Halil Riza,
the Armenian Paruir Sevak, the Ukrainian Dmytro Pavlychko and the
Belorussian Ryhor Baradulin, whose poem "My Language" begins with

---

[62] U. Karpau, "Arbitrary and Prejudiced," *Literatura i mastactva*, February 19,
1963, p. 3.
[63] See the statements by the young non-Russian writers N. Damdinov, Sh.
Rahmudov and O. Suleimenov in *Voprosy literatury*, 1962, No. 9, pp. 130, 144 and
154. At one time Smelyakov spoke of the "elder brother" and "younger brother"
(he poem "Ode," *Literaturnaya gazeta*, July 12, 1962, p. 3) but in December of the
same year he says of himself as a Russian that he is "by no means the chief, but
equal among brothers and sisters" (the poem "The Word of a Russian," *ibid.*,
December 29, 1962, p. 1).
[64] For Nekrasov, see V. Zemlyak, "Take Care of the Honor and Glory of
Soviet Literature," *Literaturna Ukrayina*, April 23, 1963, p. 3; for Yevtushenko,
see A. Malyshko, "For the Happiness and Welfare of the People," *ibid.*, April 12,
1963, p. 3; and for Shklyarevsky see Jakub Usikau, "The Political Honesty of the
Artist," *Literatura i mastactva*, March 29, 1963, p. 2.

"the statements of historians and linguists" that "the borders betwee
nations are gradually being obliterated and that the language of n
mother, the Belorussian language, must die out as an outdated survival
i.e., statements which have been canonised in the new Party program b
which the poet finds it inconvenient in this case to mention directly. Neith
the feelings nor the mind of the poet can be reconciled to such statemen
he is sure that his native language will not become a "dead Latin" an
that if it "pours into the common ocean of humanity it will flow in it li
a small Gulf Stream and my heart will be warmed by every word which
saved. For the Belorussian language is as eternal as the rye." Thus the po
ends his poem, which was begun on the mournful notes inspired by th
new Party program, with a eulogy.[65]

But long before this poem the same Baradulin, in translating th
poems of the Yiddish writer Chaim Malcinsky, who lives in Belorussi
translated with special love a poem which praises the Yiddish languag
not only doomed but at that time banned in the USSR, as a "new torch
which "may shine as bright as seven suns over the Earth day and nig
and may be like old wine in oak barrels!" In order to appreciate to the fu
the position of the author and translator of this poem, with its genui
moral intelligence and courage, one should remember that since 19
Jewish authors in the USSR writing in Yiddish have been able to publi
their works only in translation (the poem which has just been quot
begins with a bitter affirmation of this fact), and only since last ye
(after the publication of this poem in translation) has a slender journal
Yiddish, *Sovetish Heimland* (Soviet Homeland), the only one in the USS
begun to appear, as a concession to world opinion. In general, the fa
of the Yiddish language and literature in the light of the thesis regardi
the "obliteration of language differences" should serve as an eloque
reminder to all non-Russian writers, although, as we have seen, the
are poets who stubbornly and openly refuse to take it all into account.

But if young poets who display perceptible neo-fellow-traveller ten
encies defend their native language so convincingly and courageousl
refusing to reconcile themselves with the official thesis relating to
(and their) obliteration, the writers who adopt the more moderate positi
of co-existentialism, and even with a clear leaning to the side of Caes
are also beginning to regard their language as a factor of the first impc
tance in co-existence with Caesar's compulsory taxation. Thus the Georgi

---

[65] R. Baradulin, "My Language," *Cryvonaja zmiena*, January 13, 1963. I
the others, see Torossian, *op. cit.*, p. 115; S. Tekiner, "Developments in Azerba
zhan," *Studies on the Soviet Union*, Munich, Vol. II, No. 3, 1963, p. 122.

[66] Chaim Malcinski, "Like Seven Suns," *Polymia*, 1961, No. 8, p. 141. T
Azerbaidzhani poet Halil Riza also calls his language the "sun."

writer Demma Shengelaya, who soon after Khrushchev's March speech published an article in *Literaturnaya gazeta*, condemned any deviations by writers from the Party line and assured his readers:

> No, Georgian writers decisively reject all this . . . Their works are filled with a thirst to apprehend in artistic forms our life which is steadfastly directed forward; great love for man, the people and its language is felt in them. Language is of course not only a means of communication — without it, as without air, the creation of a native culture and literature is unthinkable. In works by our writers which are written in the Georgian language sounds the ardent voice of the Soviet man, the bearer of the immortal ideas of Marxism-Leninism.

The formula for co-existence, as we see, is very transparent — on the one hand the national language and literature, which is "unthinkable" without it, and on the other Marxism-Leninism.[67]

In the light of this struggle for the consolidation of the non-Russian languages the rehabilitation of the national culture of the literary language acquires particularly vital significance. In the course of such a rehabilitation the struggle itself acquires the opportunity for an active deepening and strengthening of its positions from within. The rehabilitation itself in this case was a reaction to increased Russo-Sovietisation of non-Russian languages under Stalin, the first attempts to formulate a question about it relate to the last years of his regime (for instance, the statement by the Armenian philologist V. Arakelyan in February 1952), but widespread discussion started only in 1956, after which it waxed and waned but never ceased completely (in Turkmenia, for instance, the discussion was halted only by the Party-administrative outcry after Khrushchev's March speech) and in places, such as the Ukraine, even extended to special conferences and congresses. But much more important is the fact that parallel with these discussions concrete work started and still continues in all non-Russian literatures on restoring the national elements of the lexicons and phraseologies of the non-Russian literary languages which were subjected to Russo-Sovietisation under Stalin. Such restoration does not always end with the deletion of all Russo-Sovietisms from the language; sometimes they remain to coexist with the corresponding national elements which have been restored quite in the spirit of inter-literary coexistence; sometimes attempts may be observed at a semantic differentiation of these

---

[67] D. Shengelyya, "The Light of Our Ideas," *Literaturnaya gazeta*, March 30, 1963, p. 5. Connected with this are attempts to defend the non-Russian languages by invoking the authority of Lenin as, for instance, in the pseudo-classical ode by the Belorussian poet Andrej Aleksandrovich, "I Sing of Lenin" (*Literatura i mastactva*, April 21, 1961, p. 2) and the poem by the Ukrainian poet Dmytro Pavlychko, "In Lenin's Studio" (*Prapor*, 1963, No. 1, pp. 6—7).

coexisting elements in the direction of using them as synonyms (like the differentiation of the root Anglo-Saxon and borrowed French elements in English). Nevertheless, as a result of this unceasing practical work, supported by the appearance of appropriate textbooks and dictionaries, the process of de-Russification and nationalization of the non-Russian literary languages is progressing and thereby their national character and position, and that of their literatures, is becoming ever stronger.

Such practical work in general, with the emphasis on it in language and in all fields of literature and national life which finds an outlet in it, is the outstanding present characteristic of all the non-Russian literatures of the USSR. At the same time it provides a practical answer to the threat to their existence, the dark shadow of which is thrown onto their path by the new Party program.

In 1961 in connection with the anniversary of Taras Shevchenko, the rehabilitated veteran of Belorussian poetry Uladzimier Dubouka formulated one of the most important precepts of the great Ukrainian poet "to us all, his heirs," in the words: "There is nothing in the world more terrible than inactivity, for that is not life but non-existence," and at the same time spoke of the poet's lines to the effect that "it is terrible to fall into chains to die in captivity, but much worse still to sleep, sleep and sleep in the open, and to fall asleep for all eternity, and not to leave a trace, not a single one as to whether one has lived or died."[68] Two years later, almost simultaneously with Khrushchev's March speech, the young Belorussian poet Uladzmier Karatkevich published a work reminiscent of Laurence Sterne's *A Sentimental Journey Through France and Italy* and Heine's *Die Harzreise:* this was the *Fairy Tales of the Amber Land* already cited. This, so to speak, is his national-sentimental journey to neighboring Latvia, the "Amber Land" of the Soviet West which still retains a certain flavor of the West from which it was torn by the Second World War and which, like the other western Soviet republics, is more accessible to Soviet writers than the West or even the "people's democracies." After travelling through this land, admiring the manner in which "its small people construct their great culture" ("and we are not worse, there are no untalented peoples"), acquainting himself with their history and pondering over it, the author comes to the conclusion that "no historical phenomenon disappears without leaving traces and a strong seed which is more often than not capable of life. You may destroy a people, impose alien beliefs and an alien language upon them and the seed will all the same give forth its corpse." He then draws the conclusion that "One has to sow one's

---

[68] U. Dubouka, "To Live With the Heart and To Love People," *Polymia*, 1961 No. 3, p. 156. The lines by Shevchenko are from the poem "Days Pass, Nights Pass," *Tvory* (Works), Vol. I, Kiev, 1961, p. 328).

corn rigorously, to struggle with hail and storms, to sing and to pay no attention to defeats, treachery and pain" and, re-phrasing the old Roman saying *Vae victis!* (Woe to the Vanquished!) he exclaims: *Ave victis!* (Hail to the Vanquished!). For they are not asleep, just as the shoot is not asleep in the earth. Thanks to thee, Amber Land. For all that thou hast done, thanks to thee . . . The people in thy fields will be eternally mighty. Their wise tongue will be eternal. And the *kokle* will laugh and weep in all eternity under thy old elms."[69]

Thus the most thoughtful and sincere representatives of the "vanquished" non-Russian literatures of the USSR seek justification for their hopes for their own future, thus they try to find a true answer to the *Ave Caesar!* which is officially required from them.

But if the vanquished try not to sleep, then, neither of course, will their victors sleep. In all their campaigns in the field of literature, which for some time now have begun with a "meeting with writers" in the Kremlin, they try not to forget these vanquished who are about to die. It is true that up to now not one of these campaigns has come to a "last and decisive battle" but each has ended with an implicit retreat. Many listeners are already hearing the sounds of a retreat from the last campaign, which began in December of last year and reached a high point in March of this. But, repeating what has been said about the risk of making forecasts in the present epoch of alternating "thaws" and "freeze-ups" all that remains is to wait and see how the future will develop, what victories and defeats it will bring, and to whom.

---

[69] Karatkievic, *op. cit.*, pp. 109—10, 119 and 124. The mistake in the author's Latin (it should read "Avete victi") may be attributed to the poor knowledge of Latin grammar on the part of a product of the Soviet educational system, but one may also guess at the attempt to connect the re-phrased "Vae victis" and the implicit "Ave Caesar" for the reader. The *kokle* is a Latvian flute, here a symbol of national and folk art.

GLEB STRUVE

Soviet Literature in Perspective
Some Unorthodox Reflections

In 1930, when we discussed Soviet literature at a conference in Oxford, in speaking of the earliest period of postrevolutionary literature I advanced the view that this period was essentially a period of transition and that its place was really outside the scope of Soviet literature as usually understood. This view of mine was met with sceptical smiles and several objections. I feel inclined, however, to go even farther. Although I am myself the author of the first comprehensive history of Soviet literature, a history the pioneering nature of which is nowadays admitted even by Soviet literary scholars (though they don't approve of it, of course) in looking at that literature today "in perspective," I should like to pose the question: Is there such a thing as *Soviet* literature, or more precisely, *Soviet Russian* literature (the distinction is not unimportant in as much as in the Soviet Union the term "Soviet literature" is used to denote the whole complex of multinational literatures of the Soviet Union)? Should we not rather speak of the *Soviet period* in the history of Russian literature, a period that has its ups and downs, and even some blank spells, and is in the main characterized by the continuous tension between literature *qua* literature and the literary policies of the increasingly totalitarian Communist regime, the unceasing efforts to mould literature after the image of this totalitarian regime, to make it into an instrument of the Party?

The unique position of a Soviet writer was stressed by *Literaturnaya Gazeta*, in a leading article on September 2, 1929, in connection with the campaign against Pilnyak and Zamyatin. The paper said then that in the expression a "Soviet writer" the adjective was "not a geographical but a social concept," that Soviet writers were those who associated themselves and their work with socialist reconstruction. The paper expressed the hope that the Soviet literary community and the entire Soviet society would make Pilnyak "ponder over what a Soviet writer is and what his work must be like," and for that matter his "behavior" both inside and outside the country. Many things have changed since then in the Soviet Union, this is no longer a period of "the proletariat's offensive against the vestiges of capitalism" or of "a furious resistance of the class enemies of socialism" of which *Literaturnaya Gazeta* spoke in 1929, but many of the recent statements by Soviet leaders reflect the same attitude to literature and its practitioners: it is enough to recall Khrushchev's attack on Victor Nekrasov at the June 1963 Plenum of the Central Committee and his invidious comparison between the Party member Nekrasov and the non-Party writer Fedin.

To what extent and in what sense can so-called Soviet literature be regarded as a legitimate offspring of Russian literature, a continuation of a certain tradition or traditions (assuming that there is more than one tradition in Russian literature)? In the Soviet Union the so-called theory of a "single stream" (*ediny potok*) is still regarded as a heresy, as an implied denial of the originality (*svoyeobrazie*) of Soviet literature, of its essential qualitative difference from pre-Soviet literature.

It was, of course, much easier for Communist theoreticians of literature to postulate, at least in theory, this qualitative difference in the earlier days of the Revolution, the days of the struggle between the "proletarians" and the "fellow travellers," and in those days this very formula of a "single stream" was used in a different sense: the idea was attributed by the champions of proletarian literature, by the On Guard Group, and later by the Russian Association of Proletarian Writers, to those moderate Communist critics — like Voronsky, Lezhnev, Gorbov, the *Pereval* group, and others — who advocated essential unity *within* Soviet literature. Such unity is now taken for granted, if not always as a fact, at least as a desideratum. But the same formula — "single stream" — was subsequently reintroduced to mean continuity of development as between pre-Soviet (that is, nineteenth-century, "classical") Russian literature and Soviet literature. The denial of this continuity became one of the main assumptions on which the method of Socialist Realism, with its alleged originality and novelty, was supposed to rest. At the same time, with the growing tendency, from the late 1930's on, to reject the previously widespread attitude to the literary heritage of the past, be it the iconoclastic rejection of that heritage by the Futurists and by some of the early proletarian literary groups, or its sociological reinterpretation from the Marxian standpoint by such Communist literary scholars as Pereverzev and his school (this reinterpretation was applied by Pereverzev himself to Gogol and Dostoevsky; and by Dmitri Blagoy to Pushkin; but while Pereverzev and his followers were denounced as vulgarizers of Marxism and virtually ousted from academic scholarship, or reduced to silence, Blagoy managed to adjust himself to the new line and is thriving today), this about-face with regard to the literary legacy of the past involved, and continues to involve, both the advocates and the opponents of the "single stream" in a maze of irreconcilable contradictions. Witness the recent controversy around V. Arkhipov's article on Turgenev and his *Fathers and Sons*, when Arkhipov was accused of attempting to revive the "vulgar sociologism" of the 1920's.[1] In this respect the present official attitude towards the literary heritage of the past can perhaps be best characterized by two Russian adages: *chtoby i volki byli syty i ovts tsely* and *nevinnost' soblyusti i kapital priobresti*, a compromise idiomatic English rendering of which would be "to eat one's cake and to have it."

Needless to say, this dual tendency to assert the essential novelty and originality of Soviet literature and yet to assimilate the best of the Russian nineteenth-century tradition to Soviet culture results not only in flagrant contradictions, but also in inevitable distortions which even today, in the period of relative liberalization and broadmindedness (by comparison with the late thirties and with the Zhdanov period), are the blight of Soviet literary scholarship, even in its purely historical aspect. There is no need, however, to accept the Soviet view of the continuity of cultural and literary tradition — an extremely one-sided view according to which Realism was the prevalent literary mode in Russian literature even at the beginning of the present century, and Symbolism only a temporary and unhealthy deviation (see, e.g., Konstantin Fedin's speech at the opening of the international symposium on contemporary novel in Leningrad in August 1963)[2] — in order to realize that, considered *qua* literature, the literature of the Soviet period — that is, those works in it which will survive the test of time — will one day be reintegrated into the general stream of Russian literature, and that the same will happen to the other branch of contemporary Russian literature, the emigre branch, which since 1920—21 has been diverted away from its native soil, and with the passage of time has become more severed from the stream that continued to flow at home. To some extent this process of reunification for the literature in exile has already begun (Bunin, although in an expurgated form, has been reinstated in the pantheon

---

[1] See V. Arkhipov, "Against the Theory of *A Single Stream* in *Russkaya Literatura*, 1959, No. 2, pp. 95—130. This article was a reply to a number of critics who had attacked Arkhipov's earlier article "The Creative History of the Novel *Fathers and Sons*" in the same journal (1958, No. 1). Articles attacking Arkhipov were published in *Voprosy Literatury* (by P. Pustovoit), *Novy Mir* (by G. Bialy and A. Dementyev), *Literatura v Shkole* (by S. Petrov), *Neva* (by L. Krutikova), *Literaturnaya Gazeta* (by D. Starikov), *Literatura i Zhizn* (by E. Osetrov), *Podyom* (by G. Kunitsyn). Only one author, G. Fridlender in *Russkaya Literatura*, found himself in partial agreement with Arkhipov. In this controversy the question was of the "single stream" within Russian literature of the nineteenth century, but this is closely related to the problem of continuity of tradition as between the pre-Soviet and the Soviet period. Arkhipov's view of Turgenev, supported by numerous references to the "revolutionary democrats" and to Lenin, as fundamentally a Liberal went against the now prevalent tendency to "appropriate" to Soviet culture the best of Russian literary heritage. Arkhipov showed more consistency than most of those who want to eat their cake and have it.

[2] See "Sudba romana," *Literaturnaya Gazeta*, August 6, 1963.

of Russian classics; Tsvetayeva's poetry has been reissued; even some poems by Khodasevich were recently published in a Soviet magazine), though so long as Russia continues to be ruled by the Communist regime this reunification of the two branches of contemporary Russian literature is bound to remain only limited, inasmuch as it will be influenced by all-decisive extra-literary factors. The same is true of the real, undistorted assimilation of the cultural heritage of the past in all its richness and diversity. The Soviet claim to that heritage rests on falsehood and hypocrisy, but the ground has been laid down for it, and the moment the fetters and shackles of totalitarian tyranny are thrown off the process will become rapid and spontaneous. As for the emigre branch of Russian literature, in which foreign students of contemporary Russia have shown so little interest, there is plenty of evidence that there is very real and steadily growing interest in it on the part of Soviet writers and literary scholars.

While I am on this subject I should like to quote a passage from a very fine essay by Wladimir Weidlé in the latest issue of the almanac *Vozdushnye Puti*, entitled "Vozvrashchenie na rodinu" ("Homecoming" — or should one perhaps translate it as "The Return of the Natives"?).

> . . . Russia is a spiritual, conceptual entity, changing in time and coloured for each of us in a slightly different way, yet outlined sufficiently clearly and existing not only in the past, but through the bond between the future and the past. Barbarization has distorted the image of Russia precisely by obscuring and weakening this bond. The efforts of the new generation are directed — whether it is clearly or only dimly aware of it — towards restoring this bond.

> The bond must be restored in the first place — as everybody apparently seems to feel — with the most recent past, with the 1920's, when thought and imagination had still not been completely wiped out in our country, even though they were being oppressed ever more assiduously with every year; and then, with the prerevolutionary beginning of the century, which had put an end to the provincialism of the preceding era. The restoration of tradition and continuity is impossible short of a revision of those absurd judgments which for so long have barred access to this recent past, without a careful examination of what had been done by it, as well as of what has been done by the emigration which, to the best of its ability, has continued its work. The ban has so far been lifted only from a very small part of that legacy, but the emancipation of memory has begun, however timidly. It does not mean, as everybody realises, a return to the past. Continuity does not imply a repetition of past stages. We must look to the past, not for models for imitation, nor for thoughts with which we agree in advance, but for "food for the mind." And here, in our recent past,

it will be easier to find it than anywhere else. Through this recent
past lies the road to the understanding of the more distant one.
Continuity can be re-established only in struggle, only through
assimilating some things and rejecting others. It cannot be affirmed,
prolonged, passed on to the future without something new being added
to the old. But, in order to add, one must know to what one is adding.

The underlying idea of Mr. Weidlé's essay is the same which he
developed in his excellent book *La Russie absente et présente* — the idea
of Russia's unity with Europe, of Russia as part and parcel of Europe —
and he ends his essay with the following lines:

> Russia must once again become aware of herself as both Europe
> and Russia, become once more both Europe and Russia. This, just this,
> will mean a homecoming for all of us.[3]

There is every reason to believe that if this little essay could be circulated and read today in the Soviet Union it would awaken responsive chords
in the hearts of many a Soviet intellectual, in those of the younger generation, as well as in a few of the older one who have survived the ordeals of
the Stalin era and remained true to the old banners and old ideals, who
have not prostituted them as did so many others. But even some of those
who were guilty of such prostitution in the recent past — men like Ilya
Ehrenburg — seem to have entered now on this homecoming path.

*

The *differentia specifica* of Soviet literature is determined by factors
that lie outside the sphere of literature. So-called "Soviet" literature is in
this sense a unique phenomenon in the history of world literature.
Throughout its existence we have in it a great number of works produced
by Soviet writers and within the geographical limits of the Soviet state,
which are either rejected as "un-Soviet," banned, suppressed (as an example,
one may cite the works of such a prolific and influential writer of the
1920's as Boris Pilnyak, who disappeared in 1937 and most of whose works
have not been reissued since 1929), or even remain unknown to the vast
majority of Soviet readers because their publication was never permitted
(the best-known examples of such works are Zamyatin's anti-Utopian *We*
and Pasternak's *Doctor Zhivago* and *Essay in Autobiography*), or even
never sought by their authors. I have in mind several works recently
smuggled out of Russia and published abroad — let me name only one of
them, viz. *The Tale of the Bluebottle* by Valeri Tarsis, the most uncompromising satirical indictment of Soviet totalitarianism as a pseudo-socialist

---

[3] *Vozdushnye Puti*, Almanakh III, New York, 1963, pp. 65—66.

state, as a parody on Socialism, so far to appear in print. I happen to know that, in contradistinction to some other specimens of this clandestine literature, those which, prior to their publication abroad, had been circulated in Moscow, the existence of Tarsis's novel was neither known to nor even suspected by the Soviet literary community until its publication abroad. Tarsis, who back in 1930 had published a useful biobibliographical aid entitled *Russkie pisateli* (Russian Writers), and some stories, led a very secluded life, and although he apparently retained his membership in the Union of Soviet Writers, little was known about what he was doing. His arrest and confinement to a mental home in August 1962 came as a complete surprise to those who knew him and they could think of no possible explanation.

In the Foreword to the American edition of my book on Soviet literature I wrote of the great handicaps which an outside student of Soviet literature had to overcome in his study, even though sometimes he was better off in this respect than an average Soviet reader, and I added: " . . . we can only presume, for instance, the existence of a considerable body of unprinted literature — the fact that many Soviet authors must be writing for their own inner satisfaction, without any hope of seeing their works in print, was hinted at recently . . . by such a staunch apologist of Stalin's regime as Alexander Werth, who spent the years 1941—48 in the Soviet Union and met in person many Soviet writers." What could only be surmised or hinted at then is now known to be a fact, and a fact of major significance for our evaluation of the literature of the Soviet period. There is a large and ever growing body of literature in the Soviet Union which is either circulated clandestinely or smuggled out abroad. I happen to know of several important unpublished (and in some cases at present still unpublishable) works by well-known "Soviet" writers, both living and dead. There are probably many more in existence. Some of the clandestine works published abroad anonymously are known to be by well-known writers who continue to publish their other works in Soviet magazines. There is one case, when a poem, which was first circulated from hand to hand within the Soviet Union and then appeared abroad both in translation and in original, later found its way into a Soviet publication. There may be other such works by well-known and established writers, works which they keep in their drawers in the hope of having them published one day. There may even be different versions of the same works — one for current publication and another for the future. Are such works, or are they not, part of "Soviet" literature? For that matter, are Zamyatin's *We* and Pasternak's *Doctor Zhivago* part of that literature? Back in 1946—47, two well-known Soviet literary scholars reproached me for including such "renegades" as Zamyatin and Zoshchenko in my survey of Soviet literature.[4] Perhaps they were right? Quite recently, Professor Roman Samarin (who has since been denounced by a Soviet man of letters, in a document published abroad, as an ignoramus and a Stalinist with a criminal record)[5] attacked my book on Soviet literature because my account of the development of that literature was "pivoted," he says, on such names as Zamyatin, Babel, Pilnyak, and Pasternak.[6] While there is no denying that such works as Zamyatin's *We* or Pasternak's *Doctor Zhivago* belong to the Soviet *period* of Russian literature, their exclusion from Soviet literature (together with many works that once upon a time *were* published there) is not accidental. They are émigré books by non-émigré writers, and their ultimate reintegration into the stream of Russian literature is as certain as that of the works of *bona fide* émigré writers. According to information which recently came my way, some émigré writings — for instance, critical articles about Soviet literature — even now find their way into certain clandestine publications circulating in the Soviet Union.

There is another aspect of "Soviet" literature which contributes to its uniqueness. It is a "negative" or "private" aspect, too. Soviet scholars, especially those of them who are engaged in editing and commenting upon the works of the Russian classics of the nineteenth century, pride themselves on having restored many such works to their pristine condition by reincorporating in them passages that were cut out or disfigured by "Tsarist" censorship. But, even leaving aside the fact that there was a time when the writings of the same classics were subjected to a new Communist censorship (we all know examples of this), does the history of prerevolutionary Russian literature — or of any other literature, for that matter — know of any examples of major fictional works, novels or plays, being subjected to censorship and alteration by the authors themselves, in order to make them fit in with the current Party line, as has been done by Sholokhov, Fadeyev, Slonimsky, and others? Soviet literary scholars and critics have criticized me for underrating Sholokhov and his celebrated masterpiece, *The Quiet Don*. I admit that there are many

---

[4] See Alexander Anikst, "Slander in the Guise of Scholarship," *Soviet Literature*, Moscow, 1947, No. 10, pp. 62—65, and L. Timofeyev, "Letter to the Editor," *Kultura i Zhizn*, March 9, 1947. More recently, A. Brukhansky, in a long article about the study of Soviet literature in the United States ("Study or Falsification?," *Russkay Literatura*, 1959, No. 1, pp. 204—216), repeated the same charge when he said that such writers as Zamyatin, Klychkov, and others, "who had nothing to do with [Soviet literature]," were included by me in its history (see p. 206).

[5] See "Informers and Traitors Among Soviet Writers and Scholars," *Sotsialistichesky Vestnik*, May—June 1963. The same document, emanating from a Soviet man of letters, was published in English by Forum Service, London.

[6] See R. Samarin, "The Distortion of the History of Soviet Literature in US Literary Criticism" in *Sovremennaya literatura SShA*, Moscow, 1962, pp. 211—213.

works of the Soviet period which I personally prefer to this novel, although
I do not deny its merits. But I should like to ask my critics which version
of Sholokhov's famous novel I am to regard as authentic — the original
one or the one revised on the eve of Stalin's death and praised so much at
the time by Soviet critics precisely because of those revisions — revisions
obviously dictated by extra-literary considerations and intended to meet
the demands imposed on writers by their watchful guardians, by those
vigilant Party bureaucrats whose role was castigated as early as 1921 by
Alexander Blok in his remarkable speech at the commemoration of the
anniversary of Pushkin's death, and so prophetically satirized about the
same time by Zamyatin in his novel *We?* And now that the "cult of personality" (what a characteristically hypocritical formula!) has been denounced and Stalin dethroned (and even his mortal remains demoted),
how many works, including some by highly respected Soviet writers, will
have to be revised (if they are reissued) in order to have the paeans to
Stalin (or perhaps even a bare mention of his name in a complimentary
context) removed, just as once upon a time this had to be done with the
names of Trotsky, Tukhachevsky, and other "enemies of the people"
(some of them are enemies no longer, and perhaps Nikolai Virta will be
now allowed to restore the references to Tukhachevsky in one of his
earlier novels)?! That those who did not glorify Stalin were not many was
implied as recently as 1957 by Mikola Bazhan, when at the Plenum
of the Union of Soviet Writers at which *Literaturnaya Moskva* and its
editors were torn to pieces he referred with indignation to an unnamed
Moscow writer who "boasted" of having never used the name of Stalin
in his works![7] I have always been curious to know whom Bazhan had in
mind. Since he is now probably anxious to forget that indignant outburst of
his, he is unlikely ever to reveal his "secret."

   Taking advantage of the debunking of Stalin, some Soviet writers
invite us now to read a new, hidden meaning into some of their old works.
Thus, Ilya Selvinsky, in a recent article in *Literaturnaya Gazeta*, recalled
in the following way some poems he wrote in the 1930's:

   Of course, none of us, who were remote from Stalin's life and
   its every-day routine, realized the full dimensions of the purges. Yes,
   we were carried away by the personality of Stalin, we believed that he
   alone knew how to lead the people toward Communism; but even
   during his lifetime we were from time to time puzzled by the discrepancy
   between this — so it seemed to us then — highly poetic [embodiment
   of the] ideal of Soviet man and the injustices [committed under] the
   cult of personality. With regard to Stalin the consciousness of each of
   us has had its own trajectory and many of us, in their hearts and even

---

[7] See *Literaturnaya Gazeta*, 1957.

in their creative work, vacillated between two poles. If I, for instance, as a member of the "Chelyuskin" expedition, sincerely dedicated to Stalin an enthusiastic ode in my epic poem "The Chelyuskiniad," in my lyrical poems I wrote, parallel with it, the following:

> No matter at what hour I go to bed,
> At five my eyes open of themselves;
> And my throat is again and again
> Choked with frozen tears.
> The drifting chaos of sullen wrongs,
> The moving mercury of humiliation . . .
> And one tries to make aloud, as though sobbing,
> Swallowing motions.
> But chunks of inedible pain still stick in the gullet,
> (Or do we no longer have the strength?)
> Like a black cross you lie in the dark,
> Resembling a grave in a field.

For a long time they did not forgive me those lines.[8]

*

Last year, when we were discussing the most recent developments on the Soviet literary scene, I voiced my pessimism. I disagreed with Max Hayward's evaluation of Khrushchev's speech at the Third Congress of Soviet Writers in 1959 as relatively mild and benevolent. I see now that Walter Vickery, in his recently published book *The Cult of Optimism*, also characterizes that speech as "friendly and conciliatory."[9] To me its benevolence, friendliness and good humour seemed very superficial and deceptive: both when I first read it and on rereading it again I was struck above all by its condescendingly scornful approach to literature and its practitioners. There was in it an outward bonhomie which seemed to be in contrast with the high-handed manner which Zhdanov had adopted in 1946 and which prevailed in the various literary *obiter dicta* in the period that followed. But it was a bonhomie of contempt, a purely tactical change, born of the realization that this outward "benevolence" pays, that such sops are received gratefully by some opposition-minded writers, while others are induced to stake out greater claims — later to be rapped on the knuckles. It was in December 1962, and still more so in March 1963, that Khrushchev showed his real face. The "drunken outburst" in the Moscow Manège confirmed my pessimistic forebodings of summer 1962. It is true that in between there had been some episodes which seemed to indicate

---

    [8] I. Selvinsky, "Green and Ripe," *Literaturnaya Gazeta*, June 8, 1963.
    [9] Walter N. Vickery, *The Cult of Optimism: Political and Ideological Problems of Recent Soviet Literature*, Bloomington, Indiana, University Press, 1963, p. 94.

that gentler breezes were blowing in the opposite direction, enough to encourage some optimistic wishful thinking: I have in mind the publication of Yevtushenko's "Babi Yar" and "The Heirs of Stalin," of Viktor Nekrasov's American impressions, and of Solzhenitsyn's concentration camp story. But even if they could be seen as signs of "liberalization," they were only one of those zigs in Soviet cultural policy which are invariably and inevitably followed by a zag. I am not sure, however, that the "liberal" significance of those events was not greatly exaggerated at the time. My pessimism was not dispelled by them. In 1962 I was inclined to regard Yevtushenko as a man who was becoming more and more a tool — and a useful tool at that — of the regime. I have since modified my view of Yevtushenko in the light of his *Autobiography* (though it is in many ways, in my opinion, an unpleasant document), and especially in view of the circumstances of its publication, but I am less impressed by the two poems I have mentioned. I am not sure about "Babi Yar" (in this case the poem as such must be separated from the reception it had, the effect it produced); but "The Heirs of Stalin" seemed to me to be entirely in keeping with the Party line at the time, something that almost filled the "social command" of the moment, and should therefore have pleased Khrushchev, inasmuch as it helped to build up the image he had been studiously creating for himself — that of the Great Liberator from Stalin's tyranny. If there is a cult of Khrushchev in the making (and I think there is), this sort of poetry must be grist to his mill. The Solzhenitsyn story is something different, of course. There was in it no denunciation of Khrushchev's Stalinist adversaries and potential rivals at the top of the hierarchy, or of survivals of Stalinism today. But fundamentally, as an indictment of the evils of the Stalin era, it did not contradict the official Party line. It was bound to be given a proper and acceptable interpretation, and such an interpretation was immediately forthcoming in Simonov's nauseatingly hypocritical article in *Izvestia*. The story of how Solzhenitsyn's story got published is by now well known. Some people still seem to be surprised that Khrushchev himself should have approved of its publication. But apart from what I have said already, one may perhaps look for an additional reason for this. How do we know that Tvardovsky, in submitting the story for the boss's approval, did not point out that if it were not printed in *Novy Mir*, it might find its way abroad and be published there? He might have convinced Khrushchev of the undesirability of this, as well as of the relative innocuousness of Solzhenitsyn's story and of the advantages to be gained from its "de-Stalinizing" aspects. There is no doubt I think that, in some cases at least, the possibility of a publication abroad can now be used as an effective argument in promoting the publication of certain works (such an argument was in fact used in print by Lev Ozerov in an article that will be mentioned below). Tvardovsky's efforts on behalf of Solzhenitsyn came soon after the publication in England of Tarsis's *The Bluebottle*. What is more significant, Tvardovsky's own poem "Tyorkin in the Other World" (read by the author in a revised version at Khrush-chev's Black Sea estate and printed both in *Izvestia* and in *Novy Mir*) was being circulated clandestinely at the time in Moscow and had found its way abroad, where the original version appeared in *Mosty* more than six months before its publication in Russia.[10]

It is more difficult to account for the publication of Solzhenitsyn's two other stories — "Matryona's Home" and "At the Krechetovka Station" — which appeared subsequently to the events of December 1962 — unless we look for a similar explanation. Contrary to the widespread opinion, I regard "Matryona's Home" as less interesting from the purely literary point of view than "One Day in the Life of Ivan Denisovich," but politi-cally more explosive and revealing. The same is true, I think, of Fyodor Abramov's "Round and About," the literary value of which is greatly inferior to that of any of Solzhenitsyn's stories. It is significant that both "Matryona's Home" and Abramov's story came under strong attack, and that Abramov even made an attempt to stop the publication of the English version of his story, while "One Day in the Life of Ivan Denisovich" is still accepted in the spirit of Simonov's review.

Far be it from me to deny the existence and the apparent growth, in the Soviet Union, of an opposition mood and of a spirit of independence among the intellectuals and in the younger generation. There is indeed, I believe, more of it than most of us suspect. But as it grows, the chances of any true liberalization of cultural policies diminish. On that score I remain an out-and-out pessimist. In his *Precocious Autobiography* Yevtushenko objects to the term "Thaw" introduced by Ehrenburg in his novel of that name. Yevtushenko says:

> I don't think the word "thaw," which Ilya Ehrenburg stuck so casually on this movement, is a very appropriate one. I have objected to it several times in the press and should like to object again. There is no doubt that it is spring. It is a rough spring, a difficult spring with late frosts and cold winds, a spring which takes a step to the left, then a step to the right, then a step back, but which is certain, nevertheless, to go on and take two or three steps forward. And the fact that winter should hold the earth so desperately in its grip and refuse to give it up is also quite in the order of things; but then, in the very counter-attacks of winter, one can sense its growing impotence — because times have changed.[11]

---

[10] A. Tvardovsky, "Tyorkin in the Other World," *Mosty*, Munich, No. 10, 1963, pp. 129—144.

[11] Y. Yevtushenko, *A Precocious Autobiography*, New York, 1963, pp. 99—100.

Unfortunately, so long as the Soviet regime remains what it is — a one-party totalitarian tyranny — this kind of spring, with alternating spells of *ottepel'* (thaw) and *zamorozki* (freeze-up), is the most one can expect; it will remain a sort of permanent climatic feature, the thaw spells being determined, as a rule, by policy considerations which have nothing to do with the arts. In 1962, in discussing Max Hayward's paper at the Oxford conference, I pointed out the importance of the foreign policy of the Soviet government as a factor in shaping its line of conduct on the cultural front. I want to stress it again. Whatever may be its motives (and I am by no means sure that the Soviet-Chinese dispute and rift is here the decisive factor), the Soviet government is now bent on pursuing its policy of "coexistence," and this implies so-called "cultural coexistence." Its needs may at times dictate relatively liberal policies on the literary front and result in certain concessions. But such concessions are always subject to recall, and what is more, they are less likely whenever the Soviet government scores a victory on the international front, or scores a point which it can interpret as a success. This, I think, applies to the recent test-ban treaty, and therefore the *détente*, which is optimistically assumed in the West to follow from this treaty, is not very likely to lead to a relaxation on the cultural front; rather, the other way round. The case of the Fellini film is a very characteristic illustration of this ambiguous situation. By voting for the award of the first prize at the Moscow Film Festival to Fellini, Soviet representatives demonstrated the importance attached by them to at least a semblance of cultural coexistence and accord. But no sooner was the prize awarded when Alexei Romanov, who is regarded in Moscow as one of the pillars of Stalinism among the top Party functionaries, hastened to attack the film and to emphasize its incompatibility with the Soviet outlook.

Unfortunately, there is still a fairly large section of the European intelligentsia (including writers) which accept unquestioningly the official Soviet concept of cultural coexistence and minimizes, or even dismisses as "hostile falsification," the deep-seated conflicts and tensions within Soviet society. A good illustration of this could be seen at the symposium — the first of its kind to be held in the Soviet Union — which took place last month in Leningrad under the auspices of the European Community of Writers, a decidedly pro-Soviet organization, launched a few years ago in Italy by some Italian intellectuals (including such well-known men as Piovene and Ungaretti) in conjunction with some Soviet writers (the leading part among them was played by Alexei Surkov and Mikola Bazhan). The subject of the symposium was the contemporary novel and its problems. It was attended by a number of Western writers, among whom the Italians, led by Giuseppe Ungaretti, seemed to predominate, but other literatures were represented, too (France, among others, by Alain Robbe-

Grillet and Nathalie Sarraute; England by John Lehmann and Angus Wilson; Western Germany by Hans Enzenberger and other members of the "47" Group, etc.). On the eve of the symposium its Soviet vice-president Mykola Bazhan and its Italian secretary-general Giancarlo Vigorelli gave interviews to *Pravda* (August 5, 1963). Bazhan attacked contemporary "bourgeois" writers who deny the social role of literature and regard it as a vehicle of "self-expression" and morbid introspection. He also spoke of the distortion of Soviet literature in the bourgeois press, especially of late, and expressed a hope that the Leningrad conference would help "to clear the atmosphere of the miasma of anti-Communist lies and slander." Vigorelli, for his part, emphasized the importance of the fact that the meeting was going to take place after all the hallaballoo about "some sort of crisis" in Soviet literature raised in the West on the basis of "falsified information," and stressed the fact that Western delegates to the conference represented a variety of outlooks ("Catholics, Liberals, Socialists, and Communists"), but were at one in their "anti-Fascism" and their "fight for peace." Vigorelli probably does not know, or prefers, to ignore — and it is not very likely that anyone enlightened him during this conference — that there are today many people in the Soviet Union for whom the word "Fascism" has a real topical meaning only when apllied to Stalinism and its survivals in the present Soviet regime. Vigo-relli concluded his interview by saying: "I am convinced that whoever proclaims himself an anti-Communist thereby assigns himself to the camp of Fascism. One need not be a Communist, but one cannot be an anti-Communist"; he added that this had always been the main point of the program of the European Community of Writers since its foundation. This is, of course, an attitude that can give no help and encouragement to those intellectuals in the Soviet Union who yearn for greater freedom and try to fight the periodical inroads of wintry weather, to use Yevtushenko's image.

At the symposium itself the first two speeches on behalf of the Western and Soviet delegates were made by Ungaretti and Sholokhov respectively. Sholokhov made a short and playful address, jokingly attributing the honour conferred on him to the fact that Surkov and other organizers of the meeting knew that if he were to speak after the others he might come out with something tactless. He also said it was a good thing the meeting was being held in Leningrad where it was cooler than in Moscow, and should the debate become too heated it could be moved further north, to Arkhangelsk or Murmansk. The first substantial Soviet contribution to the discussion on the novel was made by Konstantin Fedin. His speech was significant in a negative way. He stressed, of course, the continuity of the realistic tradition in Russian literature, linking up Socialist Realism with the nineteenth-century tradition and asserting that even in the present century, in the prerevolutionary period, realism played the dominant role (the two names he mentioned in this connection were those of Bunin and Kuprin, two émigré writers who are now back in favour). But he also devoted much of his speech to an attack on Symbolism and some of its offshoots (including Futurism).

Speaking of the early phase of postrevolutionary literature, Fedin singled out the names of four poets whose work, though they belonged to the movements and schools which were now irrevocably relegated to the past — Symbolism, Acmeism, Futurism, and Imaginism — will not be forgotten. These four poets were Alexander Blok, Vladimir Mayakovsky, Sergei Yesenin, and Anna Akhmatova. But in the novel these outmoded schools had left practically no trace, said Fedin. Speaking briefly of the literature of the Twenties, Fedin mentioned Boris Pilnyak and Artyom Vesyoly as the leading writers who had continued the non-realist tradition of pre-1917 literature:

> Only at the fountainhead of the Soviet novel are to be observed traces of influence of the forms which were being relegated to the past. It seems that its most striking expression is to be found in the works of Pilnyak in which one hears the rhythms of Bely or the stylized *skaz* of Remizov. The same applies to Artyom Vesyoly who came into literature later. In his prose he responded in a loud echo to the verse, based on sound effects, of the Futurists.

Of Babel, of the Serapion Brothers, of Pasternak's early prose fiction, of his own and Leonov's early novels Fedin said nothing. After paying a vague general tribute to the diversity of styles and manners within realism, he summed up the subsequent development of the Soviet novel by the following list of names: Furmanov and Alexei Tolstoy, Sholokhov and Leonov, Fadeyev, Vsevolod Ivanov, Ehrenburg and Paustovsky, and stressed their artistic "dissimilarity."

In anticipation of possible criticisms from Western participants of the conference Fedin rejected emphatically the charge of "literary isolationism," sometimes brought against Soviet literature. Its absurdity, he said, is demonstrated by the number and variety of translations from foreign writers in the Soviet Union, a field in which his country, he said, could not be matched by any other. He took some pains, however, to "explain" why such Western writers as Proust, Joyce, and Kafka were unacceptable to them:

> . . . Literature is now confronted with an attempt to hoist, nearly everywhere in the West, the banner of the traditions of Joyce, Proust, and Kafka in the novel. We decline this banner. We do not believe that, in search for innovation, one should go back to decadence of this variety.

The refusal to support such an attempt is not built on sand. It is hardly known to everybody that Marcel Proust's Collected Works were published in our country. If his reputation did not become rooted, this was not because any isolationism stood in its way. And if Soviet novel writing had followed Proust's intuitivism, it would have been logical to revive also some of our native modernists. I think that Joyce, too, is not a secret to all of our novelists. Kafka is probably known to but a few. I knew him in Germany at the time of World War I, when Dadaism was only beginning to be split into German Expressionism and French Surrealism. I do not think that since then I have sought his books. Kafka wrote, of course, with great formal elegance, and he possessed his own personal truth, but it was not then the truth for any large circle of readers. What is then the point now of trying persistently to enlarge that circle?

We come again to the very essence of the difference between a novelist who is responsible to himself for himself only, and a novelist who is responsible to all for all that he has done.[12]

Fedin's speech, aimed primarily at a sophisticated foreign audience, was moderate in tone, relatively subtle, and cleverly evasive. He abstained deliberately from crossing all the *t*'s and dotting all the *i*'s and preferred to speak of realism *tout court*, rather than of Socialist Realism, let alone of such ingredients of it as *partiinost*. But what he said of the literature of the Twenties sounded like a clear discouragement to those younger Soviet writers whose eyes turn more and more to that period, who want to explore it more thoroughly, to learn more about its various representatives, as well as about their predecessors, instead of confining themselves to a few officially permitted and sanctioned names. In the domain of poetry, this desire was clearly voiced two years ago by the young poet and critic Lev Ozerov who, in an article in *Literaturnaya Gazeta*, spoke of the necessity of opening up the hidden treasure of Russian poetry.[13] It was later echoed by the ex-Futurist Victor Pertsov who spoke of the interest shown by young Soviet writers in such poets as Mandelshtam, Tsvetayeva, Khlebnikov, and even hinted at the possible "rehabilitation" of Gumilyov.[14] The same "back-to-the-Twenties" trend was, of course,

---

[12] See note 2. It would be interesting to know whether anyone pointed out to Fedin that by 1918, when he left Germany after having been interned there during the war, he could not have read much of Kafka, little of whose work was published before 1919 (his major works appeared only after his death in 1924).

[13] See L. Ozerov, "The Land of Russian Poetry," *Literaturnaya Gazeta*, March 28, 1961.

[14] See V. Pertsov, "The Search for Something New and Great Traditions," *Literaturnaya Gazeta*, February 27, 1962. Cp. also K. Zelinsky, "Russian Poetry Today," in *Survey*, London, No. 40 (January 1962), pp. 49—67. In this article, translated from an Italian publication and apparently never published in the Soviet Union, Zelinsky, a well-known Soviet critic and an ex-Constructivist, calls Gumilyov "a fine poet" and compares his fate with that of André Chénier.

the salient feature of Ehrenburg's *Memoirs* for which he was so sharply rebuked by Khrushchev and Ilyichev. Judging by Fedin's speech, there is little chance of this trend receiving any further encouragement.

Ehrenburg himself did, however, appear at the symposium, and both his appearance and the speech he made, later printed in *Literaturnaya Gazeta*, were symptomatic. It was his first appearance in public after the attacks made on him in March 1963 by Khrushchev and Ilyichev. Reports from Moscow had it that, prior to his departure for Leningrad, he was personally received by Khrushchev, the implication being that what he was about to say had received the latter's blessing.

The most significant point in Ehrenburg's speech was his "defense" of Joyce and Kafka (to "defend" Proust he apparently thought to be beneath his dignity); and this involved him in a direct polemic with Fedin who had spoken not only for himself, but in the name of Soviet writers and even of Soviet readers. Joyce and Kafka, said Ehrenburg, were both "major writers." They were different from each other, but one could not "reject" them. "For me," said Ehrenburg, "this is the past, they are historical phenomena. I do not make a banner of them, but neither do I make of them a target to be shot at." Here Ehrenburg drew an interesting parallel with Khlebnikov, a poet, he said, whose name would mean little to the foreign participants of the symposium and about whom present-day Soviet readers knew little; a "difficult" poet, Ehrenburg went on, adding that he himself could not read more than one or two pages of Khlebnikov at one sitting. "But," said Ehrenburg, "Mayakovsky, Pasternak, and Aseyev, have told me that, without Khlebnikov, they themselves would not have existed. Many of our young poets who have never read Khlebnikov, have inherited many of his poetic discoveries from Mayakovsky, Pasternak or Zabolotsky." Although Ehrenburg did not spell this out, the implication was that Joyce and Kafka were seminal writers in a similar way. Of Joyce Ehrenburg said: "Joyce ferreted out the tiniest psychological details, discovered the mastery of inner dialogue. But an essence is not drunk in pure form, it is diluted with water. Joyce is a writers' writer." And of Kafka: "As for Kafka, he foresaw the terrible world of Fascism. His works, his diaries, his letters show that he was a seismographic station which, thanks to the sensitivity of its equipment, recorded the first rumblings. People attack him as though he were a contemporary of ours, but he is a great historical phenomenon."

On a more general plane, Ehrenburg came out in defense of experimentation in literature. He said:

It seems to me that it is unnecessary to fear experiments. In my book, I cited the words of Jean-Richard Bloch at the First Congress of Soviet Writers. He said that there should be writers for the millions and writers for five thousand readers, just as there should be pilots "who work on already tested models" as well as test pilots. One can and ought to reject charlatanism, but one ought not to reject the right of experiment in literature.[15]

On Socialist Realism Ehrenburg was vaguely brief: "...it is not worth saying that Socialist Realism is bad; after all, so many excellent books are associated with it." What these books were Ehrenburg did not specify. He went on, however, to say:

> Our writers sometimes write bad novels, not because they are tied up to socialist ideology, but because the Lord God has not endowed them with talent. We never claimed that under socialism there would be no untalented writers. We said that we would have no exploiters, and we don't have them; as for untalented writers, I daresay we have enough of them.[16]

One of the most interesting speeches made at the symposium by a Soviet writer was Leonid Leonov's. As usual, there was much in it that sounded cryptic, much that could perhaps be read between the lines. Unlike Fedin, Leonov abstained from any sallies against Proust, Joyce, and Kafka, though he probably has little use for them as a writer. He did say much that was critical of the West and of "Modernism," but his criticisms were on a moral plane, and the whole speech was imbued with moral pessimism. He hinted darkly at his own "microbes of pessimism" which have already caused him "enough professional disasters," and spoke of the disease of "excessive optimism" which befell the Soviet Union at the beginning of the war in 1941 and the effects of which are still painfully felt. In line with other Soviet participants of the symposium, he "defended" the novel and testified to its viability, or rather to its great mission. Without mentioning socialist realism once, he referred several times to the great genius of Dostoevsky. Admitting his ineradicable affection for "old tools," he included among them Dostoevsky's pen which is preserved in the Dostoevsky Museum in Moscow — "very simple, almost a school pen with which *The Brothers Karamazov* was written"; and added: "It is a sin to throw such a thing out of the window. In the hand of the genius, had it not been for his death, it could have produced more than one literary

---

[15] See I. Ehrenburg, "Defend Human Values," *Literaturnaya Gazeta*, August 1, 1963.
[16] See L. Leonov, "Praise Be to Man," *Literaturnaya Gazeta*, August 8, 1963. It is to be noted that both Leonov's and Ehrenburg's pieces were published as articles "based" on their speeches. There was no note to that effect in Fedin's case. At the same time it was obvious that Fedin's "The Fate of the Novel" was a speech addressed to the symposium. It is to be assumed that Leonov's and Ehrenburg's speeches were "edited" for publication.

treasure." "I do not believe," said Leonov, "in art which begins with drumlike manifestoes. In art one may do as one likes, on one condition — that it comes out well. The form is dictated by the practical goal of the artist, by his port of destination, which every serious master must foresee in advance. Thus, what matters is not the bottle, but the wine which we, the writers, pour into it" (formulated thus, Leonov's artistic credo was in direct contradiction with one of the early utterances of Mayakovsky the Futurist). Leonov began by warning his audience that much of what he was going to say would sound "old-fashioned and even banal," and he ended as follows: "In conclusion I beg you not to judge me for the tiresome didacticism of this speech...nor for the excessive insistence of my arguments, because even more than you I needed to convince myself of the primacy of the citizen over the artist."

The Soviet press, while reproducing several speeches by Soviet writers and critics, did not report the proceedings of the symposium in full. Ehrenburg's remarks on Socialist Realism were not published and no mention was made of the fact that many of the foreign participants spoke very critically of Socialist Realism and of present-day Soviet literature in general. The reaction of such Soviet delegates as Fedin or Professor Anisimov (who is well known for his support of Zhdanov in the post-World War II period and for his polemic with Ignazio Silone)[17] to Ehrenburg's defense of Joyce and Kafka, and of experimentation in general, remains unknown. It is to be hoped that a full and unadulterated report of the proceedings of the Leningrad symposium will be published before long — such a possibility was hinted at by one of the English delegates, Mr. John Lehmann, in an article in The London *Observer*.[18]

To regard what took place at the Leningrad symposium (including Ehrenburg's rather courageous speech) as the sign of a new "Thaw" seems to me unwarranted. Much of it was designed to keep up appearances before a Western audience, and was thus part of the "cultural coexistence" policy. The view of Joyce and Kafka, as stated by Fedin, obviously expressed the official, accepted attitude. Ehrenburg's defense of them may have been courageous, but it was accompanied by one important reservation: they belonged to the past, were a "historical phenomenon." It is therefore possible that henceforth Joyce, and especially Kafka (as a prophet of fascism), will be made accessible to Soviet readers, with appropriate warnings about their unsuitability as models. This may be a gain in itself, but a small gain, and not something that will *eo ipso* contribute to greater creative freedom of Soviet writers. It is, on the other hand, highly deplorable

---

[17] I. Anisimov, "Soviet Literature Today and Its Prospects," *Innostranaya literatura*, No. 2, February 1957, pp. 228—232.
[18] See the London *Observer*, September 8, 1963.

that some eminent representatives of Western culture who took part in the symposium thought it necessary to affix their seal of approval to the state of affairs in Soviet arts and letters and even to contribute to the incipient cult of Nikita Khrushchev. They did so in their interviews with the Soviet press. The most astonishing example (astonishing enough to make one suspect its authenticity) was the following statement by G. Ungaretti published in *Pravda* (August 16, 1963) after the delegates to the symposium had returned from Gagra where they were received by the Soviet Premier:

> This was a memorable day. We made the acquaintance of Nikita Sergeyevich Khrushchev, a simple man, a man of exceptional kind heartedness. But we saw that he could be firm and unshakeable when justice demanded this, when truth was on his side. I should like to tell you of one incident. After our warm talk my friend Giancarlo Vigorelli on behalf of all of us, expressed our thanks to the Premier of the Union of Soviet Socialist Republics, adding that, were it not for the conventions of etiquette, he would embrace Khrushchev. N. S. Khrushchev at once came up to Vigorelli and gave him a friendly hug. Standing next to Vigorelli, I said: "I feel envious and jealous." Nikita Sergeyevich Khrushchev gave me a good hug, too.

One is tempted to ask the celebrated Italian poet what was the occasion during their short stay in Gagra, which made it possible for them to realize that Khrushchev could be "firm and unshakeable" when "truth was on his side"? Or, for that matter, that he was a man of "exceptional kindheartedness"? What will Ungaretti feel like if he lives to see the day when de-Stalinization in the Soviet Union is followed by de-Khrushchevization? And does he not recall many naive Westerners who saw Stalin both as kindhearted and as firm and unshakeable when "truth" was on his side?

*

To go back where I began: Soviet literature, as it is usually understood, is, in the last analysis, largely a fiction, not to say a hypocritical humbug, a huge lie. Its "Sovietness" is composed mainly of all sorts of negative characteristics and is determined by extra-literary factors which hinder and slow down its normal, spontaneous development as literature. It was only in the 1920's that it produced a more or less significant *body* of imaginative writing (and the same is true of literary criticism). After that it was never given a chance of speaking at the top of its voice. It is significant that one of the best anthologies of Soviet poetry — published outside Russia and edited by Vladimir Markov was entitled *Priglushonnye golosa* (Muted Voices),[19] and that more recently Max Hayward had to call the selection of Soviet writings he edited jointly with Patricia Blake *Dissonant Voices in Soviet Literature*. To the Muted and Dissonant Voices should be added the Silent ones — those writings which to this day have not reached us from under the surface where they have been confined. In approaching the literature of the Soviet period we must not forget this mysterious X, the Great Unknown.

[19] I am aware that the title of this anthology was imposed on Professor Markov by his publishers, that he did not like it, and that it does not quite fit in with its contents. I think, however, that it does apply to some of the poets represented in this fine anthology and see no reason to alter the classification offered here unless one were to add to those three groups one more — that of Silenced Voices (as distinct from Silent).

MAURICE FRIEDBERG

Literary Output: 1956–1962

Even as the ancient Hebrews proudly called themselves the People of the Book, so a popularly held image of the Soviet Union is that of a nation of many books. Hardly any Russians doubt, as many Westerners accept at face value, the Soviet claim of world primacy in the production of books. No matter what one may think of the other aspects of Soviet life, the argument runs, one must admit that Soviet citizens have access to more copies of a greater variety of titles than any other people in the world, and that, furthermore, Soviet books, while admittedly less attractive in their physical appearance than books in the West, have the undeniable virtue of being reasonably priced, of being issued in a multitude of languages, and hence of being more accessible to the average Soviet reader.

Having devoted several years to the strenuous study of *Knizhnaya letopis* (Book Chronicle), the weekly Soviet index of all published material, I would be the last person to deny the impressiveness of Soviet achievements in the production of books. Next to the enormous progress in the fields of public health and industrialization (quite aside from the unnecessary human cost that was involved), gigantic strides in — though not, as Soviet spokesmen would have us believe, the complete — liquidation of illiteracy, the expansion in the physical volume of book output is probably one of the proudest Soviet achievements. What I wish to question are merely the official Soviet claims of the magnitude of progress that has been made under the Soviet regime (leaving aside the problem of whether the progress is attributable solely to the political regime in power or to other factors which would have resulted in similar advances under another political system); I would merely like to demonstrate that the Soviet reader's lot is far less happy than the official pronouncements would lead one to assume.

I would like to offer a number of observations on official Soviet figures in book publishing and to speculate on the extent to which these reflect the true availability of books in the Soviet Union. The paper itself will be confined to general observations; detailed factual data may be found in the appendices at the end.

The official Soviet figure for book publishing in 1961, a typical post-Stalin year, is 73,999 titles, an achievement the Soviet authorities like to contrast with the mere 18,060 brought out that year in the United States.

Let us consider these figures. As the official delegation of American book publishers which visited the Soviet Union in 1962 reported:

It is essential to a proper understanding of Soviet statistics on publishing to have a clear grasp of the definitions on which these statistics are based. There are four major ways in which these definitions vary from American and Western European practice. First and foremost, there is no differentiation between books, pamphlets and leaflets. All publications of five pages or more (and a few with less) are considered together as books-and-pamphlets. This contrasts with the UNESCO-recommended definition now being used in the USA which defines a pamphlet as being between five and forty-eight pages and a book as being forty-nine pages or more, not counting the covers. Secondly, in the USSR there is no clear definition of a published "title." Three entirely separate categories of publications are lumped together as "titles" in the USSR statistics: (1) entirely new books; (2) substantially revised books; (3) unchanged reprintings of old books. In the USA and most European countries only new and substantially revised books are included in the statistics of annual title production, and mere reprintings are not so included. Thirdly, all books and pamphlets are counted in the USSR, regardless by whom published, whether or not distributed through book trade, and whether or not carrying a price, including such printed publications as administrative instructions, catalogues, patents, industrial standards, descriptions of new inventions or new processes, construction plans for buildings, teaching programs for schools and other items of a similar nature for specialized audiences. In contrast, the United States book title statistics include only books intended to be sold through the book trade; they do not include local, state, or federal government publications, business and industrial publications and such items as industrial standards and patents. Fourthly, because it is a multilingual country, the USSR counts as "titles" each year translations of the same book in as many as sixty additional languages. This sort of multiplication in the counting of titles does not, of course, occur in the USA with its single national language...

...priced [Soviet] books and pamphlets now account for about two-thirds of all titles, and priced items have been increasing much more rapidly than free books and pamphlets, the number of which has remained relatively stable in the past twenty years. The 24,476 unpriced titles in 1961 are an impressive part of the title statistics...

If we take the total of priced books and pamphlets as the only figure comparable in any way with US book title statistics, we get a figure of 49,523 books and pamphlets (new editions, revised edition and mere reprintings) published in the USSR in 1961, compared with 19,060 original and revised editions of books of forty-nine pages or over in the USA book titles statistics compiled by *Publishers Weekly*. A more comparable figure for the United States might be th copyright registration of books, pamphlets and leaflets for the yea ending June 30, 1962 which amounted to 61,787. However, even thi figure does not include many thousands of state, local and federa government publications which are rarely copyrighted. In 1960 ther were over 13,000 state and local publications alone that the Librar of Congress considered important enough to list in its *Monthly Chec list of State Publications*.

The American publishers conclude, with scholarly understatemen

Thus it may be seen that no very close comparison can be made USSR and USA book title statistics — the definitions and the statistic systems are too far apart to make this possible. *It is clear, howeve that if the same definitions were used, the USSR would not be shou to publish more new and revised editions of printed publications five pages or more than the USA.*[1]

So much for the definitions themselves. Let us return to the oth aspects of Soviet book publishing statistics.

Of the 49,523 priced titles of Soviet books and pamphlets, some 25 p cent were in the languages of the non-Russian peoples of the USSR a approximately three per cent in foreign languages, i.e., books destine in the main, for export. This would leave us with roughly 39,000 titl accessible to the general Russian reader, since the other titles are, course, accessible only to speakers of each of the multitude of languag involved.

In 1913, the last peacetime year of Imperial Russia, the number titles produced (according to Soviet sources!) was 34,000. Even assumi that the prerevolutionary definition of a "title" was as all-inclusive as t Soviet (which is not very likely), there can be no doubt that the percenta of pamphlets and leaflets in the 1913 figure was significantly lov than in the USSR, for the simple reason that the tsarist authorities rar

---

[1] *Book Publishing in the USSR: Report of the Delegation of US Book Publish Visiting the USSR, August 20—September 17, 1962.* American Book Publishers Coun Inc.; American Textbook Publishers Institute, Inc., New York, N.Y., 1963, pp. 28— Italics supplied.

esorted to this type of communications with their subjects. One must remember that the percentage of purely technical books, accessible only o specialists, is much higher in the Soviet figure. Further, tsarist Russia n 1913, and the USA in 1961, were significant importers of books from broad, unlike the USSR where such traffic is by and large restricted to echnical works.

Under these conditions, one must conclude that the selection of books ccessible to the general Soviet reader is not only narrower than it is now n the United States, but is also less varied than it was in tsarist Russia. This is, among other things, a reflection of the regimentation of intellectual ife in the Soviet Union: there are very few areas of thought where harply conflicting views may appear in print simultaneously — although, o be sure, there may be serious scholarly expositions of the subject as well s popularizations. At any one time the Soviet presses produce only one istory of the sole political party, only one major encyclopedia, and only ne official textbook in any controversial field of the social sciences.

Similar caution must be exercised in appraising the number of copies. These, too, include hundreds of millions of copies of pamphlets and eaflets from four pages in length upward, and include, furthermore, all tems *printed* (or even mimeographed), rather than those actually sold or ven distributed free of charge. The official Soviet figure for 1961 is ,119,400,000. The American production in 1961, rigorously limited to ooks over 49 pages in length (exclusive of all municipal, government and ndustrial publications) and further limited to books actually *sold*, was ,113,400,000. Even with these gigantic disparities in definitions, the per apita figure was 5.55 copies in the USSR and 6.05 copies in the USA. t may be for this reason that Soviet publications prefer to cite comparative JSA-USSR figures for titles only, restricting the comparison in the umber of copies to that between the USSR and tsarist Russia: tsarist ussia's production in 1913 was 119,000,000, or some ten per cent of the oviet figure for 1961. Hence, the second Soviet claim, that of attaining ne world's largest volume of book production, is equally unfounded. ne must also bear in mind that the availability of books in the USSR is rther restricted by the fact that many books are sold out immediately fter their appearance in bookstores, and for that reason some Soviet ooks are out of print almost at the moment of their publication.

The well-publicized Soviet claim of mass publication of books in nguages of the national minorities, usually cited as proof of the Soviet olicy of fostering national cultures and counteracting assimilation, is elied by the steadily dwindling proportions of books printed in languages her than Russian. This point will be discussed below and illustrated in le appendices.

The final myth is that of the cheapness, and hence accessibility, of Soviet books. In reality, in terms of actual purchasing power, Soviet book are quite expensive. A Soviet wage-earner must work approximately on and a half times as long as his American counterpart in order to purchas a typical hard-bound novel or technical book. There are, as yet, few Sovi paperbacks, such as those which, in the USA, make it possible to purcha the same work for some fifteen per cent of its original price. Besides, th official price of the book in the West represents the *maximum* amoun of money the customer may pay for it, while in the Soviet Union th official price often represents the *minimum* amount of money the purchase must spend on the book. Books in the West may often be purchased considerable discounts through book clubs, etc., while in the USSR, Sovi newspapers inform us periodically, there is a flourishing black market books, where titles which are difficult to obtain in state bookstores a resold at exorbitant prices.

We have been comparing Soviet book publishing statistics with tho for the United States merely because Soviet sources, as a rule, resort this comparison. This does not mean that either of these countries leads t world in book production. Actually, a much higher degree of saturatio of the book market is to be found in other countries. In 1954, according a Soviet compilation of statistics (*Strany sotsializma i kapitalizma tsifrakh, statisticheskie materialy dlya propagandistov*) (Countries of Socia ism and Capitalism in Figures, Statistical Materials for Propagandis Moscow, 1957, pp. 111–12), in the number of titles printed, the wor record was held by the USSR: 54,732. As has already been pointed ou these Soviet claims must be considered highly inflated. More interesti is the fact that, even in terms of absolute figures, the United Stat (11,901 titles) was surpassed by Japan (19,837). Great Britain (19,18 and West Germany (16,240) and was closely followed by France (10,66 and Italy (8,514). Considering population differentials, it may well that, in the per capita production of titles, both Russia and the Unit States are trailing behind England, West Germany, France, Italy and Japa

Belles lettres constitute approximately eleven per cent of the numb of titles and one third of the number of copies of the entire Soviet bo output (Boris I. Gorokhoff, *Publishing in the USSR*, Bloomington, India University Press, 1959, p. 201, cites these figures for 1957, and *Bo Publishing in the USSR*, p. 54, for 1961). In 1961, literature (includi literary periodicals and children's books, but excluding textbooks) w published in 318,000,000 copies. Of this, 649 titles and 35,000,000 copi were prerevolutionary authors (Russian and minority), and 55,000,0 were translations of foreign literature (no data on the number of title A comparison with corresponding figures for one of the last Stalin yea 1950, and one of the first post-Stalin ones, 1955, reveals a steady a rapid growth in the publication of Russia's own authors (162,000,000 copies in 1950; 215,000,000 in 1955; and 293,000,000 in 1961). The fate of foreign authors has been more complex. Discriminated against during the anti-cosmopolitan witch-hunts of Stalin's declining years (only 17,000,000 copies in 1950), they quickly regained ground after the dictator's death (1955 registered the spectacular growth to 71,500,000 copies). However, by 1961 the printing of foreign writers fell again to 55,000,000 copies, perhaps a reaction against the excessive liberalism of the "thaw."

Limitations of space preclude any detailed discussion of all the many different types of imaginative literature. We shall, therefore, limit our task to a rather thorough examination of the publication of prerevolutionary Russian literature in all the languages of the USSR, hoping that this will shed some light on Soviet publishing of *belles lettre* in general. Only a few remarks will be made about the printing of writers from outside the Soviet bloc and about the publication of Soviet literature proper, as, for the time being, our findings in this area remain fragmentary and inconclusive. As for the minority literatures — Uzbek, Armenian, Tatar, etc. — interesting as the subject may be, the present writer's ignorance of them has made it advisable to avoid the problem altogether.

In surveying the publication data for contemporary Soviet literature, one is impressed first of all by the great variety of new names. Whereas in the last years of Stalin's life there were comparatively few newcomers to the writing profession, since 1954 their number has been growing by leaps and bounds. This is equally true of Russian prerevolutionary writers and of those writing in the minority languages. The typical printing of Russian language editions of new writers has been ten to fifteen thousand copies, while established authors averaged 75,000 copies per issue. In my book *Russian Classics in Soviet Jackets* (New York and London, Columbia University Press, 1962) I suggested that the enormous popularity of the prerevolutionary Russian classics during the later period of Stalin's life may have been caused to a significant extent by the unsatisfactory quality of contemporary Soviet writing, and that, in Yevgeny Zamyatin's words, as long as these conditions persist, "I am afraid that Russian literature has but one future — her past." Recent developments have vindicated Zamyatin's observations. As the "thaw" progressed and as Soviet literature became, even if not more appealing esthetically, then at least more interesting thematically, the balance between prerevolutionary Russian and Soviet literature began to shift in favor of the latter. In 1954, — i.e., a year which, though chronologically a post-Stalin one, could still be said to reflect the earlier moods, since generally there is at least a year's lag in publishing — the output (in copies) of literature of the peoples of Russia consisted of approximately 30 per cent of prerevolutionary works and 70 per cent of Soviet literature. By 1956, while both categories registered a significant increase in absolute terms, the ratio shifted to 25 per cent of prerevolutionary and 75 per cent Soviet. In 1961, the output of prerevolutionary writing fell drastically to 10 per cent, while that of Soviet literature increased to 90 per cent. Russia's prerevolutionary literary heritage thus ceased to be a means of escape from the artistic mediocrity and thematic drabness of Soviet literature, and the classics now appear to be read for their own merits and not merely because readers find Soviet literature unpalatable.

We have, of course, attempted to establish the publishing fortunes of the "liberals" as contrasted with those of the "conservatives." While our overall conclusions are still very much tentative, there is strong evidence that neither camp is particularly favored at the expense of the other if one considers nation-wide publication figures alone. However, the Ehrenburgs, the Nekrasovs, the Voznesenskys, are more widely printed in Russian, while the Kochetovs, the Sofronovs and the Surkovs tend to dominate the translations into the minority languages. It is also noteworthy that the "liberals" are better represented in translations into foreign languages, presumably in the belief that their less doctrinaire and more humanistic outlook would find greater response in the non-Soviet world, where these editions are sold, than would the more dogmatic "Stalinist" kind of writing. It is characteristic that it is the non-conformist "liberal" Yevtushenko who has been, for some years, Russia's unofficial cultural ambassador to Cuba. In the Russian-language editions the "liberal" writers were more widely printed in Moscow and Leningrad, while the "conservatives" dominated the output of the provincial publishing houses. But signs of the "thaw" may be noticed even in the outlying areas. Thus, Fyodor Sologub's *Petty Demon*, long on the Soviet index of forbidden books, was printed in Kemerovo, while the *Pages of Tarusa* edited by Konstantin Paustovsky, will, no doubt, be remembered as one of the high points of the literary "thaw."

The May-June 1963 issue of *Problems of Communism* featured an interesting article by Hugh McLean dealing with the problem of literary "rehabilitations." It should be noted that in the realm of publishing — as distinct from the mere restorations of literary reputations — these rehabilitations have, on the whole, been effected very timidly, except in the case of a few prerevolutionary Russian writers whose fortunes will be discussed below. There has been but one small book of Marina Tsvetayeva's verse in a mere 25,000 copies; one slender volume of Anna Akhmatova's, in 50,000; one of Pasternak's, in 30,000; Yuri Olesha has fared best, with 150,000 copies. It is difficult to appraise the significance of the reappearance of four editions of Mikhail Zoshchenko, since they all consist of bowdlerized texts of his tales, mutilated by Stalin's censorship and not restored under Khrushchev. The promised multivolume set of Isaac Babel has never materialized, while a number of writers have never been rehabilitated at all. Of the Soviet authors once in disfavor, only Sergei Yesenin may be said to have been fully restored to grace; numerous editions of his works have appeared, including multivolume sets. But then, the process of his reinstatement in Soviet literature was begun already under Stalin. Needless to say, no *living* emigre Russian writer has been "rehabilitated," although a number of dead ones are slowly being assimilated into the organism of Soviet culture; thus, for example, a Soviet journal recently featured a number of poems by Vladislav Khodasevich.

With regard to the publication of foreign literature, we shall, for the time being, confine ourselves to reporting the following preliminary findings.

While the availability of foreign literature has greatly improved since Stalin's day, it is still very unsatisfactory both from the qualitative and the quantitative points of view. The first and most important shortcoming is, of course, the fact that Soviet citizens, with insignificant exceptions, have no direct access to the *original* editions of foreign *belles lettres* and literary periodicals, and are thus restricted to the reading of those books which the Soviet authorities see fit to publish. In all of the USSR there is only a single bookstore in Moscow which sells French classics and works by modern French left-wing writers, all of them printed by a single publisher, Hachette, with whom the Soviet authorities have concluded a bilateral agreement (books from the people's democracies may be purchased comparatively freely, and these, particularly the Polish, are the average Soviet citizen's best "window to the West"). The single most important source of modern non-Soviet literature is the periodical *Inostrannaya Literatura* (Foreign Literature) which prints many translations of foreign fiction, poetry and drama, including such that will never be published in book form. The deep-seated suspicion of the Soviet authorities of all but purely technical books published in the West is perhaps best illustrated by the existence of special Soviet editions of foreign literature — English, American, German, French, Spanish, Latin American — *in the original languages*. These editions, obviously intended for very advanced language students, are not "readers" or "adaptations," but the original unabridged texts; they do not even have any vocabularies appended to them. Why, one may ask, have not the Soviet authorities simply imported the necessary books from abroad? Even considering the fact, that, not being signatories to international copyright agreements, Soviet authorities are not forced to pay royalties to Western authors whose works they reprint without their permission and often even without their knowledge, the cost of printing new editions would more than offset this gain. It appears that the reasons for the decision to print books in their original languages in the USSR are to be sought elsewhere.

In the first place, if original foreign editions of anthologies in foreign languages were to be imported, the selection of materials in each book would inevitably reflect the "bourgeois" tastes of Western publishers, and the books might thus include some politically undesirable writings or, conversely, not include the creations of Communist authors whose literary standing in their native lands would not entitle them to the distinction of being included in such collections. Second, the importation of original French or American or German editions would deprive the Soviet publishers of the opportunity of appending to each edition a Russian-language, politically-oriented foreword and footnotes — a "commercial," so to speak, a few well-chosen words from the sponsor whose kindness made the very appearance of the book possible.

The second shortcoming, a chronic one in the history of Soviet publishing of Western writing, is the insufficient number of copies, which never seems to satisfy the public demand for them. A poignant description of this is found in a recent story by Vera Panova, in which a group of youngsters is shown bitterly fighting over a single volume of Alexandre Dumas, and in the end the boys tear up the book into sections in order to enable them to read it at once.

For reasons mentioned above — namely, the usual nonpayment of royalties to living foreign authors or to their estates, and the extreme cheapness of reprinting the established classics from ready-made translations or even old galleys — foreign books are excellent moneymakers, and there is good reason to believe that, if given the authority to do so, Soviet publishers, who are not at all insensitive to the profit motivation, would print far more of them. Obviously, the printings of foreign literature, while most impressive in absolute figures, are limited because of other than monetary considerations. The explanation usually offered by Soviet officials is the chronic shortage of paper. This, however, is not altogether convincing. As the trade publication *Sovetskaya knizhnaya torgovlya* (Soviet Book Trade) reports, for the last several years retired persons and young people have been urged to become full-time or part-time *knigonoshi* — book peddlers — to help in the dissemination of merchandise which, obviously, cannot be easily disposed of by the bookstores alone. Furthermore, though this was officially denied by Soviet spokesmen, the 1962 delegation of American publishers came out with the distinct impression that a good many Soviet books cannot be either sold or even distributed free of charge, and must therefore be pulped.

The most important negative feature of Soviet editions of foreign literature in translation is the extremely strong ideological bias in the

election of authors and titles for publication and, once this problem is
settled, in the assigning of different sizes of printings. The word "ideolog-
cal" must be understood in the broader sense — it includes not only the
political orientation of the individual writer, or his book, but artistic
deology as well, namely the degree to which the book is in accord with
he prevailing artistic tastes of the Soviet literary authorities. However,
ince in the West the two do not always go hand in hand, and some
artists whose politics are admittedly "progressive" nevertheless espouse
"reactionary" artistic credos — the painter Picasso offers a fine example of
his unhappy situation — Soviet publishers must decide in each individual
case which of the two factors outweighs the other. As a result, some
"progressive" writers are denied publication because of the "decadent"
character of their art, and conversely, some traditional realists and natur-
lists are printed in spite of their political "backwardness." Of course,
an ideal choice is, if possible, an ideologically "progressive" writer whose
style is unexperimental and not overly "modernistic" by the standards
of readers brought up on nineteenth-century Realism and Romanticism,
and the latter-day Socialist Realism, or, as Abram Tertz would have it,
Soviet Romanticism or Neo-Classicism.

Again, the label "progressive" must not be understood to mean that
the writer in question is or was a Communist, a fellow-traveller or even
a partisan of moderate social reforms. Indeed, in surveying the critical
commentaries and introductions which are often appended to Soviet editions
of foreign *belles lettres*, one cannot escape the conclusion that, insofar as
authors no longer living are concerned, it may be said that, in the Soviet
view, all of the universally acknowledged great writers have, given the
conditions of their time and their consequently limited understanding of
social problems, been essentially "progressive." Thus the "progressives"
include Sophocles and Goethe, Shakespeare and Molière, Aristophanes and
Cervantes, Homer and Dante. One is almost tempted to establish a series
of literary "laws" used in the USSR to appraise foreign writers. The
degree of a foreign writer's "progressiveness" increases in direct proportion
to his international reputation and is inversely proportional to the date of
his death. Thus, no classical Greek poet would ever be dismissed as
"reactionary," but many a modern Greek might be; and, other factors being
equal, a deceased Nobel Prize winner would stand a far better chance
of being treated as a "progressive" figure than would a lesser-known
author.

The criteria used in evaluating foreign literature differ significantly
from those used in appraising the Soviet Union's own literature, and this
double standard may be a source of potential danger to the Soviet literary
pundits. It cannot but be somewhat confusing to the average Soviet

reader to see foreign writers hailed by the Soviet literary bureaucrats for their noble defense of the underdog and denunciation of all rulers, while reading at the same time that the rebellious young Soviet writers of the "thaw" were wrong in adopting, in essence, the same attitude. Also, one may be reasonably certain, many a non-Russian Soviet reader may wonder why the Soviet prefaces to works by contemporary Afro-Asian writers – which are now, incidentally, printed in millions of copies — hail these authors for their national and even race consciousness, mere traces of which would suffice to brand a Turkmen or a Ukrainian writer a "fascist" or, at the very best, a "bourgeois nationalist."

Since, to most Russians, foreign literature in translation is the most important source of information on life abroad, it must be pointed out that the picture of living conditions in the West emerging from these works is highly distorted. Soviet commentators, as a rule, fail to inform their readers that the lot of the British child has improved since the days of Dickens, that few American migratory workers in 1963 live under the conditions described in *Grapes of Wrath*, that life in the French country-side is less drab than it was in the era of *Madame Bovary*. On the contrary, since these works are supplemented by the writings of left-wingers, "angry young men," etc., the impression received from the reading of what foreign literature is available is that life abroad is characterized not only by material poverty and social injustice, but by spiritual emptiness and aimlessness as well.

Soviet citizens also receive a distorted image of foreign literature as such, because of — ideological considerations aside — the traditional gap between many writers' reputations at home and abroad. Thus, one would find it difficult to discover an educated Russian who does not know anything about Byron, but few Russians are familiar with Shelley and Keats. There are many Russians who have read Molière or seen performances of his plays, but who have never heard of Racine and Corneille. Judging by my own students in New York, I would venture the guess that at least ten times more Russians than Americans know Jack London. And, naturally practically every Russian knows Mayne Reid and, furthermore, considers him a great *American* writer. Of course, this process works in both directions. An acquaintance of mine, who visited Russia soon after Stalin's death, told me about a Soviet student who was surprised by the foreigner's strange interest in a minor Russian novelist named Dostoyevsky who, after all, wrote only such undistinguished lachrymose works as *Poor Folk* and *The Insulted and the Injured*. The Russian then tried to introduce the misguided American to some truly great Russian classics, such as Uspensky and Mamin-Sibiryak — a somewhat ludicrous result of Stalinist publishing politics.

Sifting through the mountains of statistical material relating to the Soviet publication of foreign writers since Stalin's death, one is struck by three phenomena. First, by the extraordinarily high printings of the giants of world literature up to the nineteenth century and of writers of social protest of all periods (though with some notable exceptions, and with the reservations made above with regard to Soviet publication figures). Second, by the total absence of a number of "modern" writers who are now in the West already considered classics — Kafka, T. S. Eliot, Proust, Joyce, and even Baudelaire, in spite of his venerable age. Third, by the huge printings of works by writers whose names cannot be found even in detailed Western reference works. Therefore, the assistance of seven specialists was enlisted. Each of them was a bona fide university professor of one of the following seven literatures: English, French, Italian, Middle Eastern, Scandinavian and Spanish. All seven of them failed to identify approximately one third of the foreign writers in their respective fields. These writers were obviously either Communists whose creations have no literary merit (unlike, for example, Louis Aragon) or else obscure third-rate realist or juvenile authors unknown in their native lands. To cite but one extreme case: the *number one* Italian bestseller in Russia, Gianni Rodari (close to 4,000,000 copies published between 1956 and 1962 in sixteen languages), is not even mentioned in the recent edition of the three-volume *Dizionario letterario Bompiani* which includes entries on six thousand Italian authors.[2]

Most of the translations of foreign literature appear in Russian, and editions in the minority languages are often translations from the Russian rather than directly from the original language, which probably reflects the technical difficulty of finding, say, a qualified translator from the Spanish into Tadzhik. It is interesting to note that some cognizance is taken of national affinities. Thus, publishers in the three Baltic republics — Latvia, Estonia and Lithuania — favor Scandinavian literature, little of which is published elsewhere, while the Central Asian republics print disproportionately large amounts of Arabic, Persian and Afro-Asian works, and little of anything else. In general, little foreign literature is printed in the minority languages, except the Baltic, Ukrainian, Armenian and Georgian. From the point of view of literary sophistication and ideological broadmindedness, translations of foreign literature may also be grouped by languages. Most "liberal" in this respect are Latvian and Estonian pub-

---

[2] The mystery of Gianni Rodari's idendity was unexpectedly solved in December of 1963, when the Moscow *Literaturnaya gazeta* reported on Rodari's visit to the Soviet Union. Rodari, it turns out, is a contributor of children's tales and verse to *Unita*, the principal newspaper of the Italian Communist Party. He is practically unknown in his country, but is by far the most widely read Italian author in the USSR.

lications, which often include works which one would not expect — for political or artistic reasons — to be printed in the USSR; Russian and Lithuanian publications are more conformist; the Ukrainian reflect even more caution in the selection of authors and titles; most conventional are Azerbaidzhani and Armenian publications, while those of Belorussia, of all the Central Asian Republics and of the smaller national groups offer an assortment that is hardly different from that of the darkest years of the Stalin era.

Curious are the several publications which acknowledge the existence abroad of emigres of various Soviet ethnic groups. Needless to say, the lot of the emigres is shown to be a cheerless one, and their compatriots in the Soviet Union are duly informed about it, in order that they may appreciate their own good furtune. Thus, the Armenians received 50,000 copies of translations of William Saroyan, and 5,000 of a book by a "progressive" Armenian American writer named Benjamin Nurikian entitled *Under Alien Skies*. The title must have pleased the Soviet editors, for it was used again, this time for a 3,000-copy printing of Lithuanian-American poetry, printed in Lithuanian. There was also a 7,000-copy Ukrainian-language book entitled *Canadian Poets: Verse by Ukrainian Worker- and Peasant-Poets*.

Between 1956 and 1962 Soviet publishing houses brought out 231,209,000 copies of works by 94 prerevolutionary Russian authors, exclusive of anthologies and textbooks. Of this number, 200,000,000 copies, or some 87 per cent, were printed in Russian, and the remainder in approximately fifty languages of the peoples of the USSR, as well as in several Western European languages. The Russian language editions are not only the most important ones in absolute figures, but in relative ones as well. For the 114,500,000 ethnic Russians, the 200,000,000 copies of the Russian classics constitute a very important — under Stalin, in fact, *the* most important — item in their reading fare, amounting to almost two copies per capita for the period under review, by far, as we shall see below, the highest figure for any language. As one would expect, most of the scholarly and multivolume editions are also printed in Russian. A list of 69 multivolume sets by 29 prerevolutionary Russian authors was in the process of being published in 1956–62. Among those completed during that period, was the most impressive Soviet publishing venture to date, the ninety-volume definitive edition of Tolstoy's complete works which was begun in the 1920's on the eve of the 1928 centennial of the novelist's birth; the ten-volume edition of Dostoyevsky, at 300,000 copies per volume, the second important Soviet issue of works of that writer, the first one having appeared in the 1920's; and the first Soviet multivolume set of Leskov, which consisted of eleven volumes at 300,000 to 350,000 copies each. The most important new venture inaugurated during that period was the twenty-eight volume set of Turgenev, the first Soviet edition of such scope.

By contrast, there have been only twenty-one multivolume editions in twelve languages of the other peoples of the USSR. It may, of course, be argued that to the Russians the editions of Russian classics are publications of *native* literature, and that consequently there should be far more of them. However, the few scholarly editions of the non-Russian peoples' *own* writers do little to compensate for the disparity. Furthermore, in translations from foreign languages, the gap between the quantities of books and types of editions made available to the Russians and those offered to the other ethnic groups was, if anything, even wider.

The years 1956–62 were marked by the restoration to the Olympus of Russian letters of the last "sinners" who had hitherto been confined to the literary Hades. At the present time, one may safely assert, there are almost no writers or works of prerevolutionary Russian *belles lettres* (exclusive of essayists etc.), of any consequence that are, so to speak, "illegal," i.e., unpublished with the sanction of the Soviet authorities. This does not mean that all of those writers and works are equally accessible to the Soviet reader. Many of those who had never been printed before have now appeared only in nominal quantities; but appear they did. Among these was Apollon Grigoryev, obviously destined to remain forever the *neudachnik* — "failure" — both in the fate of his poetry as well as that of his criticism; the recent Soviet printing of his works was restricted to 20,000 copies. The Slavophile Ivan Aksakov was discovered to have written some verse worth reprinting in 10,000 copies; A. N. Apukhtin, an unsuccessful poet, reappeared in two anthologies, a total of 60,000 copies; Archpriest Avvakum was allotted a separate book, all to himself, and thus 30,000 copies of the first Russian autobiography came to be printed; P. D. Boborykin's *Kataigorod* was reproduced in the more than respectable total of 225,000 copies; A. I. Ertel, copyright in whose works was vested in the "people" in 1918, only never to be taken advantage of, was finally printed, as if to atone for past neglect, three times, a total of 300,000 copies; S. I. Gusev-Orenburgsky's portraits of village priests were resurrected from oblivion — true, only in Ukrainian and only in 65,000 copies, but still an event worth noting, considering Gusev's themes and the aggravating circumstance of his unsavory past as an emigre in the United States where he had even edited some obscure periodicals. There were separate editions of eighteenth-century classics in the sense in which Mark Twain used the term — books which everybody wants to have read and nobody does — including those of Kapnist (29,000 copies), Kantemir (15,000) and Karamzin (200,000 copies in Russian supplemented by 20,000 copies of *Poor Liza* — in Azerbaidzhani!).

The once notorious scourge of the capitalist bourgeoisie, the Futurist Vladimir Khlebnikov, who was for a long time condemned to the status of an "un-poet" by the ruling Soviet philistines, has been reprinted in 50,000 copies; but the Soviet bourgeoisie played a grim joke on Khlebnikov: the edition contained none of his Futurist poetry. Thus, for example, the volume did not include even his "Laughter."

Then there were also 8,000 copies of the poetry of I. I. Kozlov; the impressive total of 658,000 copies of the adventure and historical novels of I. I. Lazhechnikov; 120,000 of G. A. Machtet, another writer "nationalized" in 1918 and then never published; the once tremendously popular Semyon Nadson, who happily combined the three virtues greatly cherished by the nineteenth-century Russian *obyvatel* (philistine) in his poems — namely, civic consciousness, sweet lyricism and tuberculosis — has now reapperared in 80,000 copies; I. I. Panayev, a co-editor of Nekrasov's *Sovremennik*, was brought out in 50,000 copies; A. N. Pleshcheyev, a poet who was a member of the Petrashevsky circle, the radical society made immortal by Dostoyevsky, was printed in as many as 530,000 copies; Ya. P. Polonsky, a nineteenth-century Parnassian poet who also wrote some civic verse, was published in 50,000; F. M. Reshetnikov, the chronicler of the miserable life of Perm's peasants, 575,000; S. G. Skitalets (Petrov), the early twentieth century realist influenced by Gorky, 155,000; S. M. Stepnyak-Kravchinsky, the late nineteenth-century emigre writer, Populist, and revolutionary terrorist, a writer of thrillers about the Russian revolutionary underground, in 430,000; S. N. Terpigorev-Atava, a writer who depicted the decay of the landowning class, 75,000; N. M. Yazykov, a poet and a contemporary of Pushkin, 15,000; M. N. Zagoskin, the authorship of whose patriotic novel *Yuri Miloslavsky* Khlestakov attempted to claim in Gogol's *Inspector General*, appeared in 600,000 copies; V. Zasodimsky, the Populist writer remembered for his idealized descriptions of the peasantry, 405,000; and A. M. Zhemchuzhnikov, the liberal poet and co-creator with his two brothers and his cousin A. K. Tolstoy of the celebrated nonsense verse of "Kozma Prutkov," 30,000 copies.

By far the most important "discovery" of 1956—62 was K. M. Stanyukovich. No great writer, and hardly published at all before World War II (though quite well-known before the Revolution) he was now brought out within the short span of six years in 3,512,000 copies, including a six-volume set of his collected writings. An "apolitical" author of adventure stories, tales of naval life, etc., he was presumably destined to at least partly satisfy the thirst for this type of reading matter, of which there is very little in Russian literature, and which has, in the USSR, traditionally been satisfied by the publication of translations of such authors as Jack London, Robert Louis Stevenson, and Jules Verne.

Among the major literary "rehabilitations" of the period was Ivan Bunin, Russia's only, before Pasternak, winner of the Nobel Prize for literature. Though he died abroad, an opponent of the Soviet regime, he is now often represented in prefaces to his works as a man who was about to return to the USSR and was only prevented by his death from doing so. Between 1956 and 1962, his works were printed in Russian and six other languages in a total of 2,116,000 copies, including a five-volume set at 250,000 copies per volume.

The greatest of the Symbolist poets, Alexander Blok, though never officially disowned, enjoyed a revival in the period under review. His works were printed in 1,788,000 copies, including two multivolume editions, an eight-volume set and a two-volume one. On the other hand, in spite of his much-heralded rehabilitation, Dostoyevsky, though printed in the more than impressive total of 6,985,000 copies, was not truly "rehabilitated." Aside from the multivolume editions of his works (ten volumes at 300,000 copies each), the "real" Dostoyevsky is still little published in other than the Baltic languages, or else for export. What is made available is the "innocuous" Dostoyevsky, mostly his early writings. It should also be noted that there was no Dostoyevsky *at all* in some of the important languages of the national minorities, including Belorussian, Armenian, Moldavian, Uzbek, Tadzhik, not to speak of the lesser tongues, and that the publication of Dostoyevsky in Ukrainian was restricted to 35,000 copies. Dostoyevsky's "rehabilitation," one must conclude, was a very half-hearted one. Even in Russian, aside from the multivolume set, there was only one separate issue of *Brothers Karamazov*, and none of *The Possessed*, of *The Notes from the Underground* and so forth. It is not impossible that the Balts are given access to Dostoyevsky's "dangerous" works on the assumption that they are likely to have known them anyway, having been annexed by the USSR only in 1940, and that the printing of Dostoyevsky would do more good than harm since it would make the Soviet publishing authorities appear liberal and broadminded.

A. Pisemsky, another "reactionary" writer, had some of his work printed in 3,685,000 copies, though only in Russian and English — there were no editions whatsoever in the minority languages. Unlike in the case of Dostoyevsky, his truly "reactionary" writings were not reprinted at all.

A comparison of the fifteen most widely printed prerevolutionary authors listed in order of the magnitude of printings of their works in 1918—41 and 1956—62 is quite enlightening on the changing position of the State vis-à-vis the Russian classics. The fact that the 1918—41 list includes only Russian-language editions, while that of 1956—62 includes editions in all languages, does not materially affect the picture.

1918—1941	1956—1962
Tolstoy	Tolstoy
Chekhov	Pushkin
Pushkin	Chekhov
Krylov	Lermontov
Turgenev	Turgenev
Gogol	Mamin-Sibiryak
Korolenko	Nekrasov
Saltykov-Shchedrin	Kuprin
Nekrasov	Dostoyevsky
Mamin-Sibiryak	Gogol
Lermontov	Leskov
Uspensky	Goncharov
Goncharov	Krylov
Ostrovsky	Korolenko
Dostoyevsky	Ostrovsky

The two tables reveal that Uspensky and Saltykov-Shchedrin, the two violent accusers of the *ancien regime*, and consequently traditional favorites of the orthodox Party critics, are no longer to be found on the later list. Instead of these two (Uspensky, incidentally, has slipped all the way down to the thirty-second place), we now have two writers of lesser political significance, but far greater interest as literature, namely Leskov and Kuprin. The vogue for Leskov, the unsurpassed master of the Russian narrative style, began in the late 1940's when his Russian nationalism was no longer thought objectionable, as it had been in the earlier years of the Soviet regime. Kuprin, on the other hand, is a comparative new-comer, his emigre period (he spent a considerable time abroad, returning to the USSR as a prodigal son only shortly before his death) now having been forgiven and forgotten.

Dostoyevsky has moved from the fifteenth place to the ninth, though most of the increase in the printings of his works still consists of his early writings which had once endeared him to the nineteenth century radical critics. The upgrading of Lermontov and the downgrading of Krylov probably reflect the greater literary sophistication of the Soviet reading public, although, to be sure, both authors may be read on different "levels."

An examination of the publication of the Russian classics in the minority languages reveals, in the first place, that in certain areas of the USSR non-Russian readers may find most of the treasures of Russian literature in their native tongues, and are thus not forced to abandon their own heritage — as Heinrich Heine once complained of being forced to do — in order to gain entrance into a higher culture. In other localities national minorities are deprived of this opportunity and a command of one's native tongue is quite useless as a tool for acquainting oneself with world literature. While a detailed discussion of this problem is outside the scope of the present paper, it is worth noting that the availability of translations is approximately the same in every individual case, regardless of the original language of translation; that is, that a minority language which boasts numerous translations of the Russian classics is, as a rule, similarly well supplied with translations from the Western European languages, and, conversely, a minority language in which translations of the Russian classics are inadequate qualitatively, quantitatively, or both, is similarly deficient in translations from foreign languages. The problem of translations of the Russian classics into the minority languages will be discussed in detail in the Appendices. Suffice it to say here that, on the whole, both the number of titles and copies of books printed in the minority languages are constantly declining in relationship to the Russian-language books. The national groups best supplied with translations of the Russian classics (and, consequently, also with translations of foreign literatures) are the three Baltic peoples (Latvians, Lithuanians and Estonians), Armenians, Georgians, Azerbaidzhanis, Kazakhs and Kirgiz. The most blatant case of discrimination against a particular ethnic group is, of course, that of the Soviet Jews: although in the 1960 census almost half a million of them declared Yiddish to be their native tongue, *not a single* translation from any language into Yiddish appeared between 1956 and 1962, the most clearcut case of cultural discrimination encountered. The other striking example is that of the Belorussians, with over six and a half million native speakers in whose language almost no serious translations — from Russian or from other languages — have appeared. Little was published in all of the minor Uralo-Altaic, Caucasian and Ugro-Finnic languages, with the significant exception of those minorities which inhabit the Soviet Union's border areas. This suggests the possibility that the Soviet authorities are interested in strengthening the national consciousness of peoples living close to "non-Socialist" countries, *as well as of those bordering on China,* while a conscious effort is made to assimilate minorities living, so to speak, in "Soviet encirclement." In fact, with reference to China, it is worth noting that for some years now the Soviet publishing authorities have been conducting a subtle campaign of subversion among China's own national minorities. As is known, the Uigurs and, to a lesser extent, the Kazakhs, live on both sides of the Sino-Soviet frontier. Those living in the USSR have had their alphabets changed from the Arabic to Latin, and finally from Latin to a modified form of Cyrillic, while those living in China's Sinkiang province have retained the original Arabic script. Between 1956 and 1962 Soviet publishing houses printed scores of books in Uigur, and also a number in Kazakh, in Arabic script (there were also, as

usual, those printed in the Cyrillic). There can be no doubt that the
Arabic-alphabet editions were destined for the Uigurs and Kazakhs living
in the Chinese People's Republic, to whom they were distributed free of
charge (no prices were indicated on these editions, and, usually, there was
also no indication of the sizes of printings). The aim of the step was quite
obvious: it was to make the Chinese Kazakhs and Uigurs regard the USSR,
rather than China, as their spiritual homeland. These findings seem to
support Communist China's denunciations of the Soviet Union's "imperial-
ist" acts first made public in 1963.

The fact that little is published in languages of minorities which border
only on friendly "Socialist" states is illustrated by the comparatively little
translating done in the Ukrainian language, a tongue spoken by thirty-
two million native speakers, who constitute the largest linguistic group in
the USSR, other than the Russians themselves. It should also be noted
that as a rule, the translations of the Russian classics into the minority
languages consist, by and large, of thin pamphlets comprising a single story
or a poem or two. Little "sophisticated" literature appears in the languages
of the minorities, and thus the statistics alone create a more optimistic
picture than is warranted by the facts. An interesting practice, quite
often resorted to, is the publication *in Russian* of large quantities of simple
works of prerevolutionary Russian writers, especially edited and annotated
for readers of various national backgrounds, all obviously destined to
facilitate the learning of Russian.

Should Khrushchev's avowed policy of peaceful coexistence with the
capitalist world in all spheres except for the ideological be continued, the
spoken and the printed word, and particularly books, may now become the
chief weapons in the cold war, and the quantities and qualities of books
made available to the peoples of the USSR may become subjects of far
greater importance than it has hitherto been customary to believe. A
major step in this direction may be discerned in the establishment, in
August of 1963, of a new state commission to supervise the output of the
Soviet Unions' publishing houses. According to the *New York Times* of
August 19, 1963, "Pavel G. Romanov, who had been responsible for control
of foreign correspondents' dispatches before censorship was abolished two
and a half years ago, was named to head the organization with the rank
of a Cabinet Minister. The organization will decide what literary works will
be published and what circulation they will get."

I do not think that, centuries ago, Caliph Omar was trying to display
his wit when he, a believer in the One Book, suggested that all the other
books be destroyed as either harmful or superfluous. The Moslem ruler
sensed the real danger inherent in providing the population with ex-

pressions of different viewpoints or even moods and attitudes, and tried to avert it as best as he could. This, I am convinced, was also in the minds of our own contemporaries, the Nazis, when they built bonfires of selected books, and of Stalin's efficient purgers of Soviet libraries.

It is fortunate, in my view, that with age, despotic regimes can no longer resist the allurement of assuming the pose of tolerant protectors of the arts. They thus sow, as it were, the seeds of their own impotence. In exchange for a few obsequious odes by court poets, they allow themselves to be deceived into tolerating and even promoting attitudes and ideas which, in the long run, cannot but weaken their ideological grip over their subjects. It is perhaps — to use a Soviet cliché — no "mere coincidence" that the last Roman and Byzantine rulers were philosophers, and that the last French monarchs prided themselves on being "enlightened." The subversive role of the artist in an authoritarian society was foreseen long ago by Plato in *The Republic*. The artist, the poet, need not appeal to open rebellion. They help to erode the pillars on which the old regime rests by teaching their audiences to trust not only their reason, but their feelings as well; by instructing them in the art of irreverence, by preaching that healthy measure of selfishness known as individual dignity, by demonstrating the superiority of relativity to dogma and rigidity, by re-discovering for their countrymen the dual universes of passion and detachment. The poet teaches his countrymen to think in allegorical categories and he sharpens their sensitivity and imagination. These are all seemingly innocuous lessons and are, furthermore, learned but slowly; but they have the compensating virtue of not being easily forgotten.

A century ago, the critic Belinsky remarked that, to a Russian, the arts are primarily literature, and the didactic and inspirational role of Russian art is by now common knowledge. Literary monuments of the past have enjoyed the protection of the Soviet regime since its inception, and particularly — not without some logic — since the beginning of what is now called the "cult of personality." The very reverence displayed by the Soviet authorities with regard to Russia's cultural heritage might in itself have been politically subversive. Was there not some inconsistency in condemning Nicholas I for having hounded poets to death in the 1830's, while doing exactly the same in the 1930's? Was there not something ironical in employing hundreds of literary scholars in order to restore and salvage the true texts of nineteenth-century literary works distorted by the Tsar's censorship, while at the same time paying the salaries of hundreds of *Glavlit* censors whose function was to mutilate works of twentieth-century authors? Is there not some discrepancy between praising free-thinking and opposition to established authority in dead novelists, while at the same time demanding absolute subservience of living artists?

It is a far cry since the early years of the Soviet regime when non-Soviet books — both Russian and foreign — were carefully selected for their ideological content and published in inconspicuous pamphlets on poor paper, and also supplied with long, militantly political commentaries. Such booklets have all but disappeared. They have been replaced by ornate, gilded, multivolume sets of the great classics of Russian and Western letters. Inevitably, these sets also include millions of printed pages of text which could not possibly — if merely freshly typed out on ordinary paper and submitted to a Soviet editor — appear in any Soviet periodical, so much at variance with the letter and spirit of the Soviet idea are the thoughts expressed in them. And yet the very same pages appear in the USSR and are openly sold — and even promoted and advertised — by Soviet bookstores. To be sure, many of the sets of Shakespeare and Pushkin, of Dickens and Tolstoy, of Mark Twain and Dostoyevsky, merely adorn the living rooms of the highly *kultura*-conscious Soviet bourgeoisie. Yet, inevitably, many of these books are read, often by the bourgeoisie's own rebellious offspring.

As long as these books exist — and there is every idication that their number will increase in the years to come — the Communist campaign of spiritual remolding of the New Soviet Man — joyful, robust, efficient, obedient, and uncomplicated — is, in my view, doomed to failure. A devotee of Fet and Lermontov is unlikely to heed Khrushchev's recent appeals to immerse himself in the ryhmes of Demyan Bedny; the serious reader of Balzac and Hugo is not very likely to display much enthusiasm for Nikolai Ostrovsky; the study of Shakespeare and Tolstoy is somewhat less than certain to mold one into an admirer of Kochetov and Furmanov.

There is much evidence to indicate that the often denounced rebelliousness of Yevtushenko, the objectivity of Viktor Nekrasov, the compassion of Yashin, and other similar "un-Soviet" writing have all their roots in non-Soviet literature, both Russian and foreign. This is the price an authoritarian regime must pay for the desire to appear "enlightened." Deceived by its own propaganda, it becomes oblivious of the prime characteristic of great literature — its universality, its applicability to all men at all times and in all places. Hence Ehrenburg's "Lessons of Stendhal," hence his "Rereading Chekhov." The ethical and moral values of the non-Soviet world will continue to exert a fascination on the young generation of Soviet citizens as long as there are books written by writers without the benefit of outside "guidance."

There is only one thing that may be said to the perplexed Soviet fathers who cannot understand the roots of the rebelliousness and irreverence of their better educated sons: *tu l'as voulu, Georges Dandin.*